Essentials of Management:

Ethical Values, Attitudes,

and Actions

edited by

James S. Bowman
with Introductions and Selected Readings

National University Publications

Associated Faculty Press
Port Washington, N.Y.

Manufactured in the United States of America

Published by
Associated Faculty Press
Port Washington, New York

Library of Congress Cataloging in Publication Data

Main entry under title:

Essentials of management.

(National university publications)
Includes bibliographies and index.
1. Business ethics—Addresses, essays, lectures.
2. Management—Addresses, essays, lectures. I. Bowman,
James S., 1945-   . II. Series.
HF5387.E76 1983   171'.4   83-3712
ISBN 0-8046-9316-1 (Associated Faculty Press)

To the Memory
of My Parents

Contributors

T. Edward Boling, Professor of Sociology, Wittenberg University

James S. Bowman, Professor of Public Administration, Florida State University

Steven N. Brenner, Associate Professor of Management, Portland State University

Archie B. Carroll, Professor of Management, University of Georgia

Ralph C. Chandler, Associate Professor of Political Science, Western Michigan University

John Donaldson, Faculty of Management Science, Imperial College of Science and Technology

Peter F. Drucker, Professor, Claremont Graduate School

Jarold A. Kieffer, Staff Director, White House Conference on Aging

A. Richard Konrad, Assistant Professor of Philosophy, Virginia Commonwealth University

Odd Langholm, Professor of Economics, The Norwegian School of Economics and Business Administration

Johs. Lunde, Assistant Professor of Business Ethics, The Norwegian School of Economics and Business Administration

George Cabot Lodge, Professor of Business Administration, Harvard University

Earl A. Molander, Associate Professor of Management, Portland State University

James Owens, Professor of Business, American University

Theodore V. Purcell, S.J., Professor of Social Studies, Georgetown University

John A. Rohr, Associate Professor, Virginia Polytechnic Institute and State University

Lea P. Stewart, Assistant Professor of Human Communication, Rutgers University

Mike Waller, Faculty of Management Science, Imperial Colege of Science and Technology

Deena Weinstein, Professor of Sociology, DePaul University

Contents

Abstracts of Contents

PREFACE

I. Introduction: The Study of Management Ethics

Chapter 1 — Are Management Ethics Worth Studying?
        A. Richard Konrad

By examining arguments about the study of ethics, the author advocates its pursuit as a feasible and desirable goal for students of management. Consideration of ethics in decision-making is more than "just a sop for the archaically devout" or a misguided attempt to get people to behave. Instead, the purpose should be to challenge one's thinking about values in education, management, and society.

Chapter 2 — Empirical Methods for Management Ethics Research
        Odd Langholm and Johs. Lunde

This state-of-the-art essay argues that if management ethics warrants a place in the science of administration, then only actual value concepts and ethical conduct in management can form the basis of ethics within the framework of administrative theory. Accordingly, a foundation for the empirical study of management ethics is presented by identifying appropriate fields of investigation and discussing selected research findings.

Chapter 3 — Approaches to Management Ethics
        John A. Rohr

This article contains a discussion of those areas that are not fruitful in the study of ethics by managers. A "public interest model" of ethics for organizations is then developed. Finally, the Constitution and court cases are analyzed as authoritative sources of values in administration.

Selected Readings

II. Management Ethics in Transition

Chapter 4 — *Ethics and the New Ideology*
George Cabot Lodge

The thesis of this chapter is that society's traditional definitions of ethical conduct are rapidly changing and that many of the dilemmas we now face are the result of that transition. This theme is explored by discussing the components of the country's traditional ideology and comparing them to the nation's new, emerging ideology. Many ethical issues can be better understood, if viewed in light of this transition. What stands in the way of an appropriate resolution of these issues is "a good deal of irrelevant ideology on the part of government, business, and the public in general."

Chapter 5 — *Ethics: Age-Old Ideal, Now Real*
James Owens

One mark of a professional, is his ability to comprehend ethical dilemmas. In an age of "instant information" and public insistence on moral behavior, management ethics is a practical necessity for administrators in the real world of organizational decision-making. The author presents a useful definition of ethics for managers and managers-to-be, and explores its implications. Fundamental ethical principles and historical standards are then outlined. The article concludes by recommending the continuing development and application of codes of ethics derived from these principles and standards.

Chapter 6 — *Ethical Chic*
Peter F. Drucker

Closing this section is Drucker's controversial essay which denounces business ethics as special pleading by the powerful. He contends that ethical concern is merely a fad, and is self-defeating nonsense.

Selected Readings

III. The Organization and the Individual: Ethical Dilemmas

Chapter 7 — *The Management Ethics "Crisis": An Organizational Perspective*
T. Edwin Boling

Dr. Boling provides a brief review of the literature and identifies inadequate premises for ethical guidance. In reference to major management theorists, the author develops specific principles to encourage moral behavior in organizations based on the superiority of group standards over personal ethics.

Chapter 8 — *Organizations as Political Systems: Heroism and Legalism*
Deena Weinstein

The author challenges the concept of the organization as a rational device for efficiently securing fixed ends. It is suggested that a more comprehensive perspective understands bureaucracies and organizations to be political systems. Traditional theories of organization—the administrative myth—maintain that the bureaucracy is a rational, nonpartisan, technical process. Employees cannot act politically except in disloyal opposition; dissent is a political phenomenon that occurs in organizations that are not supposed to be political systems. Ethical action punctures the myth of value-free neutrality and social concensus in administration. Opposition strategies are heroic because they require employees to challenge authority when obedience is expected, and there are very clear limits to legal reforms.

Chapter 9 — *Linking Ethics to Behavior in Organizations*
Archie B. Carroll

A framework for ethical thinking is presented followed by a discussion of seven actions that administrators can take to improve ethics. The premise of the article is that while broad social forces are important in ethical behavior, a more immediate cause—management practices and superior-subordinate relationships—affect the ethics of employees.

Selected Readings

IV. Ethical Attitudes in Government and in Business

Chapter 10 — *Ethics in the Federal Service: A Post-Watergate View*
James S. Bowman

This chapter discusses the attitudes of public executives toward moral issues in American politics and ethical practices in daily administration. The findings suggest that although managers are disposed to serve the public interest, some kind of institutional basis for professional conduct is necessary. Methods to accomplish this are suggested.

Chapter 11 — *Is the Ethics of Business Changing?*
Steven N. Brenner and Earl A. Molander

This article reports the views of 1,200 *Harvard Business Review* readers compared with the attitudes of their counterparts 15 years ago about management ethics. It concludes with a brief identification of four needed changes in managerial outlook.

Selected Readings

V. Conclusion: Actions to Deal With Ethical Problems

Chapter 12 — *Codes of Conduct and the Golden Rule*
John Donaldson and Mike Waller

In a critique of management research and practice, it is argued that moral codes are sources of commitment and are therefore sources of power and control. The Golden Rule provides compelling answers to significant questions in administration.

Chapter 13 — *Institutionalizing Ethics in Public and Corporate Governance*
Theodore V. Purcell, S.J.

The universal nature of ethical considerations in management is analyzed and documented. The author discusses strategies on how to "do" ethics in organizations, including the case for "ethics specialists." The chapter concludes by arguing against common objections to including ethical considerations in decision-making.

Chapter 14 — *Whistle blowing in Organizations*
Lea P. Stewart

This study explores whistle blowing as an organizational phenomenon, and analyzes 51 cases in order to derive a model of these incidents. Generalizations are then made about the nature of whistle blowing and how it fits into organizational communication patterns.

Chapter 15 — *Ethics and Public Policy*
Ralph C. Chandler

"How can public administrators properly plant, bring to flower, and keep weeded a personal code of ethical performance?..." This question is discussed with reference to major historical documents in American history and key issues in public administration. "The problem of administrative ethics continues to be one of discretion...and pursuit of the public good." Michigan Public Act 196 is discussed as a piece of legislation that effectively deals with the ethical dilemmas of managers.

Chapter 16 — *Recent Reforms in Government and the Case for*
an Inspector General of the United States
Jarold A. Kieffer

A federal administrator points out deficiencies in present arrangements designed to expose wrongdoing. The public learns of official deviance primarily through random and bizarre events. He recommends that systematic procedures be installed to correct this problem, beginning with the establishment of an independent office of inspector general of the United States.

Selected Readings

Preface

If management is defined as getting things done through people, it is evident that ethics can seriously affect organizational morale, recruitment, productivity, and many other daily administrative problems. Decisions about these problems, whether or not they are perceived as ethical choices, are made in the belief that something ought to be done. The administrative response is, in a word, a function of values. They are not merely inevitable, but constitute the irreducible nucleus of management.

Ethics and values have been highlighted in recent years by what is often called post-Watergate morality. Indeed, when government and business executives are involved in national scandals, the public legitimately wonders what else is happening in American institutions. Studies have documented widespread improprieties in the conduct of routine administrative activities, a fact that has led some responsible commentators to believe that corruption is now ubiquitous and systemic in American life.

Since administrators face complicated ethical issues in organizations and in society, they are finding it increasingly necessary to expand their knowledge about managerial ethics. An executive today, in fact, can hardly afford not to study the subject. There is, however, a general lack of teaching and training materials in this field. Specifically, there are few that address these questions in the public and private sectors of the economy as they affect the administrator.

By the late 1970s and early 1980s, a number of articles appeared that examined individuals and organizations encountering ethical problems. This book, therefore, does not contain separate chapters on the conventional socio-management issues and methods which tend to be either transitory or technical. Nor does it consist of inspirational essays or accusatory polemics which do little to describe or explain behavior in, and by, organizations.

Instead, this collection aims at enlarging the administrator's understanding of the nature of ethics involved in his daily work by offering analytical studies of, and meaningful guidelines for, managerial situations. If the study of ethical puzzles in organizations is to be fruitful, in other words, then it must concentrate on problems central to management. *Essentials of Management: Ethical Values,*

Attitudes, and Action, provides materials to assist managers and future managers to develop and/or maintain, personal and organizational codes of honorable performance.

The scope of this volume includes

1. Approaches to management ethics
2. Commentaries on past, transitional, and future ethical concerns of professional administrators
3. Analyses of the organization and the individual
4. Survey evidence dealing with the attitudes, values, and behavior of managers
5. Specific actions to deal with ethical dilemmas.

The emphasis is not on high elective officials, company presidents, or major scandals—such concerns lack day-to-day relevance for the majority of students and managers in business and in government. Nor is the focus on philosophical questions. Most managers-to-be, executives, and instructors, are simply not conversant in the philosophical nuances and theological distinctions of scholars. Thus, articles are chosen with the expectation that the reader would have little formal background in policy analysis or philosophy and ethics.

The focus is on the middle manager and organizational problems of immediate significance to students of administration in the classroom or office. Both the future executive and today's executive, as decision-makers, must choose among values in making policies. Therefore, the issues here are examined from a manager's point of view; values of employees and their organizations are explored, and actions that individuals and institutions can take are discussed.

The articles in this work have been compiled in such a way as to be beneficial to undergraduate and beginning graduate students. In addition, practicing administrators will find the material useful in sustaining a personal approach to management ethics. The subject matter of this book, in a word, should be part of the intellectual equipment of all managers and students who consider themselves to be enlightened and socially concerned.

Several features of the collection will facilitate its effective use. First, in selecting articles, it has been assumed that the reader has a general interest in management problems, but limited knowledge of their ethical implications. Accordingly, they are relatively free of jargon and written in a straightforward manner. Second, each part in the volume contains an introduction that will direct the reader's attention to (a) issues that underlie ethical inquiry, (b) significant aspects of the chapters, and (c) the Selected Readings at the end of the section. Third, a synopsis introduces the key ideas in each of the articles. The bibliography following the main sections in the book reflects not only the belief that students and managers should read more, but also reflects the increasing amount of excellent literature that is available.

No book of readings can "solve" moral problems in the practice of business or government; to pretend otherwise would deny all sensitive inquiry. There are no easy answers because there are no easy questions. As will be seen, however, it is too pessimistic to conclude that nothing can be done. It is precisely because fundamental problems have not been solved that thoughtful reflection is needed. In light of the ancient curiosity about ethics and contemporary ethical issues, a timely analysis of the management implications of the subject can be found in these pages. Enough government agencies and business firms are taking concrete actions against corruption and for integrity to demonstrate that the situation can be confronted with more than pious platitudes.

This anthology is one product of several recent research projects undertaken by the editor. Appreciation is extended to John A. Rohr (Virginia Polytechnic Institute and State University), Chester A. Newland (University of Southern California), Theodore V. Purcell (Georgetown University), and N. Joseph Cayer (Arizona State University) as well as to the W.K. Kellogg Foundation for its support. Marcel Dekker, Inc., granted permission to adapt small portions of a recent work of mine for use here. Most of all, my wife Ellona, and children Christopher and Andrew, endured the domestic consequences of this effort for which no satisfactory compensation has yet been devised.

James S. Bowman

Part I.
Introduction:
The Study of Management
Ethics

The study of ethics may be an established discipline, but its application and integration into contemporary business ands government management is just beginning. Although one of the exceptional characteristics of human beings is their moral behavior, there has been a general reluctance on the part of students of organizations to give appropriate consideration to this fact. There are, for instance, few analytical models of the subject to help guide one through the maze of reality, to develop generalizations, and to draw conclusions. In both practice and theory, the ethical implications of administrative conduct remain largely unexplored. Yet no one is entirely free of moral codes. Available evidence (see, for example, Part III) clearly demonstrates that managers are interested in ethics which they associate with rules and standards, morals, right and wrong, and values of honesty and integrity.

Although almost every individual has little difficulty understanding the idea of ethics, it is not easy to define. Among the numerous attempts to explain its meaning, perhaps the simplist and most useful definition is a set of standards by which human actions are determined to be right or wrong. Stated differently, ethics may be seen as the rules governing the moral conduct of the members of the organization or management profession.

This inquiry is guided by the following assumptions:

a. The practice of management generates ethical predicaments;

b. People are capable of choosing one course of action rather than another in dealing with these dilemmas;

c. Admirable behavior can be nurtured and directed in organizational settings.

"In essence," write Charles W. Powers and David Vogel (Part I, Selected Readings), "ethics is concerned with clarifying what constitutes general welfare and the kind of conduct necessary to promote it."

Over the past century, the centrality of ethics in higher education atrophied to a peripheral concern. It has only recently acquired a visible, if small and uncertain, presence in administrative studies. Therefore, in this introductory section, several topics are explored: why ethics should be studied, and how it can join the mainstream of the study of management.

A. Richard Konrad, in the initial essay, forcefully argues that management ethics are indeed worth studying today. If students, regardless of the point in their careers, are (a) establishing a level of professional competence and integrity, and (b) facing value differences in making judgments, then the ability to comprehend what is at stake is clearly the essence of management. What is needed is a perspective on one's role in society that permits one to recognize that ethics cannot be left solely to philosophers or religious leaders.

The second and third chapters examine the problems and potential of ethics research in making a contribution to the understanding of management. Odd Langholm and Johs. Lunde indicate the deficiencies in past business ethics literature, and discuss how contemporary studies can be integrated into management science. While agreeing with Konrad that a moral pattern must be implicit in the body of knowledge that each manager bases his decisions on, they disagree with Konrad (as well as Deena Weinstein, John Donaldson, and Mike Waller, in later chapters) on how this can best be accomplished. The third chapter, by John A. Rohr, examines "false starts" in the study of ethics followed by an outline of a potentially useful approach to analyzing ethics in government.

None of the contributors would dispute the notion that ethics courses and research cannot provide a panacea; it may be impossible to arrive at definitive answers to moral questions through analysis alone. Yet, Derek C. Bok (Part I, Selected Readings) maintains that there is no reason why ethical issues cannot be as rigorously pursued as many other areas in business and in government, unless it is claimed that ethical values have no intellectual basis whatsoever. The revival of the interest in ethics in the management profession might be described as a search for its soul. To paraphrase Justice Tom Clark, "What good is knowledge of administration if those who possess it are corruptible?"

The Selected Readings at the end of this section amplify these themes by investigating the state-of-the-art of management ethics teaching and research. Perhaps the most oft-quoted piece on teaching in the field is by Bok. A useful discussion of the relevant research trends can be found in Dwight Waldo's article. Recent overviews in both areas appear in the work by Joel L. Fleishman and Bruce L. Payne in public management, and by Charles W. Powers and David Vogel in business administration.

1.
Are Management Ethics Worth Studying?

A. Richard Konrad

Although I am an instructor in a philosophy department, I now teach an ethics course in a business school. An article in *Business and Society Review* by Mary Susan Miller and A. Edward Miller ("It's Too Late for Ethics Courses in Business Schools," Spring 1976), suggests that there really isn't any point in bothering with such courses. Their thesis was reinforced a few issues later in a commentary by Pat L. Burr. If I agreed with their assumptions about the purpose of ethics courses, I would pack my briefcase immediately and look for better things to do. But I believe their assumptions are wrong.

I want to argue against the belief that the purpose of a course is to teach people how to behave and that the measure of success of a course is how "good" the students were once they had taken it. Of course, it is a waste of time to lecture students about the wrongness of kickbacks, bribery, false advertising, and lawbreaking; or about the virtues of honesty, keeping your promises, promoting public welfare, and reducing waste and unemployment. Everybody knows all that without being lectured to about it. Furthermore, the knowledge of what's right and wrong seems to have little bearing on how people will act in these matters. In fact, if teaching ethics were nothing more than a listing of virtues and vices, I wouldn't bother with it myself, for it would be an utter bore.

In their article the Millers seem to assume that what would justify...ethics courses would be the reduction of widespread wrongdoing.... After all, that is the problem which worries the general public. And the solution to the problem lies in something which the Millers believe is beyond the ability of an...ethics course to teach—personal integrity. Since the Millers don't say explicitly what

3

they mean by personal integrity, I can only infer the meaning from the context, which seems to be this: having the kind of character which makes the practice of traditional ethical virtues a matter of habit. The problem, then, is with people's character, and since character is being shaped from the cradle, the Millers conclude, "a course in morality or ethics at the graduate-school level is simply too late." Burr concurs with this on the basis of this own informal surveys, which tell him that students are inclined to act in about the same way the rest of the society does (that is, not too well from the moral point of view), no matter what they might be willing to say to a university professor.

This should surprise no one. We cannot change character during forty-five class hours. The mistake lies in assuming that "bad character" is the problem. On this point, I want to come to the defense of. . .students I have known. In one sense of the word, they do not lack "integrity." That is, they are quite ready to act consistently on the basis of what they think is really important. They do have the kind of integrity of character which the Millers seem to think is lacking. The reason they are sometimes willing to lie, cheat, bribe, and break contracts when they "get out into the world," is that they really think that that is what is important—or at least that it leads to what is important, namely, business success. They know that whatever may have been said about traditional virtues is just a sop for the archaically devout. One might agree to it for prudential reasons while getting on with the real business at hand, which is building a solid business career. This kind of thinking is reinforced all around them. It is not limited to the big, bad, outside world. It permeates the. . .curriculum itself. How important *are* ethical considerations in the average course. . .? Unfortunately, lacking hard evidence, I can only guess. And my guess is that the answer would confirm what Burr asserts:. . .students reflect the culture around them, which includes the culture of the. . .school.

So what is the problem with. . .students if it is not a character defect? My suggestion is that it is to be found in the way. . .students (and the culture they reflect) *think*. And I maintain that the purpose of a university ethics course should be to challenge people's *thinking* about values. Now I know that may make the classroom a less secure place than many would like to be, but that's the price which must be paid for having a gadfly philosopher around.

The problem in teaching business ethics is to find a method which effectively challenges people's thinking about values. Let me make a few preliminary suggestions. We could start be examining in Socratic fashion, a great variety of value claims about business and ethics that are commonplace in our culture. For example, the free market system of distribution is more just than a Marxist system. There is no such thing as an unfair price; anything the market will bear is justified. Advertising does not manipulate people; all purchases reflect a free choice by the buyer. Public employees have no right to strike. We have an obligation to future generations to leave the world in a livable condition.

How would you defend, or challenge, these or any number of equally controversial claims? Doing so would mean examining a host of philosophical concepts like justice, obligation, rights, and free will. Writings on the subject are full of conflicting views on such issues. By plunging into this literature, students would be forced to think and argue through these matters and come to a decision themselves, a decision which they know might be challenged. This should force on them the realization that they are responsible for their value decisions, that there are no moral authorities to hide behind. It is not a question of the instructor teaching values to students. The process of learning values is a growth process. There is no learning it in a simple lesson. The best that can be hoped for in an academic course is to promote that process.

There is something in the Miller's article which might show how an ethics course could be important. They refer to John Mitchell's explanation that for those deeply involved in Watergate, the affirs of state seemed more important than the truth. The Millers' reaction to that is to say, "Nothing is more important than the truth." As it stands, this is little more than a platitudinous judgment. What is the real lesson to be learned from Mitchell's experience? I believe it is this: that it is *always* easy to get locked into one's own world where everything is more important than the truth. It may well be that this is the primary reason for wrongdoing in business—the affairs of business take on an overriding importance compared with everything else. So we fudge a bit on taxes, pollution control, or campaign contributions. Why should anything but business success seem important if one's whole life, starting from one's education, is immersed in business?

If we are serious about the truth and about what is truly important, the question of the method of its pursuit is all important. John Stuart Mill believed that the most effective weapon in this pursuit was free and open debate. A suppressed idea might turn out to be a true one. Even a false idea is useful in bringing out the truth by contrast. Borrowing from Mill, we could argue that a good education would stimulate one's curiosity to track down all the views on any subject, and to accept only the opinion supported by the strongest reasons. It would teach us to recognize the fallibility of our own value judgments and to keep us humble with the recognition of the problematic nature of value judgments.

It is here that the relevance of what I am talking about should be most apparent. An important function of. . .ethics courses is to show that business is *one* institution in a highly interrelated social complex. What is needed is perspective, so that the importance of what one is doing in business does not obscure the importance of society as a whole. Appreciation of this fact is necessary for understanding the notions of social responsibility and obligation, two very important ethical concepts. What must be avoided is the narrow view which allows people to think that business is a world unto itself, with its own set of rules and values, and that the rest of "ethics" are something for the religious establishment to watch over.

An ethics course cannot transform someone into a new person. It cannot hand over a new set of values to a student. But a start must be made somewhere to get students thinking about values; about what is important. If they see *only* business courses in their curriculum, the thinking process will never start; it will be obvious what is important—business! Value, in the final analysis is attributed to experience, so in education we can only hope to present the lure to new experience. Narrowness of education leads to a limitation of what looks interesting and important, and such narrowness will lead to the failure to produce fully developed individuals.

This release from a narrowness of viewpoint, this broadening of perspective, is really nothing other than the traditional goal of a liberal arts education. At best, an. . .ethics course can serve as a nexus between the tunnel vision of "economic man," and the breadth of viewpoint which has been the ideal of a liberal education. Indeed, a course in. . .ethics is too little. Whether or not it is too late depends on your perspective. It's too late to remedy many of the ills caused by insulated attitudes which have apparently given us an ethical crisis. But it is certainly not too late to begin again to respect open inquiry about what is important; to rekindle interest into value inquiry.

To avoid premature despair, we must also see that in education we are talking about a process, not a finished product. Some people believe that teaching involves putting something into students' heads, winding them up, and sending them on their way. This, of course, is rather ridiculous. We need people who can think, who welcome a challenge and recognize that seeking the truth is an unrelenting task. We need not lament that we cannot "teach" ethics, that is, that we cannot give students their values. The game is lost if we always succumb to the request, "Tell me what I need to know." A society full of information-laden automatons cannot survive. Students of. . .ethics will not be finished products, ready to do good at all times. But we can hope that they will be people who can evaluate, respond to criticism, reevaluate, and keep their eyes open for things they may have missed in the search for truth. And that's something which seems to me worth bothering about.

2.
Empirical Methods for Management Ethics Research

by Odd Langholm and Johs. Lunde

Since the second world war,...most Western countries have developed a socially oriented welfare democracy which makes great demands on the ethical attitudes and conduct of the business community. Comprehensive measures of public control have been implemented, consumer awareness has been sharpened by an active consumer council, and a new marketing law has been introduced, with the machinery necessary for its enforcement. There seems to be a growing interest in ethical values in both the general public and in the business world—a Norwegian moral philosopher, K.E. Tranoy, has even spoken of "a new moral climate." Consumerism, worker participation, factory protection acts, the protection of the environment, consideration for the developing countries, and so forth, all contribute to the formulation of constantly stricter ethical demands, some of them new, on the practical application by the business community of the theories and models developed by economic administrative research.

THE PROBLEM

Higher academic education...has only to a slight degree adjusted the instruction given and their research programs to these social and ethical developments. The tendency toward methods with a constantly stricter quantitative orientation, made even more stringent by computer techniques, has reinforced the rejection, in principle, of all noneconomic elements.

This attitude seems to have hit particularly hard that which we sum up by the

7

term. . .ethics—a field which many economists consider to be qualitatively vague, and therefore incompatible with stringent economic thinking.

This skepticism is nourished by much of the literature on the subject, both in the United States and in Europe, such literature being more likely to consist of sermons, criticism, and polemics, than of scientific studies and analyses of the economic-ethical problem complex. The authors are often only remotely concerned with economic theory and practice. They appeal more often to the conscience of the businessman or the business community rather than to a sober recognition of the ethical-social elements which form the conditions and restraints of economic thinking and conduct. Appeals to professional and personal responsibility will of course always be necessary, but until. . .ethics is recognized as a legal element in economic administrative research (and thus in academic instruction), it is unlikely that there will be any real adjustment to the value norms of the welfare democracy.

In the business community of today the individual is not as free and responsible, morally, as in the day of the small concern and the private firm. In the large modern enterprise, decisions and attitudes are usually the result of collective processes, where the responsibility of the individual is often limited to a professionally restricted partial responsibility, mercantile or technical. Employees at the different levels must act in accordance with others' directives and without having a full view of the final ethical consequences of the actions to which they are contributing. The demand for profit maximization makes it difficult to accept responsibility which is actually or apparently capable of restricting profits.

If the moral pattern is not implicit in the body of knowledge and data on which each individual employee must base his solutions for his share of the function as a whole, the employee will have small prospects of making ethical considerations or accepting ethical responsibility, even with the best will in the world.

It was against this background—and not without skepticism from those members of the scientific staff whose views are, in principle, quantitatively orientated—that The Norwegian School of Economics and Business Administration added research and instruction in. . .ethics, on a modest scale, to its program: in 1958 with the help of a visiting lecturer, and in 1966 by the establishment of an assistant professorship in the field (1958 to 1973, positions held by Johs. Lunde, the coauthor of this article).

We give the following short description of the methods involved and of some of the results attained, not because the methods are particularly original or the results particularly striking, but because we have here an example of. . .ethics research with a strictly empirical orientation, designed with a view to the greatest possible degree of integration into quantitatively determined economic-administrative research and instruction. This article is to be read as a preliminary report on what is intended to be a long-run project.

METHODS AND INVESTIGATIONS

The method of empirical investigation in. . . ethics, as in all exact or near-exact scientific investigation, must follow the cognitive process: hypothesis, investigation, postulation of theory. The method must reject points of departure for norm formulation based on theology, value-philosophy, ideologies, and the subjective views of the researcher: *theological,* because a theologically based system of ethics would be of limited relevance in a pluralistic and secularized society (such as, inter alia, Norway); *philosophical,* because operable value norms cannot be constructed from generally recognized philosophical systems; *ideological,* because this would introduce political tendencies to the value system. In the opinion of the authors, the fact that the *researcher* needs insight into economics, value philosophy, and the history of norms, does not affect this principle. The attitude must be that of "neutral goodwill." Only actual and current value concepts, and contemporary ethical conduct in market and business activities, can form the basis of empirically founded. . . ethics within the framework of the theory of business management. In the following pages we shall employ the concept of (moral) values as defined by Professor Milton Rokeach in *Beliefs; Attitudes, and Values. A Theory of Organization and Change* (to whose methods for public opinion research we shall refer later): "Values. . . transcend specific objects and specific situations: values have to do with *modes of conduct* and *end-states of existence."*

1. Hypotheses
The following hypotheses were postulated for the three main fields on which the investigations were first concentrated: ethical relations (a) in the business community, (b) between the business community and society (the consumers), and, (c) between employees and employers.

a. It should be possible to establish the ethical norms and behavior current in the business community by comparative studies of materials which document business' own ethical goals and actual business practice.

b. Similarly, it should be possible to establish the ethical relations between the business community and society (the consumers) by means of material which will document the current value concepts of the consumers, their demands and expectations with regard to the business community, and their reactions to its attitudes and conduct toward the consumers.

c. It should be possible to elucidate the ethical relations between employers and employees in the business community on the background of research into work psychology and organizational theory, analyses of material concerning organization, wage agreements and labor disputes, public debates on personnel questions, demands made with regard to the working environment, and so forth.

2. *Empirical Investigations*

The following can be given as examples of empirical investigations carried out with the fields covered by these hypotheses (a - c correspondong to these points):

a. The Norwegian business community has a sound tradition of business morality. For generations commercial organizations such as the Better Business Committees have acted as watchdogs to protect good business practice. One investigation, using as material the Opinion of the Better Business Committee of the Oslo Mercantile Association—the so-called Committee of Fifty—having the objective of throwing light upon practical commercial conduct and the conception of good business practice in Norway, from the time industrialism established itself in this country in the 1880s until the end of the 1960s, gave interesting results.

The committee's evaluation of complaints gave the ethical scale of values used, whereas the material put forward in support of the complaints, represented the empirical material used to throw light on the actual commercial conduct involved. The investigation showed that the Norwegian business community had, by and large, high and stable ethical objectives, which in spite of certain serious defaults, must be considered to be generally accepted by responsible businessmen. The analysis was summarized under the series of norms: *Truth* (Honesty, Integrity, Confidence), *Justice and Freedom* (Contribution to Society, Fairness, Moderation), and *Solidarity* (Usefulness to Society, Service, Loyalty to Society). This scale of norms was largely confirmed by an analysis of other material from the Better Business Committees—the Opinions of the Committee of Ten of the Norwegian Marketing Federation, for which analysis the "Code of Advertising Practice" drawn up by the International Chamber of Commerce, was used as the ethical scale.

Structural analyses of these investigations made it possible to draw up specified surveys of the most usual types of ethical defaults occurring in different periods, in the different links of the marketing chain, and in different lines of business.

Another project, still in progress, concerns pricing norms and may serve to demonstrate the intimate relationship between the ethical variable and such other variables which go into a comprehensive explanation of a market economy. Seeking to throw light on the apparent discrepancy between theoretical conclusions and businessmen's own practice of pricing industrial products, extensive analyses were made, by means of computer simulation, of the technological and intertemporal relations which condition cost and price decisions in multi-product firms, in order to lay bare the pricing norms actually in operation, as well as their optimality from a theoretical point of view. The conclusion managed to reconcile theory and practice up to a certain point, by taking account of such relations. But beyond this point the study itself, and the empirical research which had gone into the preparation of the model, indicated a residual which seems to be explainable only by reference to certain norms or codes of decent behavior in pricing situations. This result, which proved a surprise to nobody in the business community, is remarkable only because a heavily argued point of theoretical controversy actually seems to seek part of its solution outside the established sphere of economic analysis—in social concerns, which the conventional preoccupation with "possessive individualism" fails to recognize. Not necessarily expressing genuine ethical convictions at every behavioral link, the operation of the norms in question shows a remarkable stable acceptance of the need to conform to an expected and well-defined social consensus about pricing behavior. From this research activity...there grew a twin project of historical and empirical research, seeking to establish in more detail the origin and development of these norms as well as their actual working under present economic and social conditions. The historical part of the project, which has been supported by The Norwegian Research Council for Science and the Humanities, is approaching the publishing stage.

b. It is obvious that the ethical aspect of the pricing problem will affect the interests of the consumers as much as those of the business community. Also, the other manifestations of internal business ethics will, indirectly, affect society and the consumers. Nevertheless, we need here investigations of materials capable of directly elucidating the ethical attitudes of the consumers, and what they expect and demand of the business community.

A comprehensive and exact record of complaints would be capable of giving valuable information here. It would to a considerable degree lay bare ethical conflict situations between customer and retailer—and would thus to some extent clarify the responsibility of producers and middlemen to the final consumer. Complaints are often oral, and leave few and obscure traces. The earlier mentioned Consumer Council has, however, a special department for complaints, in which complaint material is available on special forms. These have been systematically prepared and submitted to the opposite party for his opinion, and they often include technical test reports on the article which was the subject of the claim. From the thousands of cases covered by this material, systematic and statistical analyses have been made of a number of merchandise categories—groceries, drapery goods, electrical articles, cars, and so forth—for the registration of quality defects, unreasonable pricing, failure to comply with guarantee obligations, poor service, customer information and treatment of complaints, and so forth.

Other material has been obtained from textual analyses of readers' letters and articles on poor business morality in the daily press. A Gallup study of shop service, complaint treatment, pricing and discount policy, attitude to advertising, and so forth, has also given instructive data concerning the ethical attitudes and reactions of the consumers.

It had to be borne in mind, however, that the consumers' attitude to commercial conduct was usually influenced by self-interest and colored by irritation and aggression—sometimes also by misunderstandings or ideologically determined ill will toward the business community as such. Materials from conflict situations can therefore not be expected to give a complete picture of the opinion of an uninvolved customer, and therefore of the "resting" system of values with which the unprovoked customer will meet the business community. It is, of course, this system which the business community should integrate into its objectives and conduct.

Since it must be assumed that the ethical demands and expectations of the consumers with regard to the business community are expressions of their general value concepts, adjusted to the situation, an elucidation of the value concepts of the consumers—of so-called ordinary people—should be a focal point of an ethical consumer analysis. A suitable method was found in Professor Milton Rokeach's interview scheme for public opinion research. The person interviewed is asked to rank two series of 18 socially acceptable value criteria according to the importance he places upon them, thus registering his value preferences and whole system of values. A value study of this kind, carried out on a modest scale in Oslo and in a country district, as well as among students in Bergen, has proved fruitful, in part for the constitution of a "norm-horizon" against which the results of various special investigations can be adjusted.

The study confirms that this "norm-horizon" is very largely in accord with the classical value tradition, the highest ranking norms being responsibility, honesty, helpfulness, justice, freedom, tolerance, and equality. It should be emphasized that the Rokeach method only registers the ethical norms, not the moral conduct, of the persons interviewed. Few people come close to realizing their ideals in practical life. On the other hand ethical norms are held as demands and expectations with regard to the conduct of other people. It is these demands and expectations—from business connections, employees, employers, consumers, and the community—that . . . ethics should contribute to charting and clarifying.

c. With regard to investigations of the ethical relations between employer/ employee—questions which could be summed up by the concept "ethics in personnel administration"—we are in a somewhat different position than in studies of the fields of . . . ethics touched on in the foregoing. Work psychology and personnel administration have to a far higher degree than business administration drawn ethical-social aspects into the field of research, and the need for empirical analyses of material here appears to be less urgent. It suffices to mentioned names such as those of Talcott Parsons and Chris Argyris to indicate the wealth of psychologically founded insights, often with a clear ethical orientation, that are available here. At the same time the humanistic character of work psychology builds a barrier of problems around the integration of its results into quantitative business administration theory and model construction. The methods and objectives of organization research are closer to those of business administration. It must, however, be stressed that neither of these fields is, *in principle,* ethicaly orientated—hence the need in both fields for the elucidation which could be provided by research of an ethical nature. Here again it must be a basic principle that such studies be founded on empirical material. Few of the problems in this complex have as yet been solved. Ethical analyses of organization planning; labor disputes; work instructions; working environment; cooperation; the relations between technology, rationalization, and the monitoring of efficiency on the one hand, and ethical demands for personal integrity, and so forth, on the other hand, are subjects which offer themselves for research in this field.

3. Preliminary Results

Like all knowledge, empirical research in. . .ethics is its own objective. The simple fact of its being carried on and the publication of its results cannot help but contribute to an increased awareness of the ethical realities and the ethical responsibility inherent in the relations between the business community and society.

The studies just mentioned above have been written up in Norwegian and Scandinavian scientific journals or have been published separately. On the basis of this and other material, a theory of. . .ethics has been postulated and described in books which have formed part of the course of study for students of The Norwegian School of Economics and Business Administration. A simplified version has been prepared for undergraduate business schools. Special codes of ethics have been formulated on the request of individual concerns and trade organizations. Lectures have been held for mercantile associations, business schools, and universities, in Norway and in the other Scandinavian countries.

These activities are nevertheless only at the pioneer stage, and the scale on which they have been carried on is modest. Much remains to be done before we can hope to achieve the integration of ethical and management aspects which is a sine qua non if research into. . .ethics, and academic instruction founded on this research, is to be capable of exercising a formative influence on ethical practice in trade and industry.

INTEGRATION

If. . .ethics research is considered to warrant a place in the field of administration, and if administration is considered to be an applied science, the integration of the results of such research in the theories and models constructed for. . .administration, and their use in the solution of concrete research projects which touch on personal and social questions, must be a natural objective in all future development. In our introductory discussion of the problem we emphasized the importance of the introduction of ethical elements into the science of. . .administration, and into its way of thought. A knowledge of empirical studies such as those of which we have given examples will to some degree provide a legitimate basis for such a change in professional attitude.

However, the foundations for a genuine "eco-ethical" professionalism will not be laid until ethical elements and economic elements are integrated into the research process.

Our present body of knowledge on business economy is built up of so many partial studies that the ethical factors which may have been omitted in the preparation of each study can no longer be traced in the general theory or model used as a guide for action.

Even a special study or a commissioned project is usually so complex that the elimination of ethical variables is capable of affecting the conclusions in a way which cannot be subsequently demonstrated. In other words, efforts should be made to *incorporate* the ethical corrective—which in simpler circumstances makes itself felt in the shape of an immediate moral judgment—into the economic theory, model, or investigation on which decisions and conduct are based.

If rational research data on. . . ethics are at hand, it should be possible to carry out such an integration of ethical aspects at several stages of the economic research process:

1. During the *formulation* of an economic research project the ethical conditions and requirements which may be relevant to the problem under consideration can be ascertained and can be included in the *objectives* of the project.

2. During the *postulation* of an economic theory or model the possibility of including recognized ethical aspects as variables or restraints in the actual problem complex can be ascertained.

3. In addition to the procedures mentioned under 1 and 2, or in replacement of them if they are not feasible, the ethical aspects can be discussed in the *final critical commentary,* with the modifications and/or restraints to which the results of the economic research should be subjected before they are applied in practice.

As the ethical data are the result of empirical, and to some extent statistical, investigations, they will often either be capable of direct quantification or will take the form of clear restraints. However, even in cases where they must by their very nature be subjected to critical evaluation, they can still be treated as relevant data. Economic quantification can also rest upon an approximately objective assessment.

3.
Approaches to Management Ethics

✳ by John A. Rohr

The purpose of this article is to share with the readers of *Good Government* some personal reflections on efforts to integrate questions of ethics into a training program for government managers. The reflections are based upon a year's fellowship with the General Management Training Center of the Civil Service Commission's Bureau of Training. The fellowship was sponsored by the National Association of Schools of Public Affairs and Administration (NAS-PAA) and extended from September 1975 until August 1976. The trainees came from an extremely wide range of executive departments and independent commissions; their grade range was from GS-12 to 15.

My primary responsibility during this period was to prepare a manual on ethics to be used in the management courses conducted by the General Management Training Center. After a few weeks it became apparent that the most important aspect of my task was to clarify the nature of the problem I was supposed to address. That is, *for management training purposes,* what is the salient ethical problem? I emphasize the words *for management training purposes* because they introduce some crucial qualifications. First, the problem concerns government managers—that is, career civil servants and not congress-men, judges, or politically appointed executives. Secondly, the problem is addressed within the context of a management training program rather than that of the academic curriculum. Whatever the ultimate differences between training and education may be, there is a very important difference in the pace at which the instruction must proceed. The academic seminar can move at a pace that is at once more leisurely and more comprehensive because it is spread over the thirteen to sixteen weeks of a semester with ample time for reading on the part of the students. Training courses are usually conducted within a period of three to five days, during which time many topics other than ethics will be treated—for example, management by objectives, decision-making, team-building, supervision, the budgetary process, and motivating subordinates. If ethical considerations are to be inserted into a training course, the topic usually will have to be covered in a period of from three to four and a half hours. Within this framework I established as the minimal goal of the training session a clear and persuasive definition of the ethical dimensions of governmental management. That is, I set out at least to define the problem.

FALSE STARTS

One might object that the problem is quite obvious but I do not think this is the case. The demonstrate my point, I shall devote a substantial portion of this article to a description of several "false starts" I pursued only to reject at a later date. What follows, then, is a series of examples of what I consider *not* to be the most fruitful way to address questions of ethics for government managers.

Without doubt the worst possible approach is to focus on the sins and follies of Watergate. This is somewhat paradoxical because the current interest in ethics in government is due in no small part to the Watergate scandals. I would reject a "what-can-we-learn-from-Watergate" approach to ethics for bureaucrats for the simple reason that Watergate simply was not a career civil service problem. Indeed, one might argue that the dreadful months of Watergate actually reflected considerable credit upon the career civil service. The routine business of government was conducted in a reasonably efficient manner despite a collapse in political leadership of several months' duration. The outcome of a discussion of Watergate among career bureaucrats is likely to be a justifiable sense of self-righteousness vis-a-vis their politically appointed superiors. Self-righteousness, even when justified, is not the most appropriate starting point for serious ethical reflection.

Another reason for rejecting Watergate as an entree to ethics is the need to avoid the alleged failing of military academies—training officers to fight the last war. An excessive preoccupation with the concrete details of Watergate is more likely to attune the government manager to the dangers of the past rather than the problems of the future. This is not to say that we have nothing to learn from Watergate. Obviously, we can learn and already have learned a great deal. However, the lessons of Watergate point more in the direction of institutional reform than to improving ethical standards.

A second approach tried and found wanting was to emphasize questions of conflict of interest. The reason for rejecting this approach is grounded in the close connection between management training and routine management tasks. If management training is to be practical, it must concentrate on issues that are central rather than marginal to the managerial enterprise. For example, training sessions on planning or communication are intended to influence the routine behavior of the trainees. Topics dealing with questions that arise only on extraordinary occasions are usually unsuitable for training purposes. Such questions might be quite interesting and important in themselves but they lack that day-to-day relevance that sound management training would address. On these grounds, I found conflict of interest a rather inappropriate vehicle for introducing ethical questions into the management training curriculum. When a conflict-of-interest situation arises in the life of a career civil servant, it is indeed an important event for that man or woman but, hopefully, it is a rather extraordinary event and hence one that is not particularly apt for management training.

A second reason for rejecting conflict of interest as the focus of a training session in ethics is that the subject is at times quite technical and requires the expertise of an attorney. Ethics counselors have been designated in the major agencies of the federal government. Their efforts are coordinated by the General Counsel's Office of the Civil Service Commission. Rather than focus the training session on arcane questions of conflict of interest, it seemed wiser to advise the trainees that expert legal help is readily available should a practical problem arise for themselves or their subordinates.

A final reason for not emphasizing conflict of interest is related to the legalistic character of the issue. Precisely because conflict of interest is minutely regulated by law, the questions it triggers are necessarily structured in negative terms of administrative sanctions and criminal penalties. The motive of fear and punishment is implicit in any discussion of conflict of interest. While this motive may at times be salutary, it is not a likely staging area for developing a high sense of ethical commitment in the public service. As one trainee put it, "After fifteen years of government service, I'd like to say I did a little more than just stay out of jail!"

"Resignation in protest" is another issue that inevitably surfaces in any discussion of ethics. Like conflict of interest, it is the kind of issue that is terribly important when it arises but, fortunately, it does not arise very often in the career of any single government manager. Hence, for training purposes it seemed best to touch lightly on the topic, provide references to the pertinent literature, and move on to something more closely related to the working situations of the trainees.

I found, however, that the trainees would not let me treat this issue in a manner quite so cavalier. In presenting case studies of moral dilemmas faced by career managers, I was surprised to discover how frequently the solution recommended by the trainees was resignation. After some gentle probing, however, it became quite clear that this solution was often suggested because the trainees were able to distance themselves from the people involved in the cases. When the discussion shifted from the facts of the particular case at hand to the *personal consequences* that might be visited upon those who resign in protest, the participants usually assumed a more cautious attitude. Rigid adherence to principle was tempered by questions of family responsibility and the prospects of future employment. This struck me as a healthy development because it highlighted the truly heroic virtue that is at times required by those brave souls who do resign in protest over questions of principle—especially those who do so without having a profession, or prominent family, or independent source of income to rely upon. For this reason it seems that resignation should be suggested as the ultimate weapon rather than as an opening salvo in an organizational dispute that raises serious questions of principle. This is especially true in dealing with idealistic young people. It would seem to be dreadfully irresponsible to encourage young men and women to enter government service and then advise them to resign at the first hint of a moral crisis. Precisely because resignation in protest is, and should be, an extraordinary form of behavior, I felt it was an unsuitable focal point for a training session. I found it best to let the trainees raise the issue themselves in the discussion of case studies presented for their consideration. They seldom disappointed me.

As the previous paragraph suggests, I found case studies a helpful training device but, despite their obvious utility, I did not make them the central focus of the session. The reason for this is that case studies frequently fail to yield principles of sufficiently general character to be of ethical interest. The rich and fascinating details of case studies are at once their strength and their weakness. Precisely because they are so rich in detail, case studies, while always prompting lively discussion, frequently fail to focus on one or two issues of principle that might be applied in a wide variety of administrative situations.

A final approach that I rejected was to emphasize what might be called questions of basic human decency. Lest the reader be shocked by this statement, let me hasten to explain that I have nothing against human decency—basic or otherwise. My point is that I could see little usefulness in exhorting trainees to treat their peers, supervisors, and subordinates decently because such an exhortation does not get at the ethical problems *peculiar to career government managers.* Decency and thoughtfulness are as precious to government employees as they are to anyone else in any walk of life—commercial, industrial, academic, military, or religious. To stress such universal human values as consideration for, and sensitivity to, the needs of others, runs the risk of ignoring the distinctive qualities of government employment that must be stressed in meaningful reflections on *professional* ethics.

While one might quarrel with certain self-serving aspects of the codes of ethics developed by the medical and legal professions, there is little doubt that it is the high sense of professional definition among physicians and lawyers that accounts for the clearly articulated ethical standards of their professions. They have a fairly clear idea of what it is that makes them *different* from everyone else. Ethical norms of behavior are then deduced from these differences. I would suggest that governmental managers follow a similar course and for this reason I would downplay the broad human values that we look for in every walk of life. It is quite possible for a surgeon with impeccable ethical standards in his professional life to be an absolutely irresponsible parent, a compulsive gambler, or an incorrigible lecher. Unless we are willing to acquiesce in the same possibility for government managers, I do not think we will make much progress in developing meaningful ethical standards for managers in the career civil service.

Lest the previous two paragraphs seem a bit harsh, it might be helpful to note that humane and thoughtful treatment of one's fellow workers is a salient consideration in a great deal of the literature associated with Organizational Development and Participative Management. The same might be said of the emphasis on "negotiation" in MBO literature. Profound ethical issues can surface in areas that are not labeled "ethics." The emphasis on Participative Management, OD, and MBO in management training today might well be interpreted as a harbinger of humane managerial styles. These developments should certainly be encouraged. Nevertheless, if we are to get on with the task of developing ethical standards (or at least ethical attitudes and values) that are peculiar to government managers, we must in principle reject the emphasis on basic human decency as our starting point.

I trust I have not wearied the reader with the long list of unsuccessful approaches to ethics. I trust, too, that my criticism of these methods will not be taken in a doctrinaire sense. I do not intend to banish the words *Watergate, conflict of interest,* or *resignation* from the training curriculum. My point is rather to expose the "soft underbelly" of each of these approaches and to suggest that they be used cautiously and only in passing rather than as the central focus of a training session.

THE "PUBLIC INTEREST" MODEL ✳

Let me now strike a more positive note by outlining the approach I found most helpful. To give it a name I shall call the approach a public interest model of ethics for government managers. The model is "political" in that it relies upon administrative discretion as its starting point. It should be noted that I am not using the word *political* in the relatively narrow sense of electoral, partisan politics. Rather, I am using it in its broader, more traditional and, indeed, classical sense that describes any action that promotes or retards the common good. In this sense all administrative discretion is inherently political and for this reason public administrators (including career civil servants) can be said quite properly to share in the governing, that is, political process.

To the extent that career civil servants govern, an interesting theoretical problem arises because in a democratic society those who govern are supposed to be responsible to the constituents who elect them. Yet the whole point of a personnel system based on merit is to structure the civil service on a permanent career basis and thereby remove it from electoral pressures. To the extent that career bureaucrats govern, democratic principles require that they somehow be responsive to the values of the people in whose name they govern. Since, however, they are forbidden by law from responding through the conventional institutional means of the electoral process, they must find some other means of responding. In the absence of institutional means, the problem is transformed into an ethical issue wherein the career civil servant assumes a personal obligation to examine his behavior to see if it is attuned to the values of the American people.

It will not do to dismiss the problem by saying that the career civil servant does not govern but simply executes the will of Congress, the President, and political appointees. Such a simplistic notion ignores the richness and complexity of the administrative process in general and in particular the nature of administrative discretion which confers the legal power to decide something. Anyone who decides anything of consequence in the name of government *governs*. Through the broad discretion conferred by Congress and delegated down through the ranks of the bureaucracy, the career civil servant becomes an active participant in the governing process.

This line of argument is intended to *define the peculiar problem of ethics for the career civil servant in a management position.* Its intended effect is to impress upon the career bureaucrat the significance of his routine labors and thereby to help him achieve a legitimate sense of pride in what he does. As O. Glenn Stahl has noted in *Public Personnel Administration,* on the topics of ethics, "[A] proud public servant is a good public servant. Our efforts should be directed toward building and maintaining that pride."

There are abundant concrete examples of governmental activity to support the "public interest model" herein proposed. The institutional decision-making that characterizes the activities of the regulatory agencies provides many obvious examples, for example, maintaining a "fair and orderly market," preventing "unfair competition," proscribing "impure drugs" and "substandard food," and granting licenses in the name of "the public interest, convenience, or necessity." Such value-laden decisions are not restricted to the regulatory agencies. One could cite such routine occurrences as plea bargaining in law enforcement agencies, or the discretionary judgments inherent in awarding government grants and contracts as well as the discretionary judgments made every day by compliance officers. The modern industrial state is an administrative state and, as such, is characterized by discretionary judgments on the part of managerial personnel exempt by law from the discipline of the ballot box. This, I suggest, is the most appropriate starting point for ethical reflection on the part of government managers.

In stressing the importance of administrative discretion, I do not mean to use the word only in the technical sense in which it appears in textbooks of administrative law. I refer also to the wide-ranging discretion that managers (and many of their subordinates) enjoy in participating in an agency's decision-making process. The questions one asks, the complaints one makes, the encouragement one offers, the rebukes one imposes, the advice one offers, the initiatives one assumes, the directives one chooses to enforce zealously or to quietly ignore, the decisions one postpones, the responsibilities one avoids—all these forms of behavior are discretionary and, as such, can enhance, enliven, and enrich the administrative decision-making process that promotes (or retards) the common good of our society.

I have mentioned that to the extent the manager governs he has an obligation to examine his attitudes and behavior to see if they are attuned to the values of the American people. It is far easier, of course, simply to announce this principle than to make it meaningful. There are a few things, however, that can be done to make this very broad obligation a bit more concrete. One way is to clarify the term *values of the American people* by distinguishing the popular whims of the moment from the abiding principles of the republic. It is, of course, the latter that provide the suitable background for examining one's attitudes and behavior.

ETHICS AND THE CONSTITUTION

The Constitution of the United States is the most likely place to find the inchoative expression of these abiding principles, because that document is the supreme symbol of our common life as a people organized for action in history. Broad constitutional principles are especially appropriate because they focus on a document which all government managers have taken an oath to uphold. Unfortunately, the oath of office as presently administered is all too often a meaningless and perfunctory recitation that is a most unlikely candidate for selection as a statement of high moral purpose. Nevertheless one can make the argument that *in principle,* the oath of office creates a moral community among government employees that demands a moral commitment to constitutional principles that is not required of the ordinary citizen. For training purposes this principle can be used to structure a workshop around an exercise in which trainees try to make connections between specific agency decisions in which they have participated and one of the general purposes of the United States proclaimed in the Preamble—to form a more perfect union, to establish justice, to secure the blessings of liberty for ourselves and our posterity, and so forth.

The connection between routine, specific decisions and grand constitutional principles, is admittedly a bit tenuous at times but the exercise serves at least as a symbolic reminder to managers from many different agencies that by their oath of office they have become members of a very special moral community. The task is somewhat simplified in intraagency courses where all the participants share some common occupational experiences. Here organic acts or agency mission statements can be very useful and practical sources of reflection upon the specific values a given agency is supposed to further. One dramatic example of this point is the 1924 "mission statement" issued by Attorney General Harlan Fiske Stone in defining the role of the newly created Federal Bureau of Investigation:

> There is always the possibility that a secret police may become a menace to free government and free institutions because it carries with it the possibility of abuses of power which are not always quickly apprehended or understood. . . .
> It is important that its activities by strictly limited to the performance of those functions for which it was created and that its agents themselves be not above the law or beyond its reach. . . . The Bureau of Investigation is not concerned with political or other opinions of individuals. It is concerned only with their conduct and then only with such conduct as is forbidden by the laws of the United States. When a police system passes beyond these limits, it is dangerous to the proper administration of justice and to human liberty, which it should be our first concern to cherish.

One can only speculate on what might have happened had the training sessions of the FBI emphasized this mission statement over the years but, surely, it would have been worth a try.

CONCLUSION

The purpose of this article has been to share some reflections on ethics and public management training. I think it is quite obvious that a great deal of work needs to be done in this area both at the theoretical level of what we are trying to accomplish, and the practical level of how to proceed. During the early 1950s there was a great deal of interest in the question of "ethics in government." Many fine books and learned articles were written but ethical considerations failed to become an established component of the training curriculum. One reason for this was that the literature at that time was to a considerable extent a reaction against specific abuses in the last years of the Truman administration. When the public grew tired of hearing about the abuses, they grew tired of the reforms as well. It is for this reason that I would oppose focusing contemporary discussions of ethics on Watergate. At present, it seems to me the most important issue is to establish the *legitimacy* of ethics as an integral part of management training. To do this, it is imperative that we define the central problem as clearly as possible and distinguish it from issues of only marginal relevance. Perhaps the reflections in this article will contribute to a vital dialogue on what we should be doing. Perhaps someday questions of ethics will be as commonplace in management parlance as questions of efficiency and economy.

Selected Readings
Part I.

Armstrong, DeWitt C., and Graham, George A. "Ethical Preparation for the Public Service." *The Bureaucrat.* 4 (April 1975); 5-23.

Banfield, Edward C. "Corruption as a Feature of Government Organization." *Journal of Law and Economics.* 18 (December 1975); 587-606.

Bok, Derek C. "Can Ethics Be Taught?" *Change.* 8 (October 1976); 26-30.

Bowman, James S. "Teaching Ethics in Public Administration." *Innovations in Teaching Public Affairs/Administration,* edited by Ann-Marie Rizzo and Richard Heimovics. Kansas City/Miami: Teaching Public Administration Conference, 1981: 79-90.

Denhardt, Robert B. "On the Management of Public Service Education." *Southern Review of Public Administration.* 3 (December 1979); 273-83.

Fleishman, Joel L., and Payne, Bruce L. *Ethical Dilemmas and the Education of Policy-makers.* Hastings on Hudson, N.Y.: The Hastings Center, 1980.

Grosenick, Leigh. "Problems of Teaching Ethics in American Public Administration." Paper presented at the Fourth National Conference on Teaching Public Administration, Lexington, Kentucky, May 29-30, 1980.

Heidenhiemer, Arnold J., ed. *Political Corruption: Readings in Comparative Analysis.* New York: Holt, Rinehart and Winston, 1970.

Henry, Nicholas. "Toward a Bureaucratic Ethic." In his *Public Administration and Public Affairs.* 2nd ed. Englewood Cliffs, N.J.: Prentice-Hall, 1980; Chap. Six.

Lilla, Mark T. "Ethos, 'Ethics,' and Public Service." *Public Interest.* 63 (Spring 1981); 3-17.

Newstrom, John W., and Ruch, William A. "The Ethics of Business Students: Preparation for a Career." *American Assembly of Collegiate Schools of Business Bulletin.* 12 (April 1976); 21-29.

McMahon, Thomas F. C.S.V. "Classroom Ethics: A Survey of Business School Courses." *Business and Society Review.* (Summer 1975); 21-24.

Peters, John C., and Welch, Susan. "Political Corruption in America: A Search for Definitions and a Theory. *American Political Science Review.* 72 (September 1978); 974-84.

Powers, Charles W., and Vogel, David. *Ethics in the Education of Business Managers.* Hastings-on-Hudson, N.Y.: The Hastings Center, 1980.

Rizzo, Ann-Marie, and Patka, Thomas J. "Teaching Administrative Ethics in the Public Sector." *Education for the Public Service 1979,* edited by Guthrie S. Birkhead and James D. Carroll. Syracuse, N.Y.: The Maxwell School, 1979; 45-62.

Rohr, John A. *Ethics for Bureaucrats: An Essay on Law and Values.* New York: Marcel Dekker, Inc., 1978.

Saul, George K. "Business Ethics: Where Are We Going?" *Academy of Management Review.* 6 (April 1981); 269-76.

Schorr, Philip. "Teaching Ethics in Public Affairs and Public Administration: Searching for an Ideal Model." Paper presented at the Annual Convention of the American Society for Public Administration, Detroit, April 13-15, 1981.

Waldo, Dwight. "Public Administration and Ethics: A Prologue to a Preface." in his *The Enterprise of Public Administration: A Summary View.* Novato, Calif.: Chandler and Sharp Publishers, Inc., 1980, Chap. Seven.

Part II.
Management Ethics
in Transition

One of the reasons why ethics occupies an uncertain place in the study of management, is because some people believe that in today's pluralistic society there can be no overall set of standards or sense of value. While there may be little doubt that corruption is pervasive, the fact remains that the concern for proper behavior in business and in government, can be traced back thousands of years (Caiden and Caiden, Selected Readings). Disreputable conduct has been condemned in every generation and by all societies. As Theodore V. Purcell remarks in a later chapter, core notions of right and wrong seem to be constant, and ethics is not totally subjective, situational, or personal "like the taste for lobster tails or a fancy for bow ties."

Indeed, recent headlines in business and in government, have brought to the surface the moral malaise in society, taken away the archaic pall that clings to such concerns, and stimulated an interest in ethics. The evidence demonstrates that while newspapers on almost any day report breaches of principle, Americans are clear and insistent on principle, and it usually prevails. Most people, quite simply, want and need to live a moral life (Rokeach, Selected Readings). Even in the midst of considerable immorality in government and business, managers are ready to confront ethical issues. They should, in point of fact, embody the highest standards of society and accept responsibility for their actions; professional accountability includes moral obligation.

Since ethics deals with the purpose of organizations and permeates all forms of management, conscientious men and women know what is honorable through a blend of reason, experience, intuition and leadership (cf., Boling chapter). It may be a circumstance of modern societies that the definitions of right and wrong are diverse. Yet not being able to discern right from wrong is the classic defense of insanity. It remains the difficult task of leadership to bring consensus out of the

25

natural diversity present in society's organizations. While no one knows what is right and wrong all the time, most people, certainly managers, who are more affluent and better educated than the average citizen, have this awareness most of the time.

If administrators and the organizations they manage are able to identify ethical issues and articulate thoughtful responses, it is important that they accurately gauge societal trends. George Cabot Lodge in his chapter, "Ethics and the New Ideology," argues that the "business mentality," as epitomized by the saying, "the business of America is business," has become increasingly inappropriate for the contemporary supervisor. In order to understand ethical issues, "a good deal of irrelevant ideology on the part of government, business, and the general public," needs to be replaced by an emerging set of beliefs more germane for modern organizations.

Since the mark of a professional is the ability to comprehend ethical dilemmas, James Owens contends that the "age-old ideal" of ethics is now a practical necessity in organizational decision-making. The author develops this thesis by discussing ethical principles and historical standards for the contemporary administrator. The managerial challenge posed by Lodge and Owens is to face, not merely accept, the ethical predicaments in modern society. Peter F. Drucker, however, claims that concern about ethics is "ethical chic," and is nothing more than traditional hostility toward business in a new, dangerous guise. While there may be no authoritative interpretation of management ethics—the uncertainty that pervades management includes moral issues—it is important that administrators and students accept the obligation to put themselves in touch with the concerns of the American people.

One of the ways to accomplish this is to explore the Selected Readings that follow. The considerable extent of fraud, waste, and abuse in organizations is examined in Clinard et al. regarding the business world and the Comptroller General regarding government. A useful overview of some of the issues in the following chapters appears in Albert T. Sommers's article. William M. Agee represents a dissenting viewpoint, by arguing that the "morality flap" is now under control, and has become something of a bore to the practical manager.

4.
Ethics and the New Idoeology

✳ George Cabot Lodge

Standards of right and wrong depend upon time, place, and situation. The Christian admonition to love thy neighbor as thyself and its Judaic counterpart to do justly, love mercy, and walk humbly with thy God, are universally noncontroversial. But their application, definition, and institutionalization, provoke disagreement and vary according to when, where, and under what circumstances.

Today there is much concern on all sides about...ethics,...especially about what is considered to be the wrong conduct of managers.... (It is significant that the corner grocer is nowhere near as suspect.) Is this because the number of sinners in executive suites has suddenly increased? I think not. Rather it is because the definition of sin, of right and wrong, has been changing radically and, in changing, is both unclear and controversial.

...Critics say we lack a sense of social responsibility. But just what is "responsibility"? At the least, as philosopher Charles Frankel says, it is "the product of definite social arrangements," from which flow the dos and don'ts that constitute a more or less coercive framework by which the community assesses and controls behavior.

Today, however, the framework is in disarray. Sufficient thought it may be to help identify clear-cut villainies and punish the perpetrators, it is less helpful in appraising the actions of managers who, in their own judgment and that of many of their peers, consider their conduct justifiable and well meaning, even though large segments of public opinion consider it inhuman, irresponsible, and corrupt.

In examining these different opinions, it is useful to bear in mind Frankel's "definite social arrangements"—defined here as ideology, or framework of ideas, which a community uses to define values and to make them explicit. Ideology is the source of legitimacy of institutions and the justification for the authority of those who manage them. Ideology also can be seen as a bridge, which a community uses to get from timeless, universal, noncontroversial notions such as justice, economy, self-fulfillment, and self-respect, to the application of such notions in the real world.

As the real world changes, so does its definition of values and its ideology. Frequently, however, there is a lag; society tends to linger with an old ideology even after its institutions have perforce departed from it. The status quo tends to use the old ideas to justify itself.

The real world of America is obviously vastly different today from what it was 100, 50, or even 20 years ago. Consequently, the traditional ideology of America has also changed. Living with a new reality, we are in transit from one ideology to another, and many of the ethical dilemmas we now face are the result of this transition.

Two things have happened: First, the "traditional ideology" of this country has become inconsistent with the real world. Second, great institutions have departed from the traditional ideology, thereby contributing to its subversion and replacement.

Corporate America (not the corner grocery) has outgrown the ideology to which it and the community generally have traditionally looked for its legitimacy. In structure and practice it reflects a new ideology, one that has not yet been fully articulated and is vague, confusing, and somewhat fearful.

Other institutions, especially government, have also left the old ideology behind, even though their leaders as well as society in general tend to sing the old hymns. Indeed, it almost seems that the farther the departure from the old framework of values the greater becomes our devotion to it. We are thus looking for legitimacy and authority in ideas that are becoming increasingly inconsistent with practice and reality.

THE LOCKEAN FIVE

The traditional ideology of this country is not difficult to identify. It is composed of five great ideas that were first brought to America in the eighteenth century, having been set down in seventeenth-century England by John Locke, among others, as "natural" laws. These ideas found fertile soil in the wilderness of a developing America and served well for a hundred years or more.

The Lockean Five are:

   1. *Individualism.* This is the atomistic notion that the community is no more than the sum of the individuals in it. It is the idea that fulfillment lies

in an essentially lonely struggle in what amounts to a wilderness where the fit survive—and where, if you do not survive, you are somehow unfit. Closely tied to individualism is the idea of *equality,* in the sense implied in the phrase *equal opportunity,* and the idea of *contract,* the inviolate device by which individuals are tied together as buyers and sellers.

2. *Property rights.* Traditionally, the best guarantee of individual rights was held to be the sanctity of property rights. By virtue of this concept, the individual was assureds freedom from the predatory powers of the sovereign.

3. *Competition = consumer desire.* Adam Smith most eloquently articulated the idea that the uses of property are best controlled by each individual proprietor competing in an open market to satisfy individual desires. This idea is explicit in U.S. antitrust law and practice.

4. *The limited state.* In reaction to the powerful hierarchies of medievalism, the conviction grew that the least government is the best government.

5. *Scientific specialization and fragmentation.* This is the corruption of Newtonian mechanics which states that, if we attend to the parts, as experts and specialists, the whole will take care of itself.

While it can be argued that the Lockean Five may be valid as ideals, in practice we have often departed from them. For example, history is replete with examples of business going to "the limited state" and seeking protection or favor. While this might be justified in the name of property rights, it has had the effect of forcing government into an active planning mode.

Or one might cite the many examples in America of ethnic communities with a high sense of interdependency—organic social constructs instead of the atomistic conglomerations of Locke. Immigrants did indeed bring a strong sense of community with them, but over time this sense weakened for lack of nourishment from the surrounding social system. Whatever may have been our historic inconsistencies with the traditional ideology, for most of our history it served as the principal justification for our instutional life and behavior. Departures from it were exceptional, and every effort was made to minimize their significance.

Today, however, the exceptions are overwhelming. Although many small enterprises remain comfortably and acceptably consistent with the Lockean Five and hopefully can continue so, the managers of large institutions in both the so-called private and public sectors are forced not to practice what they preach. It is this gap between the behavior of institutions and what they sometimes thoughtlessly claim as a source of authority, that causes trauma.

What then is the ideology that would legitimize the behavior of these institutions? The answer may be five counterparts to the Lockean Five.

The New Ideology

1. *Communitarianism.* The community—New York City, for example—is more than the sum of the individuals in it. It has special and urgent needs as a community, and the survival and self-respect of the individuals in it depend on the recognition of these needs. Few can get their kicks *a la* John Wayne, although many try. Individual fulfillment depends mostly on a place in a community, an identity with a whole, participation in an organic social process. Furthermore, if the group—the community, faction, or neighborhood—is well designed, its members will have a sense of identity with it. If, on the other hand, it is poorly designed, the individuals within it will be correspondingly alienated and frustrated. In the complex and highly organized America of today, few can live according to the principles John Locke had in mind.

Both corporations and unions have played leading roles in creating the circumstances that led to the erosion of the old idea of individualism and created the new framework of values. But invariably they have been ideologically unmindful of what they have done and have, therefore, tended to linger with the old forms and assumptions, even after those have been critically altered.

A central component of the old notion of individualism is the so-called Protestant ethic: hard work, thrift, delayed gratification, and obedience to authority. Business has extolled these virtues on the production side while systematically undercutting them on the marketing side. Advertising departments spend millions reminding us that the good life entails immediate gratification of our most lurid desires—gratification that we can buy now and pay for later.

Similarly, the assembly worker has been led to believe by management, early parental training, and TV, that the old idea of individual fulfillment is valid. But finding himself constrained by an inescapable work setting dramatically unlike anything that he has been led to expect, he is one day liable to strike out—perhaps violently. Or he may join the absentee lists, taking Fridays and Mondays off to eke out some spurious individualism via drugs, drink, old movies, or—if he is lucky—a walk in the hills

Paradoxically, such behavior puzzles both management and unions. They cling to the traditional, individualistic idea of the contract, long after the contract has ceased being individualistic and has become "collective," unmindful of the inevitable dissonance between the idea of contract and the new forms of consensus toward which communitarianism is leaning.

Our traditional social policy attempted to guarantee that each worker had equal opportunity. The lawyers enforcing today's equal employment legislation have taken a different tack. In the case of American Telephone & Telegraph, for example, they argued that discrimination had become institutionalized, that it, in fact, had become endemic to the AT&T community, and that women, in particular, were being slotted into certain tasks.

When this kind of argument receives acceptance, it is no longer necessary to prove individual discrimination to get redress.

Subsequently, the government moved to change the makeup of the company's workforce to provide, in effect, for equality of representation at all levels. The issue became one of *equality of result,* not of opportunity; and with that, a communitarian idea had superseded an individualistic one.

2. *Rights and duties of membership.* A curious thing has happened to private property—it has stopped being very important. What difference does it really make today whether a person owns or just enjoys property? He may get certain psychic kicks out of owning a jewel, a car, a TV set, or a house—but does it really make a difference whether he owns or rents?

Even land—that most basic element of property—has gone beyond the bounds of the traditional ideology. The United Nations Commission on Human Settlements (as quoted in the *New York Times,* June 7, 1976) said that because of the crucial role land plays in human settlements, it "cannot be treated as an ordinary asset controlled by individuals and subject to the pressures and inefficiencies of the market."

Today, a new right, which clearly supersedes property rights in political and social importance, is the right to survive—to enjoy income, health, and other rights associated with membership in the American community or in some component of that community, including a corporation.

Such rights derive not from any individualistic action or need; they do not emanate from a contract. Rather, they are communitarian rights, which public opinion holds to be consistent with a good community. This is a revolutionary departure from the old Lockean concept under which only the fit survive.

Escalating rights of membership, however, have strained the ability of governments to pay the bill. Transfer payments to pay for these rights have risen from 33 percent to of the federal budget in 1972, to 42 percent in 1975. New York City hovers on the brink of bankruptcy. Inevitably, therefore, the necessity of membership *duties* emerges, and a question follows: Who decides the duties? The individual or the state? If government is to be the employer of last resort, does that impose an ultimate obligation to work at a job prescribed by government? And what do we do with the increasing numbers of persons in the workforce who are simply not needed?

The new ideology presents us with rather ominous choices.

The utility of property as a legitimizing idea has eroded as well. It is now quite obvious that our large public corporations are not private property at all. The 1.5 million shareholders of General Motors, for example, do not and cannot control, direct, or in any real sense be responsible for, "their" company. The vast majority are investors pure and simple, and if they do not get a good return on their investment, they will put their money elsewhere.

"Campaign GM" and other similar attempts at stockholder agitation represent heroic but naively conservative strategies to force shareholders to behave like owners and thus to legitimize corporations as property. It is a peculiar irony that James Roche, as GM chairman, branded such agitation as radical, as the machinations of an "adversary culture...antagonistic to our American ideas of private property and individual responsibility." In truth, of course, GM was the radical; Ralph Nader et al. were acting as conservatives, trying to bring the corporation back into ideological line.

But if GM and the hundreds of other large corporations like it are not property, then what are they? The best we can say is that they are some sort of collective, floating in philosophic limbo, dangerously vulnerable to the charge of illegitimacy and to the charge that they are not amenable to community control. Consider how the management of this nonproprietary institution is selected. The myth is that the stockholders select the board of directors, which in turns selects the management. This is not true, however; in reality, the management selects the board, and the board, generally speaking, blesses management.

Managers thus get to be managers according to some mystical, circular process of questionable legitimacy. Under such circumstances, it is not surprising that "management's rights" are fragile and its authority waning.

3. *Community need.* It was to the notion of community need that ITT appealed in 1971 when it sought to prevent the Justice Department from divesting it of Hartford Fire Insurance. The company lawyers said, in effect:

> Don't visit that old idea of competition on us. The public interest requires ITT to be big and strong at home so it can withstand the blows of Allende in Chile, Castro in Cuba, and the Japanese in general. Before you apply the antitrust laws to us, the secretary of the treasury, the secretary of commerce, and the Council of Economic Advisers, should meet to decide what, in the light of our balance-of-payments problems, and domestic economic difficulties, the national interest is."

Here again it was the company arguing the ideologically radical case. The suggestion was obvious: ITT was a partner with the government—indeed with the Cabinet—in defining and fulfilling the community needs of the United States. This concept is radically different from the traditional idea underlying the anti-trust laws—namely that the public interest emerges naturally from free and vigorous competition among numerous aggressive, individualistic, and preferably small companies attempting to satisfy consumer desires.

In the face of serious pressures from Japanese and European business organizations, which emanate from ideological settings quite different from our

own, there will be more reason to set aside the old idea of domestic competition to organize U.S. business effectively for meeting world competition. Managers will probably welcome, if not urge, such a step; they may, however, be less willing to accept the necessary concomitant: if, in the name of efficiency, of economies of scale, and of the demands of world markets, we allow restraints on the free play of domestic market forces, then other forces will have to be used to define and preserve the public interest. These "other forces" will amount to clearer control by the political order in some form or other.

This leads to other questions, as, for example, the matter of corporate size and concentration. The confusion between consumer desire and community need is also the source of considerable criticism of business. Is the automobile industry supposed to satisfy consumer desire for large cars or serve community need for smaller ones? Can the industry decide this question, or is it up to the community acting through its government?

4. *Active, planning state.* The role of the state is changing radically; it is becoming the setter of our sights and the arbiter of community needs. Inevitably, it will take on unprecedented tasks of coordination, priority setting, and planning in the largest sense. It will need to become far more efficient and authoritative, capable of making the difficult and subtle tradeoffs that now confront us—as, for example, those of environmental purity and energy supply.

Government is already big in the United States, probably bigger in proportion to the population than in countries we call socialist. Some 16 percent of the labor force now works for one or another governmental agency, and the total tends to keep increasing. U.S. institutions more and more are living on government largess—subsidies, allowances, and contracts to farmers, corporations, and universities—and individuals benefit from social insurance, medical care, and housing allowances. The pretense of the "limited state," however, means that these huge allocations are relatively haphazard, reflecting the crisis of the moment and the power of interest groups rather than any sort of coherent and objective plan.

If the role of government were more precisely and consciously defined, the government could be smaller in size. To a great extent, the plethora of bureaucracies today is the result of a lack of focus and comprehension, an ironic bit of fallout from the old notion of the limited state. With more awareness we could also consider more fruitfully which issues are best left to local or regional planning and which, in fact, transcend the nation state and require a more global approach.

5. *Holism—interdependence.* Finally, and perhaps most fundamentally, the old idea of scientific specialization has given way to a new consciousness of the interrelatedness of all things. Spaceship earth, the limits of growth, and the fragility of our life-supporting biosphere, have dramatized the ecological and

philosophical truth that everything is related to everything else. Harmony between the works of man and the demands of nature, is no longer the romantic plea of conservationists. It is an absolute rule of survival and thus is of profound ideological significance, subverting in many ways all of the Lockean ideas.

Ethical Applications

Many of the ethical issues of our time can be better understood if we view them in the light of this ideological transition.

In the aftermath of Watergate came the disclosure that scores of America's most important corporations had violated the Corrupt Practices Act, making illegal contributions to political campaigns and payoffs to many politicians for presumed favors. While, in general, it is wrong to violate the law, there are plainly exceptions to the rule as the experience of prohibition demonstrates. There are also degrees of wrongness. Political payoffs are in a sense a perfectly natural result of the traditional ideology. If the institution of government is held in low repute, if it is indeed regarded essentially as a necessary evil, and if its direction is supposed to arise from the pulling and hauling of innumerable interest groups, then it is natural that those groups will tend to use every means, fair or foul, to work their will. It is the way the system works.

How do we change the system?

We provide government with a more revered status; we acknowledge that it has a central role in the definition of the needs of the community and in the determination of priorities and that this role requires a certain objective distance from special interests. We then restrict the practice of lobbying, insulate government from pressure groups, and charge it with the responsibility of acting coherently in the national interest.

But even as we do this we can sense the predictable threats that the communitarian state breeds: elitism, unresponsiveness, and perhaps an increasing partnership between government and large corporations, replacing the adversary relationship in the traditional ideology and evolving possibly into a form of corporate statism, which could erode the essential elements of democracy.

So without excusing the illegality of those making and receiving the payoffs or in any sense minimizing their ethical flabbiness, we must acknowledge that perhaps more important is the systemic weakness that their behavior exposed. Of equal importance is an awareness of the consequences of correcting that weakness and a precise recognition of our choices.

One of the most important uses of ideological analysis is that it helps make explicit the full range of possibilities flowing from a change in practice. There is a propensity in any society for these possibilities to be obscured or muted by those who are seeking the change, and it is perfectly possible for the United States to get the worst of communitarianism unless we are fully alert to the choices that the transition requires.

The unethical fallout of Watergate also disclosed large and questionable payments to foreign governments by many corporations. Bob R. Dorsey, Gulf's chairman, defended a payment of $3 million to Korea's ruling party in 1970 as necessary to secure the continued favor of the regime. Senators questioning him pointed out that the company's investments in Korea were fully insured by the U.S. government against expropriation and that U.S. assistance to, and influence in, South Korea, were substantial. In view of this, Dorsey was asked why he had not told the U.S. embassy about the problems he was having with the government. His answer is hard to take seriously, but at the same time is symptomatic of a larger problem. He said:

> Well, I suppose it goes back to a sort of lifetime habit, a lifetime experience of having received little help from the State Department and the American government in foreign endeavors and very often finding they had little interest and would just as soon not talk to us.

Noting that he was not talking about the embassy staff in Korea, who had always been "extremely helpful," he went on: "Maybe I was basically ashamed of what was going on, I do not know. . . ." Further on in his testimony, in speaking of American companies abroad and their relationship to the American government, he said, "They were sort of like motherless children; they had to make their way in the world . . ."

What is at stake here? First we must remember the time and place: South Korea, 1970—a government strongly supported by the United States and threatened by North Korea. The politicians from whom Gulf had received good treatment and who were friends of the United States had asked for money. It was a price of doing business, and it is understandable that he did not turn them down flat. What is not so clear is why Dorsey did not go to the embassy and report the matter; the national interest of the United States was clearly involved as was that of a U.S. corporation. Why then did he not? Some old assumptions, he said, about the relationship between government and business—vestigal remains of the limited state and property rights.

Dorsey may, in fact, be something of a hero. It seems altogether possible that throughout the 1960s the embassy, probably through the CIA, was assisting the ruling party and that Dorsey was the conduit for U.S. government funds. If this were the case, is Dorsey then perhaps to be praised for protecting his CIA connection? Or, if that is what he was doing, was he being unethical? That depends upon one's definition of the national interest and the confidence with which one leaves that definition to the institutions of government.

In either case, the issue becomes one of the relationship over time between large U.S. corporations and the U.S. government. This brings us to Dorsey's contention that, in his experience, U.S. oil companies got little help from the State Department. The record, however, seems to indicate that, quite to the

contrary, the U.S. government in the Middle East, Peru, and elsewhere, has been more than solicitious of oil company interests. Indeed, the record shows a clear, if covert, partnership between the companies and the departments of State and Defense, although there is considerable doubt about who the senior partner was.

Looking to the future and to the enormous importance of the oil companies to the community need of the United States, there will be increasing ethical difficulties as long as the terms of the partnership are not made explicit and public. Take the natural gas crisis that paralyzed the country in the winter of 1977. Who and what are to blame? Some say it is regulation; others argue that it is greedy companies seeking to maximize short-term profits. But it is pointless and superfluous to look for villains in this matter. Again, the problem is systemic. Sooner or later government will perceive the energy problem as the holistic problem it is and begin to offer some coherent leadership. Until it does, catastrophe will mount, as will unethical behavior.

Ideally, it seems that the ethical corporate executive would address reality, urge government to do the coherent planning required, offer to assist—careful not to dominate or dictate—and then proceed to implement the plan with the efficiency for which U.S. corporations are justly respected. Only in this way can the investment decisions of, for example, the oil companies be both intelligent and just.

What stands in the way of such a course of action is principally a good deal of irrelevant ideology on the part of government, business, and the public in general.

The Lockheed case raises other issues of government-business relationships. In August 1975, Lockheed, a major defense contractor, admitted it had made under-the-table payments totaling some $22 million since 1970. Part of the payments, particularly those made in Japan, were used to promote overseas sales of the L-1011 Tri-Star jet liner. Difficulties with both producing and selling the L-1011 had placed the company on the brink of bankruptcy in 1971, when Congress bailed it out by agreeing to guarantee a $250 million loan. Management defended its questionable foreign payments, arguing that they were necessary to consummate foreign sales. The company also believed that such practices were "consistent with practices engaged in by numerous other companies abroad, including many of its competitors, and are in keeping with business practices in many foreign countries."

A central issue in this case is certainly the relationship between Lockheed and the U.S. government. Lockheed is a major defense contractor. It is answerable to a Loan Guarantee Board, of which the secretary of the treasury is chairman. It is a major exporter of military aircraft. However, the evidence suggests that these relationships with government were and still are vague and unclear.

Was Lockheed acting in the national interest or its shareholders' interest? Daniel J. Haughton, then chairman of Lockheed's board, in Senate subcommittee testimony claimed the latter, but, by inference, his mention of the French as

serious competition in sales of wide-bodied aircraft, suggests he was thinking of the former.

Here, again, clarity and explicitness are essential. The question of what U.S. business sells in the way of military equipment around the world, is surely infused with the national interest. It relates to our defense posture, our diplomatic alliances, and our balance of payments. Haughton's problem, like Dorsey's may well have been as much a matter of the definition of the terms of his company's partnership with government as it was a matter of ethics.

The plight of New York City suggests a host of intriguing ethical issues for business. In 1976 the Episcopal bishop of New York chastised companies that were leaving New York for pleasanter and more secure suburban settings. Indeed, one cannot but have sympathy with such a stand—New York's principal difficulty is the erosion of its economic base.

What does the ethical...executive do? First, it would seem that ad hoc contributions to charitable causes, although worthy, are irrelevant to the problem. No amount of charity will do any good. Second, the problem must be seen as one involving all components of the New York community; it is an organic problem. Indeed, the problem extends to the suburbs of New Jersey and Connecticut and beyond. Much as some may object, New York is in many important ways a creature of the nation and of national demographic flows and pressures. What is the relevant community in this case? And what are its needs? Surely in answering these questions, the political order of the city, New York State, the several neighboring states, and the federal government will have to take leadership. Also, the city's bankers as well as the general public, will have to realize that the banks are as important politically as they are economically. They are, in fact, inextricably connected to the political order. Their distance from it has been part of the problem.

The point is that there is little that business can do alone. The solution requires a partnership with the political order, and before that can occur, the political order must become more coherent and more alert to its planning function. Until business recognizes this, it will be blamed—unfairly perhaps—but blamed nevertheless for the systemic breakdown that New York represents.

Inside the corporation, ethical questions abound concerning the proper relationship between employers and employees. Work, it is said, is dehumanizing, alienating, and boring. The old notions of managerial authority rooted in property rights and contract no longer seem to be acceptable. Consequently, many firms are moving away from the old notions to new ones of consensus and rights and duties of membership in which the right to manage actually comes from the managed. Consensual arrangements naturally threaten the old institutions attached to the contract both in management and labor. Trade unions are particularly anxious about the new development.

The new approaches will come easier—and more ethically—if we are mindful of the radical implications of what we are doing. The old institutions need to be treated gently so that their resistance will be minimized. There may after all be an important role for unions in the new consensual arrangements. Workers' participation in management can be made more effective by a properly functioning union. Both management and labor need to learn new techniques. Also, the new way is not without its own threats and dangers. The idea of the contract emerged to protect the individual from the worst abuses of ancient and medieval communitariansim. Unless we are careful, hideous injustice can be perpetrated in the name of consensus; all sorts can be excluded, for example, the weak, the black, the white, women, men, or those we merely do not like.

It is worth emphasizing that perhaps the most appalling ethical problems we may face are those associated with the new ideology. How can we preserve and protect some of the most cherished attributes of the old as we move inexorably toward the new? How can we safeguard individual rights in the face of communitarianism and the rights of privacy, choice, and liberty? How can we avoid the grim excesses of centralized, authoritarian, impersonal bureaucracy? How can we ensure democracy at all levels of our political system? How can we enliven efficiency as the definition of what is a cost and what is a benefit becomes increasingly obscure?

The general answer to these questions is alertness—consciousness of what is happening. This is no time to sing the old hymns. It is essential to compose new ones. It is, after all, not beyond the realm of possibility that we could find ourselves marching stolidly into a communitarian prison lustily singing Lockean hymns.

The specific answers must flow from specific situations. The ethical manager will be realistic about both the situation and the roles and functions of business, government, and other institutions in dealing with it. He will also bear in mind the long-term interests of the persons and communities that he affects, having the courage to place those interests above his own short-term preoccupations. He will see his problems in the context of all their relationships, employing his skills as a generalist to help produce appropriately systemic solutions.

5.
Ethics:
Age-Old Ideal, Now Real

James Owens

Scientific and technological advances in the communications field, now operating in our daily lives, have catapulted the American people, its businesses, and its other institutions, into the strange new age of "real-time" information. Computers, interesting toys just a few years ago, now make possible databanks capable of retrieving, sorting, storing, and providing anyone instantly with all known information about any person or organization. The development of telephone and similar communication has reached mature sophistication. Newspapers, magazines, radio, and television, can, in today's world of "freedom of information," "full-disclosure," and similar laws or public policies, dig out and publicize critical information about any person or organization. In any twenty-four-hour period, any person or organization can easily be "made ready," and the information fully developed (usually with entertaining and dramatic impact), for the 6:00 o'clock news. It happens every night on television, every day in the newspapers, and every week or month in magazines.

This age of "real-time" information creates some radical advantages for human beings (as in medicine, education, and daily conveniences) and some major problems as well. For example, today's managers now operate, whether they realize it or not, as though they were in a well-illuminated fishbowl, instantly under the public's scrutiny. With the advent of the late 1970s, . . . managers and their daily decisions are suddenly "on stage," carefully monitored, reported on and evaluated, and kept on "continuing file."

The full implications of databank capability and instant availability of information in general require many theoretical and practical reassessments by managers and management educators alike. These considerations, however, are beyond the scope of this article. Here we will consider only the impact of the new age of instant information upon. . .ethics.

For centuries, and especially over the past two decades, ". . .ethics" has been a popular research and conversational topic, but it was always dealt with as an "ideal" and certainly not someting to practice in the tough, real world of. . .decision-making. Today, all of a sudden,. . .ethics has become a practical necessity for all organizations and their managers.

The new age of instant information availability puts the operations and decisions of today's managers under constant public scrutiny, a condition of business life no previous American managers had to cope with or live with daily. Managers and entrepreneurs of the past in America, including U.S. presidents, operated routinely in private and secrecy, and option modern American managers understandably would relish. But the luxury of privacy, secrecy, and confidential executive decision-making no longer exists in the world of the 1970s. The issue of. . .ethics cannot be approached with mere sentimental "moralizing"; integrity and sound professional ethics are now essential conditions for practical effectiveness—even survival.

Thus, in addition to exploring other requirements of effective management, managers and their organizations must maintain an operational and continuing concern for the ethical integrity increasingly demanded by the public. Consider, for example, recent outcries in the newspapers and on television concerning misues of funds, kickbacks, collusion, corruption in public office, fraudulent use of welfare and other public funds by doctors and corporations, deceptive advertising, and so forth.

Achieving a reputation for ethical integrity, both internal and external to the organization, implies a continuing development and refinement of clear, specific, and well-publicized codes of professional ethics and persistent reference to the fundamental concepts embodied in the historical literature of philosophical ethics. It is the concepts of ethics that provide the theoretical framework and solid foundation for specific codes of ethics; without such a foundation, ethical "codes" usually degenerate into either blind reactions to current crises or flabby and meaningless generalities. This article addresses primarily these underlying concepts. I have attempted to spare the reader, as far as is possible, unnecessary jargon and theoretical trivia in order to provide a clear basis for the ongoing and much-needed development of ethical codes for managers and their organizations.

The trend toward a *profession* of management is well under way. Managers of the future, if they are to become or remain such, will be professional in the best sense of the term, including the ethical. By a kind of natural evolution, one mark of the future manager will become his unerring ability to comprehend and evaluate the ethical dimensions of his decisions; lacking this ability and sensitivity to ethical issues, he will be a net liability—and often a latent menace—to his organization.

Integrity and consequent credibility have become a practical necessity for...executives. In the current age of instant communication through telephone, computer, and television, and of supersensitivity on the part of aggressive public pressure groups, consumer advocates, and government regulators, the "new realism" dictates in fact that from a fully *practical* point of view "good ethics is good business."

"GOOD" DOCTORS AND "BAD" HUMANS

Few words suffer semantic butchery as does the word *ethical*. Some regard themselves ethical if their legal staff can keep them safely within the law. Others feel ethical if they have a generally good "feeling" toward others—at least on the Sabbath. Still others construe themselves as ethical, even within the turmoil of hard, ambiguous "business" situations, if they execute exactly the boss's (or a client's) orders (although they might concede that the boss is unethical in some of those orders).

Operationally, "ethics" can be defined as a "set of standards, or code, developed by human reason and experience, by which free, human actions are determined as humanly right or wrong, good or evil." If an action conforms to such standards, it is deemed ethical; if it does not, it is deemed unethical.

The term *humanly* in this definition, carries a special meaning and is critical. It implies and urges important distinctions among the various senses of the "good." What is *good* ethically, in the ultimate human sense of the term, transcends such common uses of the word as in *good looks, a good steak, feeling food,* or a *good automobile mechanic.* Such uses indicate what is *desirable* in terms of appearance, food tastes, personal feeling, and job performance. Ethical *good* (the *good* humanly interpreted) raises the question: What is a good human being? A doctor who demonstrates remarkable skill in experimental surgery upon healthy, unwilling prisoners is clearly a good surgeon but an evil and unethical person. Similarly, a good salesperson, manager, or lawyer, might employ tactics that are *ethically* wrong.

ETHICS AND LAW

The law is a set of imperative statements promulgated by the state and enforced by the power of the state. Thus, laws and ethics are not equatable, even though many laws tend to coincide with a particular society's ethics (as in the case of the common prohibition against lying by both law and ethics in America). But law and ethics often conflict, as in the case of the Nazi regime's laws, which violated all sense of human ethics, or the many "blue laws" in the United States that no longer represent current ethical attitudes. When a law conflicts with a person's ethics to the extent that, in good conscience, he must openly violate that law, the person is engaging in "civil disobedience." Thus, the "legal" and the "ethical" are not the same thing; but in general the formulation of law follows a society's ethical attitudes and results in a gradual merging of the two.

POSITIVE AND NEGATIVE ETHICS

Most discussions of organizational and public ethics track the more sensational and newsworthy instances of wrongdoing. The news business zeroes in upon the *un*ethical, thereby optimizing newspaper readership and subscriptions. But it is important to note that such preoccupation with wrongdoing is only one part of ethics, the *negative* part. Negative ethics centers on the analysis of what human beings do that is wrong ethically and by what standards it is judged as wrong.

The other side of ethics is *positive* ethics: the analysis of what people do that is ethically "good" and by what standards it is so judged. For example, top executives of a large firm decide to use corporate money to hire, train, and employ, a number of hard-core "unemployables" in order to better the lives of such people suffering from joblessness and little opportunity. In the development of specific ethical codes for an entire industry, the positive approach to ethics is as important as a narrow, negative approach, although both are necessary.

ETHICAL SANCTIONS

A key concept in the literature of ethics is sanctions, the rewards that prompt people toward ethical actions and the penalties that prompt them to avoid unethical actions. What prompts an executive to contribute his services one night a week to help train hard-core unemployables (positive ethics) or to avoid padding his expense account (negative ethics)? The following sanctions are common throughout the literature of philosophical ethics: personal value-systems and "conscience"; pressures of public opinion expressed in the public media, common and statute laws; religious belief and commitment; personal peace of mind; fear of retaliation—or exposure—regarding wrongdoing; fear of government intervention and regulation in the absence of ethical codes initiated (generally more sensibly and realistically) by industry people themselves; and an organization's rules, policies, and codes that are realistically enforced upon members. Any organizational code of ethics must incorporate these sanction considerations into its code or rightly anticipate failure or, at best, superficial compliance.

ETHICAL PRINCIPLES AND STANDARDS

"Principles of ethics" involve the most theoretical—and controversial—aspects of philosophical ethics. Fortunately, they are unnecessary in a practical treatment of ethics, as space does not permit us to discuss them here. The standards of ethics, derived from most "principle-oriented" and "ethical-system" approaches, happen to coincide with the most common historical standards of ethics. Several major ethical standards that are viable and have survived many hundreds of years of human experience are listed here, not necessarily in order of importance or validity:

Treat all human beings with fairness. This is the rule of justice and an inspiring maxim. However, it requires careful analysis of the rights of all parties in situations involving conflicting interests. "Fairness" to stockholders is perceived differently than fairness to employees, customers, or suppliers.

Do unto others as you would have them do unto you. The golden rule is among the most enduring of ethical standards. With slight variations in phrasing (for example, the Chinese version by Confucius in the sixth century B.C.: "What you do not want done to yourself, do not do to others"), the golden rule has been a prominent ethical force in Buddhism, ancient Greek philosophy, Hinduism, Judaism, Christianity, and many other systems of thought.

The long-range utility standard states: "So act that your act will produce, over the long range, maximum personal happiness." In explicitly stated form, this standard can be found throughout history from the ancient Greek philosophers up to American pragmatists William James and John Dewey. William James, reacting against what he interpreted as the noble-sounding but literally useless generalities of idealists, attempted to popularize the long-range utility standard as "solid ethics" and as the clear and realistic approach. This standard requires that actions be judged as ethical or unethical according to their ultimate long-range consequences for the individual. Thus, breaking a promise might be expedient in a present situation but greatly risks bad reputation—and consequent failure—for the long-term future, and is therefore judged to be unethical.

A consultant, accepting an assignment that he knows is beyond his capability, may ease immediate financial pressures; but when his mediocre performance becomes known, his reputation and success for the long-term are jeopardized. Also unethical by the long-rage utility standard are practices that, although currently convenient and profitable for an organization, lead to stiff and excessive government regulation. In essence, this standard builds ethics upon a realistic foundation of enlightened self-interest, intelligent self-interest, mutual self-interest, and similar expressions to be found in the literature of pragmatism.

The general law standard states: So act that your act could be made a general law which could be proved, from human experience, to work toward general human and social success. We have the German philosopher Immanuel Kant and, later, the American pragmatists to thank for the general law standard; it serves as a most interesting—and usually quite revealing—test of the basic ethicalness of any contemplated action or decision. The general law standard requires that we judge action as ethical or unethical by asking, "Suppose *everybody* did this." For example, suppose a securities broker is sorely tempted to misrepresent certain stocks and has, in his mind, just about "justified" it for reasons of personal problems and pressures; then he calls upon the general law standard and puts his contemplated action to the test by saying, "Suppose *everybody* did this." Assuming any degree of objectivity, reasonableness, and realism on his part, he would have to conclude that if everybody misrepresented securities, obviously a vital social structure would simply collapse, Hence, the act is clearly unethical. The act of a consultant accepting an assignment for which he is not really qualified also fails to pass the test of the general law standard.

 ## ETHICAL CODES

Using the two terms in the strict sense, as conventionally employed in the literature of ethics, ethical *standards* are general maxims and ethical *codes* are very specific statements of what is regarded as right or wrong within a particular situation in the here and now. Of course, whether or not such a code is enforced is another question, which was discussed in the section on ethical sanctions. The concept of a code of ethics is precise; it is a set of specific statements indicating actions considered ethical (positive), and actions considered unethical (negative). Such statements are developed by the realistic application of general ethical standards to current situations and environment. For example, a consulting organization might adopt, as part of its ethical code, the statement that "no member consultant shall accept an assignment when there is any doubt about his qualifications to attempt the assignment," such statements representing a clear application of the golden rule, long-range utility, and general law standards.

A written code of ethics provides quick and clear-cut ethical criteria for day-to-day actions, as well as the determination of the ethicalness of such actions. A clear, specific code of ethics (or the lack thereof) patently demonstrates any organization's serious interest (or lack thereof) in a professional ethical posture.

The most critical, and difficult, part of ethical analysis is this *application* of general ethical standards in an attempt to develop specific norms for ethical action within an organization and to determine the true ethical quality of a particular action in a concrete situation. The most common errors in ethical analysis occur in this area of application:

An organization code of ethics is developed that is carelessly or deliberately vague and too general to apply.

Ethical standards are applied to a specific issue or concrete case in which the factual situation is inadequately or inaccurately understood. For example, is it unethical for the consultant to accept a job when he has informed the client of some limitation in qualification and, despite this, the client asks him to "at least try?"

In attempting to conduct intelligent ethical analysis, vague or no reference is made to any theoretical and systematic framework—most importantly to the broad ethical standards.

No sanctions, or vague or unrealistic sanctions, are adopted for an ethical code. Sanctions, such as rules, policies, managerial control systems, and appropriate rewards for compliance and penalties for noncompliance, are essential to the enforcement of an ethical code.

In summary, a new age of instant information and public insistence on ethical behavior has transformed . . . ethics from an ideal condition to a reality, from a luxury to a practical necessity for the survival and success of organizations. The central instrument for making ethics operational and real in an organization is a written code of ethics which is specific, is both positive and negative in its ethical content, is based upon general ethical standards, and is enforceable by appropriate sanctions.

6.
Ethical Chic
Peter F. Drucker

Ethics is rapidly becoming the "in" subject, replacing yesterday's "social responsibilities." "Business ethics" is now being taught in departments of philosophy, business schools, and theological seminaries. There are countless seminars on it, speeches, articles, conferences and books, not to mention the many earnest attempts to write "business ethics" into the law. But what precisely is "business ethics"? And what could, or should, it be? Is it just another fad, and only the latest round in the hoary American blood sport of business baiting? Is there more to "ethics" than the revivalist preacher's call to the sinner to repent? And if there is indeed something that one could call "business ethics" and could take seriously, what could it be?

BUSINESS ETHICS AND THE WESTERN TRADITION

To the moralist of the Western tradition "business ethics" would make no sense. Indeed, the very term would to him be most objectionable, and reeking of moral laxity. The authorities on ethics disagreed, of course, on what constitutes the grounds of morality—whether they be divine, human nature or the needs of society. They equally disagreed on the specific rules of ethical behavior; that sternest set of moral rules, the Ten Commandments, for instance, thunders "Thou shalt not covet thy neighbor's. . . maidservant." But it says nothing about "sexual harassment" of "one's own" women employees, though it was surely just as common then as now.

All authorities of the Western tradition—from the Old Testament prophets all the way to Spinoza in the 17th century, Kant in the 18th century, Kierkegaard in the 19th century and, in this century, the Englishman F.H. Bradley *(Ethical*

47

Studies) or the American Edmond Cahn *(The Moral Decision)*—are, however, in complete agreement on one point: There is only one ethics, one set of rules of morality, one code—that of *individual* behavior in which the same rules apply to everyone alike.

A pagan could say, *"Quod licet Jovi non licet bovi."* He could thus hold that different rules of behavior apply to Jupiter from those that apply to the ox. A Jew or a Christian would have to reject such differentiation in ethics—and precisely because all experience shows that it always leads to exempting the "Jupiters," the great, powerful and rich, from the rules that "the oxen," the humble and poor, have to abide by.

The only differences between what is ethically right and ethically wrong behavior that traditional moralists, almost without exception, would accept—would indeed insist on—are differences grounded in social or cultural mores, and then only in respect to "venial" offenses. That is, the way things are done rather than the substance of behavior. Even in the most licentious society, fidelity to the marriage vow is meritorious, all moralists would agree; but the sexual license of an extremely "permissive" society, say, 17th-century Restoration England or late 20th-century America, might be considered an "extenuating circumstance" for the sexual transgressor. And even the sternest moralist has always insisted that, excepting only true "matters of conscience," practices that are of questionable morality in one place and culture might be perfectly acceptable—and indeed might be quite ethical—in another cultural surrounding. Nepotism may be considered of dubious morality in one culture, in today's U.S., for instance. In other cultures, a traditional Chinese one, for example, it may be the very essence of ethical behavior, both by satisfying the moral obligation to one's family and by making disinterested service to the public a little more likely.

But—and this is the crucial point—these are qualifications to the fundamental axiom on which the Western tradition of ethics has always been based: There is only one code of ethics, that of individual behavior, for prince and pauper, for rich and poor, for the mighty and the meek alike. Ethics, in the Judeo-Christian tradition, is the affirmation that all men and women are alike creatures—whether the Creator be called God, Nature or Society.

And this fundamental axiom "business ethics" denies. Viewed from the mainstream of traditional ethics, "business ethics" is not ethics at all, whatever else it may be. For it asserts that acts that are not immoral or illegal if done by ordinary folk become immoral or illegal if done by "business."

One blatant example is the treatment of extortion in the current discussions of "business ethics." No one ever has had a good word to say for extortion, or has advocated paying it. But if you and I are found to have paid extortion money under threat of physical or material harm, we are not considered to have behaved immorally or illegally. The extortioner is both immoral and a criminal. If a business submits to extortion, however, current "business ethics" considers it to have acted unethically. There is no speech, article, book or conference on "business ethics," for instance, which does not point an accusing finger in great indignation at Lockheed for giving in to a Japanese airline company that extorted money as a prerequisite to considering the purchase of Lockheed's faltering L-1011 jet plane. There was very little difference between Lockheed's paying the Japanese and the pedestrian in New York's Central Park handing his wallet over to a mugger. Yet no one would consider the pedestrian to have acted "unethically."

Similarly, in Senate confirmation hearings, one of President Reagan's Cabinet appointees was accused of "unethical practices" and investigated for weeks because his New Jersey construction company was alleged to have paid money to union goons under the threat of their beating up the employees, sabotaging the trucks and vandalizing the building sites. The accusers were self-confessed labor racketeers; no one seemed to have worried about their "ethics."

One can argue that both Lockheed and the New Jersey builder were stupid to pay the holdup men. But as the old saying has it: "Stupidity is not a court-martial offense." Under the new "business ethics," it does become exactly that, however. And this is not compatible with what "ethics" always was supposed to be.

The new "business ethics" also denies to business the adaptation to cultural mores that has always been considered a moral duty in the traditional approach to ethics. It is now considered "grossly unethical"—indeed it may even be a "questionable practice," if not criminal offense—for an American business operating in Japan to retain as a "counselor" the distinguished civil servant who retires from his official position in the Japanese government. Yet the business that does not do this is considered in Japan to behave antisocially and to violate its clear ethical duties. Business taking care of retired senior civil servants, the Japanese hold, makes possible two practices they consider essential to the public interest: that a civil servant past age 45 must retire as soon as he is outranked by anyone younger than he; and that governmental salaries and retirement pensions—and with them the burden of the bureaucracy on the taxpayer—be kept low, with the difference between what a first-rate man gets in government service and what he might earn in private employment made up after his retirement through his "counselor's fees." The Japanese maintain that the expectation of later on being a "counselor" encourages a civil servant to remain incorruptible, impartial and objective, and thus to serve only the public good; his counselorships are obtained for him by his former ministry, and its recommendation depends on his rating by his colleagues as a public servant. The Germans, who follow a somewhat similar practice—with senior civil servants expected to be "taken care of" through appointment as industry-association executives—share this conviction.

Yet, despite the fact that both the Japanese and the German systems seem to serve their respective societies well and indeed honorably, and even despite the fact that it is considered perfectly "ethical" for American civil servants of equal rank and caliber to move into well-paid executive jobs in business and foundations and into even more lucrative law practices, the American company in Japan that abides by a practice the Japanese consider the very essence of "social responsibility" is pilloried in the present discussion of "business ethics" as a horrible example of "unethical practices."

Surely "business ethics"assumes that for some reason the ordinary rules of ethics do not apply to business. "Business ethics," in other words, is not "ethics" at all, as the term has commonly been used by Western philosophers and Western theologians. What is it, then?

CASUISTRY: THE ETHICS OF SOCIAL RESPONSIBILITY

"It's casuistry," the historian of Western philosophy would answer. Casuistry asserted that rulers, because of their responsibility, have to strike a balance between the ordinary demands of ethics that apply to them as individuals and their "social responsibility" to their subjects, their kingdom—or their company.

"Casuistry" was first propounded in Calvin's *Institutes,* then taken over by the Catholic theologians of the Counter-Reformation (St. Robert Bellarmine, for instance, or St. Charles Borromeo) and developed into a "political ethics" by their Jesuit disciples in the 17th century.

"Casuistry" was the first attempt to think through "social responsibility" and to embed in it a set of special ethics for those in power. In this respect, "business ethics" tries to do exactly what the Casuists did 400 years ago. And it must end the same way. If "business ethics" continues to be "casuistry" its speedy demise in a cloud of ill repute can be confidently predicted.

To the Casuist the "social responsibility" inherent in being a "ruler"—that is, someone whose actions have impact on others—is by itself an ethical imperative. As such, the ruler has a duty, as Calvin first laid down, to subordinate his individual behavior and his individual conscience to the demands of his social responsibility.

The *locus classicus* of casuistry is Henry VIII and his first marriage, to Catherine of Aragon. A consummated marriage—and Catherine of Aragon had a daughter by Henry, the future "Bloody Mary"—could not be dissolved except by death, both Catholic and Protestant theologians agreed. In casuistry, however, as both Catholics and Protestants agreed, Henry VIII had an ethical duty to seek annulment of the marriage. Until his father, well within living memory, had snatched the Crown by force of arms, England had suffered a century of blody and destructive civil war because of the lack of a legitimate male heir. Without annulment of his marriage, Henry VIII, in other words, exposed his country and its people to mortal danger, well beyond anything he could in conscience justify. The one point on which Protestants and Catholics disagreed was whether the Pope also had a social, and thereby an ethical, responsibility to grant Henry's request. By not granting it, he drove the King and his English subjects out of the Catholic Church. But had he granted the annulment, the

Catholic Casuists argued, the Pope would have driven Catherine's uncle, the Holy Roman Emperor, out of the Church and into the waiting arms of an emerging Protestantism; and that would have meant that instead of assigning a few million Englishmen to heresy, perdition and hell-fire, many times more souls—all the people in all the lands controlled by the Emperor, that is, in most of Europe—could have been consigned to everlasting perdition.

This may be considered a quaint example—but only because our time measures behavior in economic rather than theological absolutes. The example illustrates what is wrong with casuistry and indeed why it must fail as an approach to ethics. In the first place casuistry must end up becoming politicized, precisely because it considers social responsibility an ethical absolute. In giving primacy to political values and goals it subordinates ethics to politics. Clearly this is the approach "business ethics" today is taking. Its very origin is in politics rather than in ethics. It expresses a belief that the responsibility which business and the business executive have, precisely because they have social impact, must determine ethics—and this is a political rather than an ethical imperative.

Equally important, the Casuist inevitably becomes the apologist for the ruler, the powerful. Casuistry starts out with the insight that the behavior of "rulers" affects more than themselves and their families. It thus starts out by making demands on the ruler—the starting point for both Calvin and his Catholic disciples in the Counter-Reformation 50 years later. It then concludes that "rulers" must, therefore, in conscience and ethics, subordinate their interests, including their individual morality, to their social responsibility. But this implies that the rules that decide what is ethical for ordinary people do not apply equally, if at all, to those with social responsibility. Ethics for them is insted a cost-benefit calculation involving the demands of individual conscience and the demands of position—and that means the "rulers" are exempt from the demands of ethics, if only their behavior can be argued to confer benefits on other people. And this is precisely how "business ethics" is going.

Indeed, under a Casuist's analysis the ethical violations that to most present proponents of "business ethics" seems the most heinous crimes turn out to have been practically saintly.

Take Lockheed's bribe story, for instance. Lockheed was led into paying extortion money to a Japanese airline by the collapse of the suplier of the engines for its wide-bodied L-1011 passenger jet, the English Rolls-Royce Co. At that time Lockheed employed some 25,000 people making L-1011s, most of them in southern California, which then (1972-73) was suffering substantial unemployment from sharp cutbacks in defense orders in the aerospace industry. To safeguard the 25,000 jobs, Lockheed got a large government subsidy. But to be able to maintain these jobs, Lockheed needed at least one large L-1011 order from one major airline. The only one among the major airlines not then committed to a competitor's plane was All-Nippon Airways in Japan. The self-interest of Lockheed Corp. and of its stockholders would clearly have demanded speedy abandonment of the L-1011. It was certain that it would never make money—and it has not made a penny yet. Jettisoning the L-1011 would immediately have boosted Lockheed's earnings—maybe doubled them—and Lockheed's share price. Stock market analysts and investment bankers pleaded with the firm to get rid of the albatross. If Lockheed had abandoned the L-1011, instead of paying extortion money to the Japanese for ordering a few planes and thus keeping the project alive, the company's earnings, its stock price and the bonuses and stock options of top management would immediately have risen sharply. Not to have paid extortion money to the Japanese would to a Casuist have been self-serving. To a Casuist, paying the extortion money was a duty and social responsibility to which the self-interest of the company, its shareholders and its executives had to be subordinated. It was the discharge of social responsibility of the "ruler" to keep alive the jobs of 25,000 people at a time when jobs in the aircraft industry in southern California were scarce indeed.

Similarly, the other great "horror story" of "business ethics" would, to the Casuist, appear as an example of "business virtue," if not of unselfish "business martyrdom." In the "electrical apparatus conspiracy" of the late 1950s, several high-ranking General Electric executives were sent to jail. They were found guilty of a criminal conspiracy in violation of antitrust laws because orders for heavy generating equipment, such as turbines, were parceled out among the three electrical apparatus manufacturers in the U.S.—General Electric, Westinghouse, and Allis-Chalmers. But this "criminal conspiracy" only served to reduce General Electric's sales, its profits and the bonuses and stock options of the General Electric executives who took part in the conspiracy. Since the electric apparatus cartel was destroyed by the criminal prosecution of the General Electric executives, General Electric sales and profits in the heavy apparatus field have sharply increased, as has market penetration by the company, which how has what amounts to a near-monopoly. The purpose of the cartel—which incidentally was started under federal government pressure in the Depression years to fight unemployment—was the protection of the weakest and most dependent of the companies, Allis-Chalmers (which is located in Milwaukee, a depressed and declining old industrial area). As soon as government action destroyed the cartel, Allis-Chalmbers had to go out of the turbine business and had to lay off several thousand people. And while there is still abundant competition in the world market for heavy electric apparatus, General Electric now enjoys such market dominance in the home market that the U.S., in case of war, would not have major alternative suppliers of so critical a product as turbines.

The Casuist would agree that cartels are both illegal and considered immoral in the U.S.—although not necessarily anyplace else in the world. But he would also argue that the General Electric executive who violated U.S. law had an ethical duty to do so under the "higher law" of social responsibility to safeguard both employment in the Milwaukee area and the defense-production base of the U.S.

The only thing surprising about these examples is that business has not yet used them to climb on the Casuist bandwagon of "business ethics." For just as almost any behavior indulged in by the 17th-century ruler could be shown to be an ethical duty by the 17th-century disciples of Calvin, of Bellarmine and of Borromeo, so almost any behavior of the executive in organizations today—whether in a business, a hospital, a university or a government agency—could be shown to be his ethical duty under the casuistic cost-benefit analysis between individual ethics and the demands of social responsibility. There are indeed signs aplenty that the most apolitical of "rulers," the American business executive, is waking up to the political potential of "business ethics." Some of the advertisements that large companies—Mobil Oil, for example—are now running to counter the attacks made on them in the name of "social responsibility" and "business ethics" clearly use the casuist approach to defend business, and indeed to counterattack. But if "business ethics" becomes a tool to defend as "ethical" acts on the part of executives that would be condemned if committed by anyone else, the present proponents of "business ethics," like their Casuist predecessors 400 years ago, will have no one to blame but themselves.

Casuistry started out as high morality. In the end, its ethics came to be summed up in two well-known pieces of cynicism. "An ambassador is an honest man, lying abroad for the good of his country" went an 18th-century pun. And a hundred years later, Bismarck said, "What a scoundrel a minister would be if, in his own private life, he did half the things he has a duty to do to be true to his oath of office."

THE ETHICS OF PRUDENCE AND SELF—DEVELOPMENT

There is one, other major tradition of ethics in the West, the Ethics of Prudence. It goes all the way back to Aristotle and his enthronement of Prudence as a cardinal virtue. It continued for almost 2,000 years in the popular literary tradition of the "Education of the Christian Prince," which reached its ultimate triumph and its reduction to absurdity in Machiavelli's *The Prince*. Its spirit can best be summed up by the advice that then-Senator Harry Truman gave to an Army witness before his committee in the early years of World War II: "Generals should never do anything that needs to be explained to a Senate committee—there is nothing one can explain to a Senate committee."

"Generals," whether the organization is an army, a corporation or a university, are highly visible. They must expect their behavior to be seen, scrutinized, analyzed, discussed and questioned. Prudence thus demands that they shun actions that cannot easily be understood, explained or justified. But "Generals," being visible, are also examples. They are "leaders" by their very position and visibility. Their choice is whether their example leads others to right action or to wrong action, between direction and misdirection, between leadership and misleadership. They thus have an ethical obligation to give the example of right behavior and to avoid giving the example of wrong behavior.

The Ethics of Prudence do not spell out what "right" behavior is. They assume that what is wrong behavior is clear enough—and if there is any doubt, it is "questionable" and to be avoided. Prudence makes it an ethical duty for the leader to exemplify the precepts of ethics in his own behavior.

And by following Prudence, everyone regardless of status becomes a "leader," a "superior man," and will "fulfill himself," to use the contemporary idiom. One becomes the "superior man" by avoiding any act that would make one the kind of person one does not want to be, does not respect, does not accept as superior. "If you don't want to see a pimp when you look in the shaving mirror in the morning, don't hire call girls the night before to entertain congressmen, customers or salesmen." On any other basis, hiring call girls may be condemned as vulgar and tasteless and may be shunned as something fastidious people do not do. It may be frowned upon as uncouth. It may even be illegal. But only in Prudence is it ethically relevant. This is what Kierkegaard, the sternest moralist of the 19th century, meant when he said that aesthetics is the true ethics.

The Ethics of Prudence can easily degenerate. Concern with that one can justify becomes, only too easily, concern with appearances—Machiavelli was by no means the first to point out that in a "Prince," that is, in someone in authority and high visibility, appearances may matter more than substance. The Ethics of Prudence thus easily decay into the hypocrisy of "public relations."

Yet, despite these degenerative tendencies, the Ethics of Prudence is surely appropriate to a society of organizations. Of course, it will not be "business ethics"—it makes absolutely no difference in the Ethics of Prudence whether the executive is a general in the Army, a bureau chief in the Treasury Department in Washington, a senator, a judge, a senior vice president in a bank or a hospital administrator. But a "society of organizations" is a society in which an extraordinarily large number of people are in positions of high visibility, if only within one organization. They enjoy this visibility not, like the "Christian Prince," by virtue of birth, nor by virtue of wealth—that is, not because they are "personages." They are "functionaries" and important only through their responsibility to take right action. But this is exactly what the Ethics of Prudence is all about.

Similarly, executives set examples, whatever the organization. They "set the tone," "create the spirit," "decide the values" for an organization and for the people in it. They lead or mislead, in other words. And they have no choice but to do one or the other. Above all, the ethics or aesthetics of self-development would seem to be tailor-made for the specific dilemma of the executive in the modern organization. By himself he is a nobody and indeed anonymous. A week after he has retired and left that big corner office on the twenty-sixth floor of his company's skyscraper or the Secretary's six-room corner suite on Constitution Avenue, no one in the building even recognizes him anymore. Yet collectively these anonymous executives are the "leaders" in a modern society. Their function demands the self-discipline and the self-respect of the "superior man." To live up to the performance expectations society makes upon them, they have to strive for self-fulfillment rather than be content with lackadaisical mediocrity.

One would therefore expect the discussion of "business ethics" to focus on the Ethics of Prudence. Some of the words, such as to "fulfill oneself," indeed sound the same, though they mean something quite different. But by and large, the discussion of "business ethics," even if more sensibly concerning itself with the "ethics of organization," will have nothing to do with prudence.

The reason is clearly that the Ethics of Prudence is the ethics of authority. And while today's discussion of "business ethics" (or of the ethics of university administration, of hospital administration or of government) clamors for responsibility, it rejects out of hand any "authority" and, of course, particularly any authority of the business executive. Authority is not "legitimate"; it is "elitism." But there can be no responsibility where authority is denied. To deny it is not "anarchism" nor "radicalism," let alone "socialism." In a child, it is called a temper tantrum.

THE ETHICS OF INTERDEPENDENCE

Casuistry was so thoroughly discredited that the only mention of it to be found in most textbooks on the history of philosophy is in connection with its ultimate adversaries—Spinoza and Pascal. Indeed, only 10 or 15 years ago, few if any philosophers would have thought it possible for anything like "business ethics" to emerge. "Particularist ethics," a set of ethics that postulates that this or that group is different in its ethical responsibilities from everyone else, would have been considered doomed forever by the failure of casuistry. Ethics, almost anyone in the West would have considered axiomatic, would surely always be ethics of the individual and independent of rank and station.

But there is another non-Western ethics that is situational. It is the most successful and most durable ethics of them all: the Confucian ethics of interdependence.

Confucian ethics elegantly side-steps the trap into which the Casuists fell; it is a universal ethic in which the same rules and imperatives of behavior hold for every individual. There is no "social responsibility" overriding individual conscience, no cost-benefit calculation, no greater good or higher measure than the individual and his behavior, and altogether no casuistry. In the Confucian ethics, the rules are the same for all. But there are different general rules, according to the five basic relationships of interdependence, which for the Confucian embrace the totality of individual interactions in civil society: superior and subordinate (or master and servant); father and child; husband and wife; oldest brother and sibling; friend and friend. Right behavior—which in the English translation of

Confucian ethics is usually called "sincerity"[1]—is that individual behavior which is truly appropriate to the specific relationship of mutual dependence because it optimizes benefits for both parties. Other behavior is "insincere" and therefore wrong behavior and unethical. It creates dissonance instead of harmony, exploitation instead of benefits, manipulation instead of trust.

An example of the Confucian approach to the ethical problems discussed under the heading of "business ethics" would be "sexual harassment." To the Confucian it is clearly unethical behavior because it injects power into a relationship that is based on function. This makes it exploitation. That this "insincere"—that is, grossly unethical—behavior on the part of a superior takes place within a business or any other kind of organization is basically irrelevant. The master/servant or superior/subordinant relationship is one between individuals. Hence, the Confucian would make no distinction between a general manager forcing his secretary into sexual intercourse and Mr. Samuel Pepys, England's famous 17th-century diarist, forcing his wife's maids to submits to his amorous advances. It would not even make much difference to the Confucian that today's secretary can, as a rule, quit without suffering more than inconvenience if she does not want to submit, whereas the poor wretches in Mrs. Pepys' employ ended up as prostitutes, either because they did not submit and were fired and out on the street, or because they did submit and were fired when they got pregnant. Nor would the Confucian see much difference between a corporation vice president engaging in "sexual harassment" and a college professor seducing coeds with implied promised to raise their grades.

And finally, it would be immaterial to the Confucian that the particular "insincerity" involves sexual relations. The superior would be equally guilty of grossly unethical behavior and violation of fundamental rules of conduct if, as a good many of the proponents of "business ethics" ardently advocate, he were to set himself up as a mental therapist for his subordinates and help them to "adjust." No matter how benevolent his intentions, this is equally incompatible with the integrity of the superior/subordinate relationship. It equally abuses rank based on function and imposes power. It is therefore exploitation whether done because of lust for power or manipulation or done out of benevolence— either way it is unethical and destructive. Both sexual relations and the healer/ patient relationship must be free of rank to be effective, harmonious and ethically correct. They are constructive only as "friend to friend" or as "husband to wife" relations, in which differences in function confer no rank whatever.

This example makes it clear, I would say, that virtually all the concerns of "business ethics," indeed almost everything "business ethics" considers a problem, have to do with relationships of interdependence, whether that between the organization and the employee, the manufacturer and the customer, the hospital and the patient, the university and the student, and so on.

But in today's American—and European—discussion of "business ethics," ethics means that one side has obligations and the other side has rights, if not "entitlements." This is not compatible with the ethics of interdependence and indeed with any ethics at all. It is the politics of power, and indeed the politics of naked exploitation and repression. And within the context of interdependence the "exploiters" and the "oppressors" are not the "bosses" but the ones who assert their "rights" rather than accept mutual obligation, and with it, equality.

To illustrate: Today's "ethics of organization" debate pays great attention to the duty to be a "whistle-blower" and to the protection of the "whistle-blower" against retaliation or suppression by his boss or by his organization. This sounds high-minded. Surely, the subordinate has a right, if not indeed a duty, to bring to public attention and remedial action his superior's misdeeds, let alone violation of the law on the part of a superior or of his employing organization. But in the context of the ethics of interdependence, "whistle-blowing" is ethically quite ambiguous. To be sure, there are misdeeds of the superior or of the employing organization that so grossly violate propriety and laws that the subordinate (or the friend, or the child or even the wife) cannot remain silent. This is, after all, what the word "felony" implies; one becomes a partner to a felony and criminally liable by not reporting, and thus "compounding," it. But otherwise? It is not primarily that to encourage "whistle-blowing" corrodes the bond of trust that ties the superior to the subordinate. Encouraging the "whistle-blower" must make the subordinate lose his trust in the superior's willingness and ability to "protect his people." They simply are no longer "his people" and become potential enemies or political pawns. And in the end, encouraging and indeed even permitting "whistleblowers" always makes the weaker one—that is, the subordinate—powerless against the unscrupulous superior, simply because the superior no longer can recognize or meet his obligation to the subordinate.

"Whistle-blowing," after all, is simply another word for "informing." And perhaps it is not quite irrelevant that the only societies in Western history that encouraged informers were bloody and infamous tyrannies—Tiberius and Nero in Rome, the Inquisition in the Spain of Philip II, the French Terror and Stalin. It may also be no accident that Mao, when he tried to establish dictatorship in China, organized "whistle-blowing" on a massive scale. For under "whistle-blowing," under the regime of the "informer," no mutual trust, no interdependencies and no ethics are possible. And Mao only followed history's first "totalitarians," the "Legalists" of the 3rd century B.C., who suppressed Confucius and burned his books because he had taught ethics and had rejected the absolutism of political power.

Discussion of "business ethics" today tends to assert that in relations of interdependence one side has all the duties and the other one all the rights. But this is the assertion of the Legalist, the assertion of the totalitarians who shortly end up by denying all ethics. It must also mean that ethics becomes the tool of the powerful. If a set of ethics is one-sided, then the rules are written by those that have the position, the power, the wealth. If interdependence is not equality of obligations, it becomes domination.

"ETHICAL CHIC" OR ETHICS

"Business ethics," this discussion should have made clear, is to ethics what soft porn is to the Platonic Eros; soft porn, too, talks of something it calls "love." And insofar as "business ethics" comes even close to ethics, it comes close to casuistry and will, predictably, end up as a fig leaf for the shameless and as special pleading for the powerful and the wealthy.

Clearly, one major element of the peculiar stew that goes by the name of "business ethics" is plain old-fashioned hostility to business and to economic activity altogether—one of the oldest of American traditions and perhaps the only still-potent ingredient in the Puritan heritage. Otherwise, we would not even talk of "business ethics."

But one explanation for the popularity of "business ethics" is surely also the human frailty of which Pascal accused the Casuists of his day: the lust for power and prominence of a clerisy sworn to humility. "Business ethics" is fashionable, and provides speeches at conferences, lecture fees, consulting assignments and lots of publicity. And surely "business ethics," with its tales of wrongdoing in high places, caters also to the age-old enjoyment of "society" gossip and to the prurience that (it was, I believe, Rabelais who said it) makes it fornication when a peasant has a toss in the hay and romance when the prince does it.

Althogether, "business ethics" might well be called "ethical chic" rather than ethics—and indeed might be considered more a media event than philosophy or morals.

But this discussion of the major approaches to ethics and of their concerns surely also shows that ethics has as much to say to the individual in our society of organizations as it ever had to say to the individual in earlier societies. It is just as important and just as needed nowadays. And it certainly requires hard and serious work.

A society of organizations is a society of interdependence. The specific relationship that the Confucian philosopher postulated as universal and basic may not be adequate, or even appropriate, to modern society and to the ethical problems within the modern organization and between the modern organization and its clients, customers and constituents. But the fundamental concepts surely are. Indeed, if there ever is a viable "ethics of organization," it will almost certainly have to adopt the key concepts that have made Confucian ethics both durable and effective:

• clear definition of the fundamental relationships;

• universal and general rules of conduct—that is, rules that are binding on any one person or organization, acording to its rules, function and relationships;

• focus on right behavior rather than on avoiding wrongdoing, and on behavior rather than on motives or intentions;

• an effective oganization ethic, indeed an organization ethic that deserves to be seriously considered as "ethics," will have to define right behavior as the behavior that optimizes each party's benefits and thus makes the relationship harmonious, constructive and mutually beneficial.

But a society of organizations is also a society in which a great many people are unimportant and indeed anonymous by themselves, yet are highly visible, and matter as "leaders" in society. And thus it is a society that must stress the Ethics of Prudence and self-development. It must expect its managers, executives and professionals to demand of themselves that they shun behavior they would not respect in others, and instead practice behavior appropriate to the sort of person they would want to see "in the mirror in the morning."

---

[1] No word has caused more misunderstanding in East/West relations than "sincerity." To a Westerner, "sincerity" means "words that are true to conviction and feelings"; to an Easterner, "sincerity" means "actions that are appropriate to a specific relationship and make it harmonious and of optimum mutual benefit." For the Westerner, "sincerity" has to do with intentions, that is, with morality; to the Easterner, "sincerity" has to do with behavior, that is, with ethics.

Selected Readings
Part II.

Agee, William M. "The Moral and Ethical Climate in Today's Business World." *Michigan State University Business Topics*. 26 (Winter 1978); 16-19.

"Big Crusade of the '80's: More Rights for Workers." *U.S. News and World Report*. 86 (March 26, 1976); 86-87.

Bowman, James S., ed. "Special Issue on Ethics in Government."*Public Personnel Management*. 10 (1981); entire.

Caiden, Gerald E., and Caiden, Naomi J. "Administration Corruption." *Public Administration Review*. 37 (May/June 1977); 301-9.

———. "Coping with Administrative Corruption: An Academic Perspective." In *Dynamics of Development: An International Perspective*, edited by S.K. Shama. New Delhi: Concept Publishing, 1979, pp. 478-94.

Clinard, Marshall B. et al. *Illegal Corporate Behavior*. Washington, D.C.: National Institute of Law Enforcement and Criminal Justice, 1979.

Comptroller General. *Fraud in Government Programs: How Extensive Is it? Can it Be Controlled?* Vol. 1. Washington, D.C.: General Accounting Office, 1981.

D'Aprix, Roger M. *In Search of a Corporate Soul*. New York: AMACON, 1976.

Fulmer, Robert M. "Ethics and the Executive." In his *The New Management*. 2nd ed. New York: MacMillan Publishing Co., Inc., 1978, Chap. 20.

Hoffmann, W. Michael, ed. *Proceedings of the Second National Conference on Business Ethics: Power and Responsibility in the American Business System:* Washington, D.C.: University Press of America, 1979.

Lerner, Max. "Business Ethics at Home and Abroad." *Personnel Administration*. 22 (August 1977); 13-16, 24.

Miller, William Lee. *Of Thee, Nevertheless, I Sing: An Essay in American Political Values*. New York: Harcourt, Brace Jovanovich, Inc., 1975.

———. "Political Ethics—Then and Now." *Center Magazine*. 8 (July/August 1975): 63-68.

Ross, Irwin. "How Lawless Are Big Companies?" *Fortune*. 102 (December 1, 1980); 57ff.

Rokeach, Milton. *The Nature of Human Values*. New York: The Free Press, 1978.

Sethi, P. Prakash. *Crime in the Executive Suites: Executive Criminal Liability for Corporate Law Violations*. Cambridge, Mass: Oelgeschlager, Gunn, and Hain, Inc., 1981.

Snyder, David P. "The Uncivil Servant." *The Bureaucrat*. 2 (Fall 1973): 310-14.

Sobel, Lester A., ed. *Post-Watergate Morality*. New York: Facts on File, 1978.

———. *Corruption in Business*. New York: Facts on File, 1977.

Sommers, Albert T. "A Collection of Ethics and Economics." *Across the Board*. 15 (July 1978): 14-19.

Walton, Clarence C., ed. *The Ethics of Corporate Conduct*. Englewood Cliffs, N.J.: Prentice-Hall, Inc., 1977.

Part III.
The Organization and the Individual: Ethical Dilemmas

Democracy relies heavily upon personal integrity as well as trust, and confidence between the public and its institutions. The citizenry, in fact, has been able to depend on the professional self-discipline of the majority of executives. Since each employee has the opportunity every day to take steps towards engaging in ethical behavior, many Americans intuitively believe that improper conduct can be explained principally in terms of individual morality and personal deficiencies.

However, to the extent that organizations put people in situations where they have discretion, a number of administrators may find it difficult to determine what is appropriate conduct. Very real dilemmas arise for the manager when a collective consensus is lacking. In addition, the tendency to blame individuals accomplishes little to affect lasting change. It is for these reasons that an exclusive emphasis on the individual is an inadequate foundation for an understanding of managerial ethics (for excellent statements of this position see Robert F. Allen; T. Edwin Boling; and James G. Waters in the Selected Readings).

The public's unhappiness about ethical transgressions demonstrates the need to clarify standards. Although many people have a sense of right and wrong, only when a large number of individuals come together, can common expectations be established and achieved. That is, while behavior is a function of personal values, organizations, through their actions, endorse certain types of activity. Individual conduct takes place in a social context. Employees may make decisions based upon personal standards, but institutions define and control the situations in which these decisions are made. People's value systems, as a consequence, adapt to the environment in which they find themselves.

While private companies and government agencies resent being embarrassed by the disclosure of wrongdoing, they do not always act to discourage future improprieties from occurring. When interactions among people and institutions no longer provide normal opportunities for the exercise of integrity, organizations must assume at least partial responsibility for the conduct of their employees. It is not simply a question of employing saints in industry and in government. Instead, structural approaches to controlling power and preventing untoward behavior are necessary. A lack of clarity of an institution's normative ethos is serious since modern organizations are major agencies of social values. A fundamental change in the passive philosophy underlying ethical standards in bureaucracies must be fostered (Comptroller General, Selected Readings).

The chapters in this section explore the role of the individual and organizations in promoting ethical behavior. T. Edwin Boling begins by examining the ethics crisis from an organizational perspective. After discussing inadequate bases for understanding ethics (compare the chapters by Rohr and Lodge), he presents three principles that form a foundation for collective action. Pointing out the institutional context in which scandals have occurred in the last decade, Deena Weinstein abandons the traditional, *unitary* (in the words of Donaldson and Waller, chapter 11) view of organizations in favor of understanding them as political systems. Ethical action reveals their political nature since it punctures the myth of value free neutrality and social consensus in administrative theory.

Archie B. Carroll offers a global framework for ethical thinking, but then specifically identifies the immediate cause of the concerns described by Boling and Weinstein: management practices and superior-subordinate relations. He then previews actions to improve ethics that will be examined later in the book.

The Selected Readings for this unit provide a rich resource for additional exploration. Robert F. Allen draws an unattractive analogy between the behavior of many managers and that of the members of the Ik, a tribe in Africa, who exhibit a loss of humanity as a result of their desperate struggle for survival. Obedience in organizations, at socially dangerous levels, is analyzed by Gordon H. Fitch and Charles B. Saunders. An account of the unintended consequences of organizational operational and control systems is given by James A. Waters. Taking the traditional approach to ethics in bureaucracies, Susan Wakefield argues that the first line of defense against immoral conduct is individually developed values.

7.
The Management Ethics "Crisis": An Organizational Perspective

T. Edwin Boling

Because of recent scandals, business is under general condemnation for what one writer has called moral abhorrence. Media popularization of moral issues has increased public awareness and concern for ethical practices. Under pressure from public and government sources, business has begun to react, with tighter controls, stricter codes of conduct, penalties, and even ethics seminars. Max Ways, vol. 89, No. 5, *Fortune,* noted that managers remain unequivocally unprepared to deal with ethical problems, an assumption which tends to be supported by empirical evidence. Steven N. Brenner and Earl A. Mollander, both professors at Portland State University, examined the behavior and attitudes of 1,227 readers of the *Harvard Business Review.* Generally, the executives studied experienced ethical conflicts. They believed that while ethics constituted good business, most executives would tend to be unethical in much of their business behavior.

An interpretation of this behavior-attitude study exposes the dilemma of management toward the...ethics problem. Managers feel that most of the blame for unethical behavior may be placed upon individual failure and not upon the lack of organizational controls. Executives say that there ought to be an absolute social standard and that peer behavior should not be that standard. But, "when faced with ethical dilemmas, (the executives) refer to their immediate organizational framework for guidance." Consequently, somewhere between organizational dependence upon individual standards set by indoctrination, and the dependence of individuals upon organizational guidance, ethical behavior slips to scandalous dimensions.

This article suggests that the cause for such confusion may be related to the inadequacy of old ethical systems. The nature of these systems is examined and the analysis leads to theoretical and practical suggestions for a solution to management's ethical dilemma.

INADEQUATE ETHICAL BASES

Perhaps a question should be raised about whether there is an ethics "crisis" in business. Since there is more order in business than disorder, social scientists may contend that there is no crisis, and ethical practices *do* far out-number the unethical. Yet, even prior to recent "scandals," Thomas A. Petit, in *The Moral Crisis in Management,* declared that there was a "moral crisis in management," defined as a conflict between classical business ideology—an operational ethic which calls for profit through economic action—and managerial ideology, an ethic which stresses social responsibility. Perhaps this conflict between practice and ideology creates an *ethical lag,* if not a crisis. The lag is enhanced by structural change which tends to outdistance ideology (ethics). When craft production was replaced by family owned companies (which in turn were replaced by manager operated corporations), the complexities of human interaction were radically increased, creating more complex ethical concerns. But ethical guidelines remained those of the craft era.

Theistic Individualism

The first inadequate base for the ethical guidelines of business is a "theistic" approach which centers in Judaic-Christian morality. The theistic perspective is supported by biblical tradition and personal obligation to God. Although managers seem to fear such a "Sunday-schoolish" focus, a recent article stressed moving the ethics-business balance back to Medieval thought—responsibility to society and God.

In American society the theistic approach has been extended into a civil religion—a secular religiosity expressed in common beliefs, symbols, and rituals. At the heart of civil religion is the idea that this is the promised land. America is viewed as dedicated to order, law, justice, and as destined to a divine mission. But civil religion does not identify God, the Bible, or the Church, as sources of ethical behavior, nor does it reduce ethical behavior to a set of rules.

Common to both the theistic and civil religion orientations is a trust in individualism, demonstrated by personal integrity and individual achievement. Ethical practices are supposed to arise out of individual character shaped by commitment to religious, social, and philosophical beliefs. At the point of decision, one is to be guided by *his own* moral sense.

Ethical Legalism

A second inadequate base for managerial ethics may be called ethical legalism. This claim to ethical concern is represented by the well-worn phrase, "Our company abides by the law," which by interpretation often means, "We are ethical." Compliance is identified with what is "right," and right in this sense is a legal code. The role of law is to define the facts of social situations, to establish means for resolving contention and conflict, and to institute compromise toward a provisional solution of problems. For this purpose, laws are specific rules for behavior and sanctions. But since laws cannot prescribe all that ethical conduct should be for everyone in all situations, social mores are necessary to serve as the leading edge of laws. One may fully abide by the law and still remain unethical. The purpose of ethics should not be to identify or sanction the violation of rules, but should be to question the social, cultural, and personal impact of broken rules (moral or legal). In the strictest sense, ethical legalism falls short of a true ethical approach to business.

Ethics based upon theistic individualism or ethical legalism seems inappropriate for complex organizations in a changing society. As interactive systems, organizations are more than the sum of the individuals who interact within them. Equally, organizational ethics are more than the sum of personal codes or beliefs about personal integrity. Even as societal indoctrination produces unique personalities, so it produces a variety of ethical orientations. Because of this variety, theism is an inadequate base for managerial ethics. The principle of diversity necessitates the recognition of ethics as *organizational properties.* An organization should establish its own conduct standards, systematize its ethical obligations into clear, concise statements, and socialize its members toward understanding and conformity.

A SOCIAL ORGANIZATION APPROACH
TO MANAGERIAL ETHICS

Over twenty-five years ago, Chester Barnard in *Organization and Management,* expressed concern with the role of morality in the maintenance of organizations. Based upon a social science approach to morality, Barnard suggested the limitations of personal Judaic-Christian ethics and advocated the necessity of *organizational norms* of ethical quality. He believed that it was necessary for individual and organization interests to coincide. Although projecting an organizational dimension, his ideas are bound by the individualism of Judaic-Christian ideology.

Executive Codes of Conduct

Barnard's primary moral concern, in practice and theory, was *executive codes of conduct,* not *organizational norms.* In spite of his emphasis upon cooperative systems, codes of conduct are actually created by moralistic executives while workers cooperatively grant or accept this authority. This approach is no more than a personal code applicable to the collective through model leaders. Barnard called for an emulation of moral leaders similar to Judaic-Christian ideology. Moral rules are authoritative because of the power of charismatic leaders. George Strothers, vol. 1, no. 2, *The Academy of Management Reviews,* suggested that we harken back to Barnard for theoretical implications toward ethics could mean that management will remain in an ethical morass of contradiction and conflict.

Cooperative Social Relations

In contrast to Barnard and individualistic theism, Herbert A. Simon's theory in *Administrative Behavior,* implies an organizational ethic. He viewed individuals as having personal goals which do not always coincide with the organization. One makes a decision based upon personal standards; but an organization can control standards and define situations in which decisions are made. To shape behavior, the organization determines "premises of decision-making," premises found in the vocabulary, the structure of communication, the rules of regulations, and the programs of the organization.

Individual choices take place in the environment of such planned and highly structured premises. Although individuals may modify the environment, modification is mostlfy an organizational matter (for example, organizations put individuals in psychological environments that force adaptation of decisions to organizational objectives). Through training and indoctrination, individuals can be led to make decisions that are in compliance with organizational goals. Simon, in *Administrative Behavior* concludes:

> . . .the individual must in his decisions be subject to the influence of the organized group. His decisions must not only be the product of his own mental processes, but also reflect the broader considerations to which it is the function of the organized group to give effect.

Simon's theory implies that organization decision-making can set the stage for, and give direction to, moral development. Supporting this position, Piaget, a Swiss psychologist, theorizes that types of individual morality derive from the types of social structures in which individuals are involved. In explaining this thesis, Piaget holds that "autonomous" moral judgments are internalized on the basis of *cooperative social relations.* Given the necessity of autonomous moral action with demands for a "situation ethic," organizations may expect more effective moral decisions through cooperative social relations, or "social contract."

COOPERATIVE ETHICAL CONTRACTS

Three principles form a theoretical base for practical action toward a solution of the management ethics lag: (a) organizations establish ethical premises; (b) individual moral judgments reflect the norms of social groups; and (c) moral action is a matter of cooperative social relations. Refleclting the need for theory to be linked with practice, Ways contends in vol. 89, no. 5, *Fortune,* that:

> Old approaches to morality cannot build a bridge for two-way traffic of ethics building activity between business. . . and the larger society. . . (This) calls for visible, deliberate construction of ethical norms that make sense on both sides of the bridge.

Since ethical norms are group properties, ethics building is an organization function. Support for this principle of superiority of *group standards* over *personal ethics* is established in Robert A. Fulmer's study of national associations, vol. 19, *Association Management.* He shows how business has profited from conduct standards set forth in associational codes of ethics. According to this research, associations are much more effective than individuals would be in identifying ethical problems which call for standards of conduct. Fulmer also finds that ethical behavior is encouraged by associational solidarity, identification, and pressure. Finally, he reports that as sociations provide a source of ethical pronouncements which managers are likely to view as more respectable than the opinions of religious, political, and academic leaders.

Principle One

The first theoretical principle for an organizational ethic—*organizations establish ethical premises*—demands mechanisms of constancy which establish a continuity of standards. Some companies, quite serious about bridging the ethics gap, have recorded their expectations for cooperative moral judgments and have socialized their employees by the use of codes of ethics. Armco Steel Corporation adopted a code of ethics on December 12, 1919 (Armco Policies). This code made ethics *an organization policy* through a specific statement of conduct applicable to all levels of the organization. The code includes organizational commitment to quality production of products, the best of service to customers, opportunities for employee self-actualization, an even application of company rules, the nullification of conflicts of interest, and response to community needs. Implications are that individuals are components of the organization; there is little or no reference to dependence upon "individual integrity." While many companies reject the idea of a code, Armco has implemented its code through a specific program of socialization. A film and training manual are used for teaching the ideological and practical significance of the code, and studies are conducted to determine its effect.

Principle Two

The second theoretical principle of organizational ethics—*individual moral judgments reflect the norms of social groups*—is social psychological in nature. This principle indicates that individuals do not have ethics apart from socialization into group standards. Cooperation and patterned responses depend upon the continuance of social memory and the inheritance of ideas. Clarity and consistency are important for this internalization of performance standards. The substance of this social psychological approach is demonstrated in the code of ethical conduct adopted by International Harvester Company, January 19, 1961. This code identifies ethics in terms of *individual actions in an organizational context.* It was developed at the corporate headquarters and expresses company expectations for employees in relation to a number of specific rules, especially rules pertaining to conflict of interest. This instrument states company guidelines and permeates the vocabulary, communications, and programs of International Harvester Company. Individuals are expected to internalize these conduct standards, incorporating them into their own normative judgments. To guarantee this internalization, the company has its managers sign a statement each year which indicates understanding and compliance with the code.

Principle Three

The third principle for organizational ethics—*moral action is a matter of cooperative social relations*—represents an ideal as old as society itself, but toward which management seems suspicious. In a recent seminar on organizational ethics, the author proposed a democratic orientation toward ethical procedures. The proposal was met with a general attitude represented in a question by one participant, "What do you expect, that an army should vote before charging the hill?" Such an unrelated response reflects misguided sensitivity which is no doubt influenced by the Barnard view of ethics that management sets the rules. In contrast to this authoritarian approach, Fulmer's study of national associations identifies membership participation—a voice in formulation of rules—as a major factor in the success of conduct standards. He states in vol. 19, *Association Management:*

> Representatives of all segments within an organization should be asked to approve both the procedure and the content of a code at each stage of its development.

Codes serve as regulatory devices, diminishing the amount of police action which is needed for maintenance of order. Some feel that regulation, even by codes, should be coopted by persons or groups with powers of control. But the principle of cooperative social relations allows those who are controlled to become involved in setting their own controls. Although a basic principle in macro society, this notion may be applied at a micro level—the company. This application can remove sole dependence upon "individual integrity" as a model for ethical behavior, replacing it with a sense of social obligation. Although some managers depend upon rules of arbitration for control, these rules are insufficient for prescribing all ethical conduct.

Evidence is mounting in support of company and industry codes of ethics. In their study of managers, Brenner and Molander found that seventy-five percent of their respondents believed that codes of ethics would "help executives to: (a) raise the ethical level of their industry; (b) define the limits of acceptable conduct; and (c) refuse unethical requests." The researchers concluded that "the mere existence of a code, specific or general, can raise the ethical level of business behavior because it clarifies what is meant by ethical conduct." Successful experiments in participative industrial democracy point to the strengthening of organizational ethics with uniformly high product quality, lower absentees, virtually no thefts and property misuse, and so forth.

CONCLUSION

By establishing the fact that ethics are group properties,...ethics may be removed from the theistic, or "Sunday schoolish" notion. Perhaps because of this notion, business has an ethical lag—craft ethics in a bureaucratic era.

Traditionally, ethical standards for business have been treated as internalized "givens" which individuals derive from Judaic-Christian belief systems and civil religion. Watergate, the Lockheed scandal, the Securities and Exchange Commission investigations, and a host of other incidents, have demonstrated the inadequacy of his dependence. Corporations can no longer depend upon the trickling down of ethical standards from authorities to subordinates or an executive cannot be placed entirely upon personal integrity derived through theistic individualism. New technology, new moral questions, and new organizational dimensions, call for moral judgments that have been internalized through cooperatively developed codes of ethics. Just as organizations have shown concern for the continuous development of production skills and effective management, concern should now turn to cooperative codes of ethics which will serve as vehicles for shaping organizational morality.

8.
Organizations As Political Systems: Heroism and Legalism

Deena Weinstein

Although it might be comforting to believe that organizations do not commit abuses, the stress of news stories exposing misdeeds during the past decade should shatter such complacency for even those who pay little attention to public affiars. It might also be soothing to believe that when abuses do occur in organizations, those who identify them and attempt to rectify them, are honored. Again, comfort would be misplaced. Efforts to alleviate such conditions by employees who do not have authority, phenomena called here bureaucratic oppositions, are often interpreted as instances of psychopathology rather than as rational and morally legitimate activities. The notion is also widespread that those who oppose their superiors violate the essence of the employment contract, which is remuneration in exchange for obedient labor. According to this viewpoint, employees who encounter conditions that they judge to be abusive should resign themselves to those conditions or should terminate their employment: "If you can't stand the heat get out of the kitchen."

THE ORGANIZATION AS POLITICAL SYSTEM

The concept of the organization as a rational device for securing fixed ends efficiently, and "artifical system," has little utility for understanding organizational abuses or attempts by employees to eliminate them. For functionalist theory, opposition and its grounds are anomalies, best comprehended as deviant behavior. The persistence of functionalist analysiš in organization studies when it has been abandoned or modified in other areas of social science, may partly be explained by noting that the view of the organization as a rational system legitimates leadership groups. A more fruitful and comprehensive perspective on organizations, and one which is particularly suited to interpret bureaucratic oppositions, understands supposedly administrative units to be political systems. From this standpoint, the concept of the organization as a rational device serves the same function for contemporary elites as the myth of "divine right" performed for absolute monarchs.

The political process, whether it occurs in an organization or in a state, involves opposition when some members of an authority system do not acquiesce in decisions that have been made, in the procedures for making them, or in their implementation. With regard to opposition, the essential structural difference between authority systems is whether they have institutionalized procedures for dissent, or have not recognized the legitimacy of dissent. Representative systems, in the contemporary world democratic states, institutionalize dissent by allowing for "loyal" oppositions which do not violate constitutional procedures, while authoritarian systems do not make such provisions. Most complex organizations have an authoritarian structure or at least severely limit representative decision-making; oppositions within them will be more similar to those in authoritarian states than to those in democracies. The more authoritarian the system of decision is, the more heroism is required of those who mount oppositions. Where it has been institutionalized, sometimes as the result of previous opposition, dissent, though not routine, is a more legalistic and less heroic endeavor.

Where political processes are repressed and elites manipulate the myth of neutral and efficient administration, employees who do not have authority can act politically only as a disloyal opposition. At a minimum, such an opposition criticizes some decision, policy, or practice, and, therefore, punctures the myth of neutrality and consensus. Criticism presupposes an act that is fundamental to any dissent, though it is often ignored in the literature concerning opposition to the state—recognition of the abuse itself. There are many psychological mechanisms which protect people from acknowledging evils in their situations. The terms vicious naivete, bad faith, and cognitive dissonance, name some of these processes. Particularly when someone's self-image is involved with the work they do or when defining the condition as evil would be a stimulus to risky action, the person has an interest in maintaining ignorance.

Abuses, when they are identified, are relative to the ideals brought to bear on concrete situations. Many bureaucratic oppositions are grounded in resistance to violations of purely technical-rational norms, such as those defined by Max Weber in his description of the ideal-typical bureaucracy. According to the Weberian scheme, each of the rules is supposed to contribute to the overall efficiency and effectiveness of the organization. For example, duties are supposed to be discharged "without regard for person." Injustice, such as discrimination against, or dishonor of, a client or subordinate, violates this norm of universalism. Similarly, offices are not personal property and officials are remunerated at a fixed salary. When administrators accept kickbacks or bribes this norm is breached. As a final example, appointment to office and presumably retention, is supposed to be based on merit: "...only persons who have the generally regulated qualifications to serve are employed." Thus, instances of incompetence, whatever their cause, are grounds for opposition, whether the case results in harm to clients or in impaired working conditions for subordinates.

Often opposition against violations of instrumental norms leads dissenters to the discovery that such infractions are integral to organizational policy. The opposition then is directed against abusive policies, not against individual violators. Policies may be judged as objectionable, not only because they are contrary to formal criteria (efficiency), but also because they are inconsistent with the particular goals that differentiate the organization from others (effectiveness), or because they are contrary to general moral standards. The problems encountered by students or organizations when they attempt to identify the goal of a bureaucracy are mirrored in disputes about effectiveness among participants in conflict. Even when multiple goals are acknowledged there may still be disagreements over priorities and emphases. Is the goal of a corporation profits or production? Is the norm of production quantity or quality? Should the CIA provide intelligence reports or overturn ("destabilize") governments? Should the university educate students or produce research? Such questions reflect possible disputes about an organization's self-definition. Policies may also be opposed because they are judged to violate general moral standards rooted in religious tradition, the culture at large, or some transcendental position.

Opposition to abuse depends not only on defining a situation as evil, but on some confidence that resistance will make some practical difference. Unlike political revolutions and social movements, in which individuals can be swept into action as parts of a crowd, bureaucratic oppositions are generally effected by only a few people and often by a single employee. In addition to having feelings of efficacy, those who attempt to make changes without the authority to do so must, in the manner of Locke, believe that there are occasions in which one is not obliged to obey an unjust superior. In order to initiate action, inertia based on loyalty to organizational leadership, habit, cooptation, and fear, must be overcome. The obstacles to initiating opposition are particularly great when a coordinated effort among several participants is necessary or desired. An opposition group requires members to risk trusting one another, which is difficult enough in a society permeated with possessive-individualist ideology, but even more demanding in highly competitive bureaucracies, as Joseph Heller illustrated starkly in *Something Happened*. Both tactically and emotionally, it is advantageous for oppositions to be groupal rather than individual. If there are more participants there are generally more resources such as ideas, knowledge, and contacts within and outside of the organization. Also, a group is less likely to be successfully labeled as "emotionally disturbed," than is an individual dissenter.

The formation and coordination of individuals into opposition groups is the result of the interplay between the ever-present grounds for struggle and the organizational conditions which inhibit dissent. That the countervailing conditions against conflict can be overcome is evidenced by the appearance of oppositions, but that these circumstances pose difficult obstacles is shown by the normally brief duration, localized scope, face-to-face nature, and lack of division of labor of opposition groups. Although the members of an opposition may have multiple and even conflicting motives for their participation, they unite around the cause of making the organization live up to its own standards or those of the wider social environment. However, the grounding of an opposition merely gives it an ideology. Grounds do not translate directly into plans of action or structural roles for participants. Oppositions are relatively unstructured activities just because they are not accorded legitimacy. Unlike generals who have been trained in military matters, oppositionists must create strategies, often *de novo*.

OPPOSITION STRATEGIES

General plans of action are divided into two types. The first, not only in order of discussion, but also usually in the temporal process of opposition, is an informing strategy in which information about perceived abuses is given to organizational authorities, outside agencies, or news media. The second type of strategy involves taking direct action against the abuse, such as harassing the offender or disrupting the routine of work.

Informing

The informing strategy is most widely employed, perhaps because it does not appear to be political; it does not seem to commit one to a conflict. The informer often makes the naive assumption, as did Frank Serpico in his battle against corruption in the New York City Police Department, that if those in positions of responsibility knew that infractions had occurred, they would be grateful for the knowledge and promptly go about setting things right. Informing also seems to be less costly than direct action because it leaves the decision to effect change with the authorities and, so, avoids the appearance of rebellion

Informers break with business as usual only by violating the chain of command, not by challenging the principle of command itself. Using an informing strategy requires finding appropriate recipients for the report. The search for a listener often results in a catch-22 predicament, in which the immediate superior is both the source of the abuse and the only administrator to whom the oppositionists may speak. When a Federal Aviation Administration employee, P.I. Ryther, found that his supervisor has held up his report about air charter abuses, he went above the immediate supervisor to the deputy administrator, who, in turn, took no action. Ryther tried to contact the administrator of the agency, who gave him no response. Shortly afterward Ryther was forced to resign when he was "...called on the carpet at a special meeting of his supervisors for ignoring proper channels." Antony Jay in *The Corporation Man*, summarizes some of the reasons why such informing is not likely to be an effective strategy:

> ...the hardest and most thankless task is to tell the higher managers in the corporation that your immediate boss is no good. In the first place, they appointed him, so you are implicitly criticizing their judgment. In the second place, maintenance of corporate authority demands that they take his word against yours.

The negative image of the informer in society at large, exemplified by such epithets as *snitch, squealer, tattler,* and *fink,* is a barrier to initiating this strategy and also gives administrators social leverage over the dissenter. Charges tend to be treated more seriously when several informers come forth rather than only a single individual, and when the group members have high status and long service. Credibility is also influenced by the nature of the evidence used to support the charges. "Hard" evidence, such as memoranda, bookkeeping records, and tape recordings, is more compelling than unsupported recall. Some abuses, particularly incompetence and sexual harassment, are difficult to demonstrate convincingly, so one opposition tactic is to inform on a easily proven misdeed rather than the one which impels the dissent. Other useful tactics within the informing strategy are rhetorical appeals to norms such as efficiency and persistent nagging.

If the first attempt at informing is not deemed successful by the oppositionists, they may inform elsewhere or shift to direct action. In the former case there are three directions for initiative. The dissenters can appeal to higher levels of their own organization, they can try to gain support laterally, for example, from a union, or they can take their complaints to a public agency or to the press.

Lateral groups, such as the Civil Service Commission, unions, or professional associations, are more or less independent of the organizational heirarchy and potentially can contribute various resources to bureaucratic oppositionists. However, the abstract potential of lateral groups is drastically limited because their elites often share the viewpoints of upper administrators in the organization and because the functions of these groups are defined so as to exclude correction of many abuses. For example, professional associations are often confined to disseminating information relevant to their specialty and do not intervene in the working conditions of their members. Unions, particularly in the United States, direct most of their efforts to obtaining decent wages and benefits. Thus, getting a lateral group to act against organizational abuse often amounts to making a bureaucratic opposition within that very group. When lateral groups are directly incorporated into the bureaucracy their effectiveness in remediating abuses is even more strictly limited. For example, such devices as the Inspector General in the armed services are only as effective as the top echelon which empowers them allows them to be.

When informing is done outside of the organization, not to lateral groups but to those with a public dimension (governmental authorities or communications media), the tactic is popularly called whistle blowing. Oppositions using this tactic are the most widely known because the press is often involved in publicizing them. Among all opposition tactics, whistle blowing is the one that organizational authorities deem the most treasonous because it strikes most directly against their autonomy. Dissenters generally do not use this tactic initially, but work up to it after internal and/or lateral informing have failed. Problems encountered in gaining credibility for the opposition in earlier stages of informing arise again when it goes public. Congressional committees, regulatory agencies, and the press, are immediately suspicious of those who do not have official legitimacy. Legislative hearings, however, do seem to provide would-be whistle blowers with once-in-a-lifetime opportunities to gain receptive audiences for their revelations.

The courts can be a resource for bureaucratic oppositionists if they can convince a prosecutor that an abuse violates a law or if a lateral organization takes up their complaint as a cause. The Good Humor employee who blew the whistle to the Brooklyn district attorney, charging the company with producing ice cream containing illegally high bacteria counts, is an example of opposition through the legal system. The final court of appeal for the dissenter, however, is public opinion, reached through the mass media. As is the case for all forms of whistle blowing, recourse to the press is only appropriate in particular cases, especially where the abuse has significance for widely shared interests. Providing information to the press is often a way of pressuring public officials to take complaints, which may simultaneously be revealed to them, seriously. Access to the press has been increased by the prestige of the Woodward and Bernstein exposes, which brought "investigative reporting" to the forefront of journalism.

Mounting an opposition through the informing strategy focuses attention on the ground of the opposition, the nature of the abuse. The underlying assumption of informing is that "the facts speak for themselves." When the recipient of "the facts" fails to take action the oppositionists may search for another listener, become disillusioned and give up, or explore direct-action strategies. The informing strategy presupposes that the recipients of revelations about abuses share a formal if not a personal commitment to the norms or values which are contradicted by the abuse. The assumption of such commitment is often unwarranted and, so, dissenters must contrive ways of exerting influence or power more directly.

Direct Action

The types of direct action are as varied as the means of power that oppositionists can deploy. Once the myth that the only leverage for effecting change is through the official heirarchy has been shattered the only limit on possible tactics is imagination. For example, two secretaries, who felt demeaned by their boss's remarks about their bodies, believed that the abuse would not be taken seriously by higher authorities. A flash of insight suggested a course of action that they could undertake themselves. Whenever they looked at their boss they stared directly and continuously at his crotch. He became flustered almost immediately but it took him several days to make the connection between their stares and his own behavior toward them. Nothing was said, but he no longer made the offensive comments.

Verbal threats are a form of direct action in which oppositionists let superiors know that if certain abusive behaviors and policies are not corrected, measures ranging from informing through resignation to physical violence will be taken. The suspicion which pervades many bureaucracies causes even the appearance of trouble, any hint that an administrator cannot maintain order, to jeopardize that official's upward mobility. Even when there is no actual jeopardy administrators may believe that they must retain the semblance of smooth functioning at any cost. Verbal threats, however, may backfire if the bluff is called and the threats are not carried out. But threatening a superior does, at least, breach the myth of obedience to authority and the trust that is needed to conduct daily business without uncertainty and tension. Certain nonverbal political tactics, such as withholding information vital to accomplishing tasks or undermining superiors by making it appear that they are incompetent, often avoid the consequences of increasing overt tension and of directly challenging the myth of obedience.

The most obvious source of subordinate power is control over aspects of the work process itself and direct action which disrupts this process is widely used. For example, the formal work rules often need to be "bent" in order to achieve efficiency and/or effectiveness. Workers who object to some policy can exert pressure for change by the seemingly innocent tactic of obeying the rules to the letter. Known as *greve de zele*, this form of direct action can bring all operations to a halt, as the air traffic controllers have often demonstrated. There seems to be an inner satisfaction associated with the use of work-by-rule, stemming in part from the sense of retributive justice involved in showing that "If you treat me as less than human, I will behave accordingly."

Work stoppages are similar to work-by-rule tactics in that both require widespread support; the opposition group must be composed of a significant proportion of the relevant employees. Strikes and slowdowns have been extensively used by subordinates whose purpose was to establish collective bargaining and, so, to change the organization's policy. Although strikes called by national unions are best understood as interorganizational conflicts and not as bureaucratic oppositions, wildcat strikes are direct-action tactics, sometimes aimed against union abuses. Work slowdowns and stoppages are highly visible protests which sharply define a conflict situation. Abusive policies can also be challenged by open, self-conscious, and conspicuous disobedience to an organizatonal rule. Unmistakable defiance also needs a broad based opposition group to have any possibility of succeeding.

The host of tactics open to those mounting oppositions against organizational abuses, whether by informing or direct-action strategies, do not assure success. There is no way of estimating what percentage of oppositions achieve their goals of eliminating an abuse administrator or policy. Some movements are swiftly defeated; others may escalate from the use of less-costly tactics to ones involving greater risks. A few oppositionists try to become permanent by formally organizing.

REPRISALS

According to the administrative myth there should be no grounds for conflict within a bureaucracy, because employees have no rights to dispute the organization's public aims and administrators are motivated to achieve those aims efficiently and in consonance with the rules. The ubiquity of bureaucratic oppositions and the even greater prevalence of organizational abuses show that organizations are not politically neutral. Bureaucracies are, instead, seedbeds of conflict in which overt struggle is often muted by repression, just as it is in authoritarian states which also often claim to have dispensed with politics. Once an overt political process has been unleashed in a bureaucracy the first concerns of the authorities are to contain it within the organization, reassert the chain of command, and refurbish the administrative myth. They may also attempt to correct the abuse, but usually without openly admitting to its existence. Thus, officials are not likely to reward oppositionists and tend to punish them even if they believeive that the dissent was warranted.

The "bureaucratic genius for retaliation" is at its most creative in devising reprisals against those who mount oppositions. Such retaliation may take the forms of personal attacks or of measures that damage the careers or adversely affect the work situations of the dissenters. Severe physical attacks have been documented, but job-related sanctions are much more readily applied by administrators bent on revenge. Demotion and dismissal, whether or not the latter is accompanied by blacklisting, are obvious reprisals, although their use may be limited by threat of legal action. A more insidious measure is informal harassment which "can interfere with an employee's ability to do his (sic) work and result in disillusionment, resignation, or grounds for formal removal." Dissidents can be transferred to undesirable locations or have perquisites which confer status withdrawn. Career opportunities, such as promotions and raises, can be severely restricted or eliminated altogether. The wide range of sanctions available to superiors shows that the reward and punishment systems of bureaucracies function as political instruments of control and not merely as tools for securing efficiency and effectiveness.

POLICY: THE ROUTINIZATION OF HEROISM

The paradigm cases of bureacratic opposition are heroic because they require participants to transcend the everyday world by naming abuses where none are supposed to exist, by challenging authority when obedience is required, by overcoming narrow self-interest, and by inventing and creating novel ways of achieving their goals. Dissenters must shatter the solidity of the bureaucratically fabricated life-world and risk damaging reprisals. The need for heroism is reduced by the provision of regularized and legitimate means for alleviating or eliminating evils. The various proposals for diminishing the need for heroic bureaucratic oppositions have been aimed at either the abuses themselves or at legitimating the means to combat them.

Proposals aimed at eliminating the sources of abuse are the most radical and, not surprisingly, are given no serious consideration by higher authorities. Among measures that strike at the heart of the matter are the elimination of the organization because its very aim is considered to be abusive, or destructuring the organizational heirarchy. Far more widespread than such drastic approaches are legalistic modes of reform intended to routinize opposition. The mere fact that a bureaucratic opposition has occurred and has become known tends to make future efforts of the same kind less extraordinary and unpredictable. Information about tactics is disseminated and, even more importantly, the very possibility that abuses exist and can be identified as such need not be discovered anew. Oppositional precedent may be more effective than any formal instrument of remediation and planned reforms may be undertaken just so that such precedent does not get out of hand.

The most limited melioristic reform and one which has recently been implemented for federal employees aims at eliminating the reprisals suffered by whistle blowers. Included in the Civil Service Reform Act of 1978 is the Merit Systems Protection Board, in which "an independent Special Council. . .will have the power to investigate charges of prohibited personnel practices, including reprisals against whistle blowers. . ." Claiming responsibility for this provision, Public Citizen, a Nader organization, asserts optimistically: "This assures that serious whistle blower complaints will be subject to serious investigation and that agency personnel decisions can be overruled when necessary." More cautiously, the article concludes that protection depends upon the appointment of a "vigorous special counsel." One may doubt that the Merit Board will effectively protect dissenters. Firstly, the special counsel must judge the merits of the case and no protection will be given if the counsel does not decide that it is warranted. Secondly, protection can only cover the obvious formal reprisals and cannot prevent harassment and career blockage.

Another set of melioristic measures for reducing heroism and routinizing dissent concerns providing formal recourse for oppositionists. There is a host of federal regulations and enforcing agencies to which employees who perceive abuses may turn. Although remedies for all possible abuses have not yet been instituted, examples of regularization cover a range from discrimination against certain categories of employees (EEOC) through unsafe working conditions (OSHA) to the production of dangerous foods or drugs (FDA). Insofar as the relevant agencies concur with the oppositionists that an actionable abuse has occurred, some rectification is possible and anonymity of the informers may be preserved. Informing to an agency, of course, may involve risks, particularly if the regulators are not sympathetic. In order to bypass the obstacles involved in gaining access to regulatory agencies, a law professsor suggests that organizations should include within their structure full-time "probation officers" appointed by regulatory agencies, "who are designated to receive 'bad news.' "

Another way of providing formal recourse to oppositionists is through creating departments internal to the organization which are supposed to investigate charges of abuse. The Office of Inspector General has existed in the United States armed services for more than a hundred fifty years and in 1978 similar offices were instituted in twelve federal agencies. They are supposed to ". . .serve as the advance troops in the war against fraud, abuse, mismanagement, error, theft, and all the other ways the government wastes money." Both private and public agencies have instituted ombuds offices which are supposed to process complaints from clients and employees. The effectiveness of such internal investigators, particularly their ability to lessen the need for heroism in undertaking opposition, is questionable. "Bah," said A. Ernest Fitzgerald, the king of the whistle blowers, when he was asked about the new push for inspectors general in government: "They won't do any good. They're on the other side."

There are several limitations on the effectiveness of internal investigators. Those who work in the federal offices do so on a temporary basis, having come from the regular administrative heirarchy and intending to return to it as their careers advance. Thus, their sympathies and interests lie with the chain of command rather than with dissenting employees. Secondly, the investigators pursue their inquiries with the help of administrators and, so, cannot antagonize them to the degree of jeopardizing future inquests. Thirdly, complaint officers are circumscribed because they lack independent power. They can merely recommend action; the responsiblity to implement proposals is with the administrative heirarchy. Of course, if internal investigation divisions functioned as they are officially supposed to, they would institutionalize bureaucratic opposition and make it routine and not heroic at all.

All of the proposed reforms of bureaucratic abuses within the present system confront a basic dilemma. The ground of heirarchical administrative authority is that a specific group of officials should be held responsible for the conduct and performance of the organizaiton. The chain of command is a way of fixing responsibility and of localizing it. The presence of abuses within organizations shows that in many cases the officials cannot or will not behave responsibly, or that their interpretation of responsible behavior differs from that of other groups of individuals. Reform of organizations concentrates on making officials accountable to other agencies. Such accountability amount to increased competition for organizational control, and as such, either weakens the autonomy of officials or, in the case of co-option, allows them to be even more abusive and less accountable than they were before. Reform within the system, then, diffuses responsibility and gives officials excuses for their failures. Yet the call for reform responds to a situation in which the competitive controls which supposedly undergird organizational society have failed. This is, indeed, a vicious circle. Officials may actually become so hedged by regulations and pressures that they cannot act effectively, or they may be able to blame other agencies for their own misdeeds. Meanwhile there is no guarantee that subordinates and publics will suffer any fewer abuses. There are clear limits, then, to legal reform. It is one of the stubborn tragedies of the human condition that resistance to abuses demands heroism.

9.
Linking Ethics to Behavior in Organizations

Archie B. Carroll

It is not easy to document whether the state of ethics...has gone downhill over the past decade, or whether rejuvenated interest in ethics has been stimulated by such events as Watergate, the Lockheed scandal, and the outpouring of confessions of international payoffs that appear almost daily. Beginning with revelations of illegal business donations traceable to the 1972 presidential election, news accounts have surfaced on a regular basis, identifying unscrupulous business practices ranging from kickbacks and fraud, to bribery of foreign officials in order to induce business abroad.

Our intent, however, is not to document further the state of ...ethics in America, for that has already been ably done. Our interest here is to address the issue of the linkage between ethics and the behavior of workers in organizations.

ETHICAL PROBLEMS AND THE MANAGERIAL ENVIRONMENT

Many have felt that ethics are shaped by the broad social values and attitudes in existence at a given point in time. These broad social forces cause behavior to become more or less ethical as the social climate changes. But more immediate causes affect the ethics of workers' behavior in organizations. Recent studies have demonstrated that these immediate causes of behavior may be traced to modern management practices and superior-subordinate relationships.

These studies suggest that the behavior of managers—the expectations they communicate to subordinates—results in perceived or actual pressures toward unethical employee behavior. A survey of managerial ethics conducted by the author, for example, showed this. When respondents were asked to evaluate the proposition "managers today feel under pressure to compromise personal standards to achieve company goals," 65 percent of those surveyed agreed with the statement. Further examination of the data also revealed that this feeling was more widely felt at the middle and lower management levels.

Managers in the study were also asked to respond to the proposition, "I can conceive of a situation where you have sound ethics running from top to bottom, but because of pressures from the top to achieve results, the person down the line compromises." Seventy-eight percent of the respondents agreed with this statement. They were then asked to respond to the proposition, "The junior members of Nixon's reelection committee who confessed that they went along with their bosses to show their loyalty is just what young managers have done in business." In a strikingly similar pattern to the findings presented earlier, 37 percent of the top managers agreed with the proposition, 61 percent of the middle managers agreed with it, and 85 percent of the lower managers did likewise. When linked with the earlier findings, these data suggested not only that subordinate managers perceived pressure toward unethical behavior, but that the pressure seemed to be felt the most at the lower end of the management hierarchy.

One other recent survey showed that the pressure to behave unethically is traceable in part to the management hierarchy. Steven N. Brenner and Earl A. Molander concluded that "relations with superiors are the primary category of ethical conflict." From their survey of managers, they found that respondents "frequently complained of superiors' pressure to support incorrect viewpoints, sign false documents, overlook supervisors' wrongdoing, and do business with superiors' friends."

Henry P. Sims and W. Harvey Hegarty concluded from their research that "it is clear that ethical behavior can be influenced by both contingent rewards and clearly stated organizational policies."

Taken together, these studies point in the direction of superior-subordinate relationships as the source of much pressure to engage in unethical behavior, and they justify a more careful examination of how managers deal with employees and subordinate managers.

A FRAMEWORK FOR ETHICAL THINKING

To illustrate how a social issue can be viewed as a managerial issue, it is useful to set forth a frame of reference—or model—that can aid us in conceptualizing the various levels upon which the issue can be examined, and the relationship of these levels to one another. As a point of departure for our thinking, let us suggest that there are at least five different levels at which the issue of improving . . . ethics can be addressed. In other words, we can take actions at five increasingly more comprehensive levels to improve ethical conditions and behavior in our society. First is the level of the *individual,* for questions of ethics ultimately reside with the individual decision maker. Second, moving in a more inclusive systems direction, is the level of the *organization.* The third level is the level of *associations*—groups of organizations that have banned together for mutual benefits. Examples of such groups would include the Retail Merchants Association, the Association of Builders and Contractors, and the National Association of Professional Accountants. A frequent action taken at this level is the creation of industrywide codes of ethics.

Next is the *societal* level. In addition to broad and elusive changes in public values about acceptability, new laws would be illustrative of action steps that could be taken at this broadest of levels. Remaining somewhat within the context of societal initiatives, the *international* level could then be considered. Apropos here might be multinational agreements on standards of acceptable business conduct.

MANAGEMENT ACTIONS TO IMPROVE ETHICS

As we move from the individual to the international level, it becomes increasingly difficult to pinpoint actions managers can take to affect. . .ethics. But there are specific actions they can take to improve behavior in organizations.

The widely held view for many years has been that ethics are personal, that ethics cannot be legislated, and that ethics cannot be managed. But couldn't managers, by their actions, help channel employee behavior in ethical directions?

We believe that there are some general areas in which management might take the initiative to bring about an improved ethical climate.

• *Realistic objectives set at the top.* Organizational action flows from objectives that have been set at the top. Assuring that proper and realistic goals have been established for all personnel is an important first step management can take in developing an ethical organization.

Fred T. Allen, chairman and president of Pitney-Bowes, Inc., makes this point quite firmly:

> Top management must establish sales and profit goals that are realistic— goals that can be achieved with current business practices. Under the pressure of unrealistic goals, otherwise responsible subordinates will often take the attitude that "anything goes" in order to comply with the chief executive's target.

Managers do not usually think about the effect that unrealistically high goals might have on the ethics of subordinates. But if goals are unrealistically high, employees are inclined to do whatever is necessary (including unethical acts) to achieve them. The temptation is strong for managers to set goals high, especially when research suggests that higher goals lead to higher performance, but consideration needs to be given to the problem suggested here lest managers create conditions that may unintentionally be conducive to unethical behavior on the part of subordinates.

• *Leadership from top management.* The moral tone of the organization is set by those at the top. In this connection, the Fifty-second American Assembly, which met to consider the ethics of corporate conduct, concluded:

> The corporation itself is a moral community; therefore, all measures such as compensation, working conditions, and pension programs that contribute to the dignity of work and respect for the individual must be fostered.

This view suggests that the many operational matters affected by top management contribute to improving the organization's ethical behavior. Carrying this point even further, L.W. Foy, chairman of Bethlehem Steel Corporation, has asserted:

> It is a primary responsibility of business management to instruct, motivate, and inspire their employees to conduct themselves with honesty, probity, and fairness. Starting at the top, management has to set an example for all the others to follow.

Foy elaborates "... management has to make company policy absolutely clear to all employees. People have to be told and retold in unmistakable terms that the company is firmly committed to integrity in all its activities." Fred T. Allen summarizes this point well. "It is up to the leader to make sure that ethical behavior permeates the entire company." Organizational ethical policy must be clearly and systematically established at the top, for if it is not, it will be set haphazardly and as the need arises lower in the organization.

• *Establish codes of ethics.* Codes of ethics have been around for quite some time and have been abused by many organizations, but a thoughtfully designed and carefully articulated code still has merit and is favored by managers. The acid test is to make the codes "living documents," not just platitudinous public relations statements that find themselves in the bottom of a file draw after dissemination. As Theodore Purcell of Georgetown University has noted, "Ethical codes are no panacea . . . but they can help to clarify ethical thinking and to encourage ethical behavior." Most important, codes of ethics should embody the thinking and policy beliefs that management and employees alike feel should prevail in the organization, and, as such, they should represent sincere communication efforts that guide employee acts and behavior in questionable situations.

• **Discipline violators of ethical standards.** To bring about ethical standards that all organizational personnel will adhere to, management must discipline violators of generally accepted ethical norms. One of the reasons the public—and indeed employees in many organizations—have questioned . . . the sincerity in desiring a more ethical environment has been the . . . unwillingness to discipline violators. There are numerous cases where top management personnel have behaved unethically but were retained in their positions by the organization's board of directors. And at lower levels there have been cases of top management failing to discipline unethical behavior of managers or employees. These evidences of inaction on management's or the board's part constitute, in the minds of many, implicit approval of the individual's acts or behavior.

Allen argues that the organization should react forcefully to the individual who is guilty of deliberately or flagrantly violating its code of ethics:

> From the pinnacle of the corporate pyramid to its base there can only be one course of action: dismissal. And should actual criminality be involved, there should be total cooperation with law enforcement authorities.

Phillip Blumberg supports this line of reasoning. He asserts that "there should be effective sanctions for violations so that there is no doubt that the code really represents corporate policy and that the effort is more than a public relations charade."

• **Create an "ethical advocate's" role.** An imaginative proposal by Theodore Purcell is that each organization hire an "ethical devil's advocate"—a top-level . . . executive whose responsibility it is to serve as an ethical catalytic agent for management by constantly asking probing questions regarding the organization's actions and posture. For example, whereas a strategic planner might ask, "What would our market share be?" or "What would our discounted cash flow be?" the ethical advocate might ask, "How will a given decision affect the rights of our employees versus the rights of the corporation?"

One possibly serious problem with this is that managers might be inclined to delegate ethical concerns to the advocate and not worry about these themselves. That must be carefully guarded against. Very little experience exists as to how the ethical advocate concept might work in practice; however, it does suggest a way managements might take actions to improve the ethical climate in their organizations.

- **_Provide a whistle-blowing mechanism._** One of the reasons unethical acts are covered up by persons in the organization is that they do not know how to behave when they observe questionable practices taking place. An effective ethical climate is contingent upon employees being able to blow the whistle on violators, with the backing of top management. Allen has summarized this point well: "Employees must know exactly what is expected of them in the moral arena and how to respond to warped ethics."

Frequently, unethical practices or, indeed, crimes come to the attention of staff farther down in the organization's hierarchy. John J. McCloy, who served as chairman of the special review committee to study the use of corporate funds by Gulf Oil Corporation, reports that some boards of directors of companies have "adopted and disseminated throughout their companies a policy that encourages any employee who observes a criminal practice to report the incident to his superior. If the superior is not responsive, the employee then has direct access to the board, usually through its audit committee." This illustrates how a whistle-blowing mechanism might function.

- **_Train managers in business ethics._** There has been some controversy over whether managerial ethics can, and should be, taught. One school of thought argues that ethics are personal, already embedded in the manager, and hence not alterable or teachable. But a growing school of thought argues that instruction in business ethics should be made a part of management training, executive development programs, and seminars.

In fact, this latter course of action is taking place in a number of organizations in the United States today. Ron Zemke has argued that the purposes of such ethics training are to increase the manager's sensitivity to ethical problems, to encourage critical evaluation of value priorities, to increase awareness toward organizational and social realities, and to improve understanding of the importance of public image and public/society relations. To this list might be added the desirability of examining the ethical facets of. . .decision-making, bringing about a greater degree of fairness and honesty in the workplace, and more completely responding to the organization's social responsibilities.

Although there are difficulties in training managers in such an amorphous subject as ethics, these difficulties should not preclude experimentation with case studies, incidents, role playing, and discussion of crucial ethical issues. For, as John Adair has said, "A good teacher can help managers to become generally aware of their values and to compare them with the consensus of value judgments in a particular company, industry, or profession."

Management training and development in ethics should be considered a viable alternative for achieving more ethical organizational behavior.

CONCLUSION

The strategies presented are some of the possibilities available to managements for improving the ethical climate in organizations. They should serve as a point of departure for thinking about management's role in this increasingly important area.

Selected Readings
Part III.

Allen, Robert F. "The IK in the Office." *Organizational Dynamics.* 8 (Winter 1980); 26-41.

Boling, T. Edwin. "Organizational Ethics: Rules, Creativity, and Idealism." in *Management Handbook for Public Administrators,* edited by John W. Sutherland. New York: Van Nostrand Reinhold Co., 1978, Chap. Three.

Comptroller General. *Federal Agency Standards of Employee Conduct Need Improvement.* Washington, D.C.: General Accounting Office, 1979.

Cooper, Terry L. *The Responsible Administrator: Ethics for the Administrative Role.* Port Washington, N.Y.: Kennikat Press Corp., 1982.

Davis, Louis E. "Individuals and the Organization." *California Management Review.* 22 (Spring, 1980); 5-14.

Dobel, J. Patrick. "The Corruption of the State." *American Political Science Review.* 72 (September 1978); 958-73.

Eddy, William B. "Credibility of the Public Managers: A Personal/Professional Issue." *The Bureaucrat.* 9 (Fall 1980); 11-16.

Ewing, David W. *Freedom Inside the Organization.* New York: E.P. Dutton and Co., Inc. 1977.

Fitch, Gordon H., and Saunders, Charles B. "Obedience in Organizations." *Business and Society.* 17 (Fall 1976); 5-14.

Hanan, Mack. "Make Way for the New Organization Man." *Harvard Business Review.* 49 (July/August 1971); 128-38.

Thompson, Dennis F. "Moral Responsibility of Public Officials: The Problem of Many Hands." *American Political Science Review.* 74 (December 1980); 905-16.

Wakefield, Susan. "Ethics and the Public Service: A Case for Individual Responsibility." *Public Administration Review.* 36 (November/December 1976); 661-66.

Walzer, Michael. "Political Action: The Problem of Dirty Hands." *Philosophy and Public Affairs.* 2 (Spring 1973); 160-80.

Waters, James A. "Catch 20.5: Corporate Morality as an Organizational Phenomenon." *Organizational Dynamics* 6 (Spring 1978); 3-19.

Part IV.
Ethical Attitudes in
Business and in Government

In Part III it was pointed out that individual conduct occurs in an organizational setting. The difficulty is that most administrators feel that organizations do not foster ethical behavior. Robert F. Allen (Part III, Selected Readings) reports:

> Of the 1,500 respondents to our surveys, taken in a wide variety of organizations,...less than 10 percent felt that the organizations in our society tend to encourage their members to behave ethically, honestly, and humanely. In fact, more than 65 percent agreed with the opposite statement—that [they] "tend to encourage their members to behave unethically, dishonestly, and inhumanely...

Managers perceive the bureaucratic environment to be less ethical than their own values and beliefs, that they are under pressure to compromise personal standards to achieve organizational goals, and that their supervisors are only interested in results, not how they were obtained.

The next two chapters document the depth of concern over ethics on the part of public officials and business executives. The editor of the present collection surveys the attitudes of government managers toward moral issues in American politics and ethical practices in daily administration. While the respondents demonstrate a high level of concern, it is concluded that an organizational foundation for individual conduct is needed. In a comparison of the opinions of business people in the early 1960s, Steven N. Brenner and Earl A. Molander report that ethics is higher today than it was then. Areas probed include frequent ethical dilemmas, standard business practices, economic pressure in decision-making, and contemporary societal trends.

In light of these results and the surveys cited in the Selected Readings, one might expect that those with high moral character would be unable to operate effectively in many organizations. While it is true that empirical research only registers norms, not necessarily actual conduct of those surveyed (Langholm and Lunde chapter), it is these norms, ideals, and societal expectations that management ethics should strive to nurture. A bridge must be built between the ethics of the individual and those of the organization, the topic of the last section in this volume.

10.
Ethics in the Federal Service: A Post-Watergate View

James S. Bowman

It is well-known that public confidence in governmental institutions has been severely shaken as a result of the traumatic events in American life during the last decade. Bitter disputes over domestic and foreign policy in recent years have engendered a new skepticism of government and have played upon, and deepened, popular suspicions of politics. The revelations, allegations, and investigations of the Watergate scandal, represented merely a symptom of deeper and more profound loss of trust in democratic government. The point has long been reached that to say that there is a crisis of confidence in America is simply to repeat a well-worn cliche.

In a democracy, it is evident that not only must government trust the people, but also the people must have confidence that government will protect the public interest. Since ethical concerns embrace all forms of governmental behavior, they penetrate many of the dimensions of the crisis of confidence today. Ethics, according to Webster, is concerned with judgments about what is right and wrong and whether or not these judgments are good or bad. Since the effective conduct of public business requires a significant degree of administrative discretion, career civil servants must continually face such questions as, "What constitutes ethical and moral behavior in exercising the public trust?" Data presented in this paper reveal that officials are interested in, and sensitive to, such problems. The purpose of this study, then, is to examine the attitudes of federal executives with respect to contemporary ethical practices in government.

Despite the fundamental importance of questions of purpose, ethics, and integrity in the public service, the study of public administration historically has tended to overlook such problems. The acceptance of the politics-administration dichotomy in the early part of this century, and the prevalence of "value free" scientific research since World War II, discouraged sustained attention to the political significance of normative values in administration. The increasing and obvious importance of politics in administration and the social climate of the 1960s, challenged the complacency in the profession.

As a result, many fundamental questions began to be raised about democratic control and administrative responsibility in American government. The apparent weakness of external political controls (congressional investigations, executive orders, court decisions) has led to an emphasis on internal controls necessary to keep public bureaucracy responsive in a democratic society. There has been discussion in recent years, for example, about general ethical problems, value systems of public administrators toward democracy, and how to inculcate democratic norms into future public managers. Few studies, however, have examined official attitudes toward contemporary ethical behavior in the conduct of public affairs.

With so much controversy and interest in normative issues we are interested in how federal executives around the nation perceive the state of ethics today. Since public administrators are key actors in the allocation of resources in American politics, it should be instructive to learn how they think about ethics in government in relation to national political issues and daily operations of public agencies. Now that the emotional reverberations surrounding Watergate have subsided, this paper documents executive perspectives and attitudes about this subject.

THE RESEARCH STUDY

In an attempt to obtain systematic data on this problem, a survey was conducted of public managers employed by the federal government. The sample was chosen at random from the membership files of a nationwide professional society of public administrators. Five hundred questionnaires were mailed in the winter of 1975-76, of which 343 were returned for a 69 percent response rate.

A wide range of managerial ranks, educational levels, and age groups are included in the sample; the "typical" respondent is a middle-aged, middle manager with a master's degree. The majority of the administrators are self-identified liberals, most of whom are affiliated with the Democratic party and voted for George McGovern in 1972. A broad variety of federal agencies and occupational professions are represented in the study, as indicated in the following list:

Executive Office of the President
U.S. House of Representatives
Department of Agriculture
Treasury Department
Department of Labor
General Services Administration
Department of Housing and
  Urban Development
National Aeronautics and Space
  Administration
Interstate Commerce Commission
Environmental Protection Agency

Department of Defense
Department of Commerce
Department of Health, Education, and
  Welfare
Department of Transportation
State Department
U.S. Civil Service Commission
Veterans Administration
Department of Justice
Department of Interior
National Science Foundation
Energy Research and Development
  Administration

The questionnaire consisted of two parts. The first two sections of this paper report the results from a series of agree-disagree statements from Part 1 of the survey about various general ethical issues and events in American government. The third section discusses the findings from Part 2 of the questionnaire concerning specific ethical practices in day-to-day administration. Thus, this study explores ethical problems both at the macro level in government, and at the micro level in the internal operations of public agencies. The final section of the paper discusses the implications of the findings and briefly considers avenues for change.

STATE OF ETHICAL CONCERN IN GOVERNMENT

Since the first part of the questionnaire requested individuals to indicate their agreement or disagreement with various statements, the findings will be presented on a proposition by proposition basis. The statements were designed to probe managerial attitudes concerning ethical problems in general, and in relation to well-known events and public policies. All of the propositions used have been topics of discussion that have appeared in widely read newspapers and magazines.

Several questions were asked of executives in order to determine their present degree of ethical interest and awareness. As the data indicate, public managers do not feel "morally exhausted" or resigned to apathy in the post-Watergate era. Over 60 percent of the respondents disputed the statement that government practices suffer from a moral numbness due to the events of the 1960s and early 1970s. This feeling was expressed by several respondents who argued that "government and politics is not a moral wasteland" and that while controversial events involved top officials, "there are many truly dedicated, ethical public administrators."

These convictions appeared to be largely independent of the respondent's age, sex, education, and political outlook. However, the manager's organizational rank did influence his views: Senior executives were more likely to agree with the proposition than were other managers. This finding probably reflects the personal and emotional anguish experienced by these executives during the many years of protest against public policy. On the whole, however, public administrators, like the American populace, have a remarkably high degree of faith in themselves and the nation despite the crisis of confidence in American institutions.

This finding is further substantiated by the results from the second statement. Nearly 90 percent of the public officials believe that government can be a moral force in the country. There is a consensus on this idea across all political and ideological beliefs as well as organizational and personal characteristics of the administrators. Only a small minority of the respondents (11 percent) were undecided or disagreed with the statement.

Insofar as career managers have a special and sensitive role in protecting and supporting democratic processes, it would be unsettling if the results were otherwise. The fact that an overwhelming majority of the civil servants see government as a moral force in democrary is encouraging. If public administrators did not see government as a potential leader in ethical conduct, public confidence in American institutions would probably be lower than it is.

Not only do managers see government as a source of moral leadership in the country, but they also seem to be ready to address such issues. Over 60 percent of the sample do not believe that "discussing ethics...is difficult because...it appears to be...too idealistic." Even taking into account that the managers returning the questionnaire may be more ethically sensitive than those who did not, we find that most respondents are prepared to talk about ethics in managerial circles.

Indeed, managers seem ready to examine these issues despite the fact that traditionally they were considered to be unfashionable and evoked ennui or embarassment. Although one administrator wrote, "I personally have never seen ethics or morality considered or discussed in relation to my job," the majority viewpoint was represented by another executive who said, "I strongly support the current reemphasis on political morality today." Again, while most of the variables examined had no effect on these attitudes, highly educated and senior level administrators were more likely to agree with the statement than were their organizational counterparts. Given the high degree of ethical concern that the responses to these three statements demonstrate, what are some dimensions of the problem? The next several items from the questionnaire posed more specific ethical issues in American government and administrative responsibility.

ETHICAL PROBLEMS AND ISSUES

The investigations, indictments, and trials of federal officials, as well as those in states such as Illinois, New Jersey, and Maryland, have led some to say that official behavior is getting worse. The findings here reveal, however, that a plurality of executives believe that ethics today are superior to those of earlier periods; more managers agree with the fourth statement (39.4 percent) than disagree (30.0 percent). The large percentage of the sample that is undecided (30.3 percent) may suggest uncertainty about the quality of contemporary ethics or how they compare to the ethics of other times. In any case, many government employees disagree with the popular, negative view of government morality and seem to concur with Elmer Staats, Comptroller General of the United States, who recently concluded that, "There's perhaps greater sensitivity about ethics and conduct in the public service than there has been at any time in my career in government."

In view of the widespread suspicion of politics today, one can possibly agree with the survey respondents if one considers, for example, that government ethics during the investigations of Watergate were generally superior to similar practices in the McCarthy era. As a middle manager in the Department of Health, Education, and Welfare commented, "Overall, ethical practices have been consistently higher in recent years. Government does not begin to tolerate practices that used to be accepted."

The findings from the next statement place these results in comparative perspective with respect to ethics in the world of business. A majority of the respondents appear to endorse Arnold Toynbee's comment about Watergate that, "One cause of the decline of political morality in America is that it has now sunk to the lowest level of American business morality." The data show that public managers are quite prepared to admit that political morality is as low as business morality.

This was found to be especially true for the disillusioned Nixon voter. Apparently, when an administration fell that prided itself as the sturdy champion of old-fashioned American virtues and private enterprise, these individuals simply resigned themselves to the notion that governmental and commercial ethics are a good deal less than salutary. Only one third of the civil servants indicated that professional conduct in government was better than that of the business community. In related questions it was found that a majority of the public officials (59 percent) believe that "big business was mixed up in the whole constellation of events labeled 'Watergate,'" and that "business suffered from Watergate because it lowered public confidence in business as well as in the political system." Perhaps these views stem from the general lack of confidence in American institutions.

If the responses to these statements generally suggest a low level of administrative morality in America (despite the belief that standards today are higher than those of earlier periods), the findings indicate that a majority of the executives feel pressure to compromise their standards in order to achieve organizational goals. This belief is especially prevalent in middle and lower management levels. Only about one third of the respondents do not experience such influences, most of whom, not surprisingly, are senior managers. The only other factor affecting this view was education. Generally, the higher the education of the executive, the less likely he is to experience this stress. Yet, even among individuals with Ph.D. degrees, more than half have this type of pressure in their work. One respondent captured the pervasiveness of this problem by saying, "I resigned from an agency in part due to ethics. As a result, I have been penalized for lack of 'loyalty' and now suffer in any job-seeking effort."

The seventh proposition is "I can conceive of a situation where you have good ethics running from top to bottom, but because of pressures from the top to achieve results persons down the line compromise their beliefs." As one Treasury Department official stated, "It is not the people per se, but rather the structure of large organizations and the ruthless competition in them that develops unethical conduct." If managers' actions resemble their responses to this hypothetical statement, the implications for understanding the depth of the ethical problem in organizations are startling. This is especially true since there is a consensus across all age, rank, and educational levels. The data suggest that all managers, including senior officials, acknowledge this type of situation, which is an important starting point in dealing with the problems. The next several statements from the survey deal with more specific ethical issues in national politics.

Nearly half of the executives believe that, "The illegal uses of the CIA, FBI, and IRS during Watergate are realistic examples of the ethics of politics today." Approximately 40 percent did not agree and the remainder were undecided. Variables such as age, party affiliation, and education, had no apparent influence on these views. In a companion questions, it was found that nearly 75 percent of the sample feel that the illegal business campaign contributions of recent years are illustrative examples of contemporary business ethics. Thus, even in the post-Watergate era, public managers have a very pessimistic view of ethical practices. No doubt this attitude has been kept alive in light of more recent disclosures of questionable activities on the part of the CIA, FBI, and multinational corporations.

The final statement reads, "Such issues as trade with South Africa, coping with racial discrimination, and making weapons, are ethical concerns of public administrators." The classical view of the role of public employees would lead one to expect that the responses would be at odds with this statement. It is still established doctrine in many government agencies that civil servants "don't make policy." As one respondent indicated, "It is our role to implement current public policy, whether we agree with it or not, whether it is 'moral' or not; 'ours is not to question why; ours is but to do or die.'" No doubt it is for reasons such as these that ethical questions in government have traditionally been limited to issues of conflict of interest, equity in personnel decisions, and the like.

In the context of these orthodox views, the responses are interesting. Over 70 percent support the statement, while less than 20 percent hold the more traditional view of the separation between politics and administration. Classical attitudes toward policy issues are clearly on the wane. The majority position is especially true for those managers who are self-identified liberals and have higher levels of education. One might hypothesize that a difference would exist between younger and older managers, but this was not the case.

In summary, the data presented here show that public administrators have considerable interest in civil service ethics. A majority of public executives dispute the idea that "government practices suffer from a moral numbness" as a result of events during the last decade. Indeed, nearly 90 percent of the respondents still believe that government can be a moral force in the nation. Two thirds of the sample are prepared to discuss ethical issues despite the fact that in the machismo culture of administration they have been seen as platitudinous, preachy, and stultifying. Perhaps one reason for this interest is that many individuals believe that political (and business) ethics leave a good deal to be desired even though they also believe that ethics today are superior to those of earlier times. For example, the findings from two propositions revealed that managers feel they are under so much pressure to achieve results that they may need to compromise their integrity. Similarly, nearly half of the executives agreed that examples of illegal use of government agencies during Watergate are realistic examples of contemporary political ethics. Concern about this situation was documented when over 70 percent of the officials perceived political issues to be professional concerns of public administrators. While additional research is needed, the evidence presented here indicates that many of the popular assumptions about morality in government require reevaluation.

These findings suggest that ethical convictions on the part of public managers should not be regarded as evidence of depravity in the administration of government. On the contrary, the respondents seem to be saying that if today's election or tomorrow's contract is won by corrupt practices, the victory does not compensate for the resulting loss of self-respect and public confidence. The business of government can be carried out far more effectively when honorable people are dealing with one another. Yet, how deep and personal are these beliefs? That is, does concern about ethics in government policy affect attitudes and behavior in day-to-day operations in public agencies? Are nationally publicized scandals only symptoms of more extensive ethical problems that arise in daily managerial behavior?

ETHICS IN DAILY OPERATIONS OF GOVERNMENT

In an effort to deal with some of these questions, this section of the study explores the "gray area" of ethical behavior inside public agencies. Incidents of outright criminality are excluded from analysis since nearly all executives regard such behavior as unacceptable. A wide variety of behavior that is regarded as perfectly acceptable by most people is also excluded. What we are interested in is those activities and situations of dubious propriety that give rise to suspicion on the part of the public, temptation on the part of the employee, and general distrust of governmental processes.

To probe this sensitive gray area of managerial behavior, data were elicited to determine what managers believe about their own ethics and the ethical practices of others in their department. A broad range of these behaviors was presented to the respondents. Some activities vary by the overt nature of the behavior, some vary on an active-passive involvement of dimension, and other vary between the involvement of a single person versus a collaboration between several people. Although the words in the phrases are not necessarily precise terms that call for absolute answers, they are sufficiently clear to be meaningful in the context of the question. In order to obtain cross-perceptual data, the questionnaire required subjects to respond to each item by indicating (1) whether they considered the behavior to be unethical, (2) whether their peers would consider it to be unethical, and (3) whether top management would believe it to be unethical. Answers to these types of questions should provide a point of departure in understanding the nature and extent of ethical problems at the micro level in public organizations.

The data indicate that individual managers do, in general, proclaim a fairly ethical set of beliefs. Nearly all of the tested behaviors were seen as basically unethical. However, these are some interesting variations in the responses to the statements. For example, five of the items received universal or near universal recognition as improper activities. Passing blame to others, falsification of reports, claiming credit for someone else's work, padding expenses over ten percent, and accepting favors in exchange for preferential treatment, were seen as unbecoming behaviors by over 90 percent of all respondents. Very small numbers of executives were willing to consider these types of conduct to be acceptable, despite the popularity of "situational ethics" in recent years.

Four forms of action were claimed to be unethical by approximately 80 percent of the public managers. That is, a substantial majority of the employees believe that divulging confidential information, giving favors in exchange for preferential treatment, padding expenses up to 10 percent, pilfering supplies, and using agency services for personal benefit, are unethical practices. The data also reveal that approximately 70 percent of the managers said that authorizing a subordinate to violate rules, calling in sick to take a day off, concealing one's errors, and taking longer than necessary to do a job, are not defensible behaviors.

Finally, between 58 and 48 percent of the managers considered the following activities to be unsuitable: doing personal business on agency time, taking extra personal time, and not reporting others' violations of policy.

When these results were cross-tabulated against management level, age, and education, an interesting pattern emerged. Generally speaking, younger age groups, lower levels of education, and junior managerial rank, all correlated with relatively low ethical standards. Although the data do not show dramatic differences, the finding is consistent on nearly all questions. Younger employees, for instance, are found to be more willing to falsify reports, claim undue credit, misuse agency time, pad expenses, and the like, than older employees. This was anticipated by one 35-year-old General Accounting Office executive who wrote:

> There is a contrast between the values of my peer group and those of our newly hired personnel. Many of the people who now join our office think nothing of using their position of trust for personal gain. . .
>
> This disdain of traditional values seemed to come with the post-Vietnam hirees. Their attitude seems to be that the government owes them a living. We (the nation) have cultivated that attitude in our minority and female personnel, but I'm puzzled by the same attitudes in some of the white males we've hired. Fortunately some of the new staff, including minority and female personnel, have the highest moral and ethical standards. My hope is that we are able to retain them.

In general, it appears that action-oriented and overt behavior such as blaming others, falsifying reports, claiming undue credit and extensive padding of expenses, are repugnant to the sample group. More covert, passive, and personal behavior involving the misuse of agency time, but not supplies and services, are more acceptable. For example, calling in sick to take a day off was referred to by one official as a "mental health day." Another manager said that, "While we may do personal business on agency time, we more often do agency business on personal time, without charging or requesting compensatory time." Finally, more than half of the respondents consider it acceptable to fail to report others' violations of official policy. On the whole, people junior in rank, education, and age seem to be more willing to engage in and tolerate dubious forms of managerial activities.

In comparing the managers' self-proclaimed ethical standards against what they think their peers believe to be proper behavior, several observations are in order. Generally, the items are in the same rank order as just discussed. However, administrators see their colleagues as having a looser set of managerial ethics on all of the tested behaviors (particularly personal and covert actions) except one—reporting others' violations of regulations. As one respondent wrote, "Managers are very likely to take a 'holier than thou' attitude and are not altogether trusting of people that they must compete with for promotions."

The third data set shows managers' perceptions of the ethical practices of their superiors. In stark contrast to this study of corporate managers, it was found that both individual ethics and perceptions of peer group ethics are superior to comparable practices of top management. For nearly half of the items, senior executives in government were viewed as having lower ethical standards then managerial peers or individuals. In a number of cases, top executives were seen as having higher standards than peer groups, but not as high as the ideals of the individual officials. In only one case (reporting others' violations) were top managers perceived as practicing better ethical behavior than anyone else. This very negative view of the ethics of responsible policy-makers was summed up by a respondent who said, "If you want to look at ethics, look at the politically appointed administrators in high positions. They stink from top to bottom." Thus, while such findings may not be surprising in light of the Watergate scandal, they suggest that even in the post-Watergate era, individual exemplary acts of leadership have not been very influential and that top executives do not serve as a key reference group in ethical behavior.

In summary, if managers believe, as these data indicate, that they are more ethical than their peers and their superiors, they may easily justify some indiscretions on the basis that "everyone's doing it," or "what I'm doing is not as bad as what others are doing." They may be erroneous in their veiws, but if they decide they are the only ones buying supplies for personal use, they may begin pilfering organizational supplies. If everyone shares this belief, the loss could be very significant. One implication of this could be that those who exaggerate the incidence of immoral conduct may unwittingly encougage more transgressions than they prevent.

The data presented in this section extend and add new emphasis to the findings of the John W. Newstrom and William A. Ruch study of business managers in *MSU Business Topics*. Several observations seem warranted. First, the fact that even the most repugnant activities are acceptable to some suggests that everyone has an individual set of standards that can be adjusted to various types of situations. Secondly, managers believe that their colleagues are more suspect than they themselves claim to be. If peer group behavior typically provides a strong reference model for individual behavior, in ethical problems it appears to be a consistently negative model. Finally, relatively few civil servants look to their superiors for guidance in ethical behavior. This implies that something more than honest and exemplary behavior on the part of senior public officials is necessary to encourage proper conduct in governmental affairs.

CONCLUSIONS

The evidence discussed in this paper permits several conclusions. First, even in the current decline of public service prestige, public administrators demonstrate a high degree of concern about the ethical dimensions of American government and public policy issues. Secondly, the respondents also profess a fairly high set of ethical practices in everyday management operations. If careerists are expected to have a moral imperative to protect the public interest, these administrators appear to be worthy of this trust. It is not sufficient, however, for the civil employee to be convinced of his own rectitude and integrity—if it were we could all then go our own self-righteous ways in peace.

Instead, the data imply that although the vast majority of executives are conscientiously disposed to serve the public interest, some kind of institutional basis for professional conduct is necessary. Without it, individual conscience can be paralyzed when morally right actions are ignored and morally wrong actions are rewarded because the rules of the organization are inadequate to support personal morality. Ethical conduct cannot be based upon informal standards and peer group values; given administrators' views about their colleagues, it would be a short step from the perceived prevalence of others' behavior (everyone's doing it) to excusing the behavior altogether. As American government moves into the last quarter of this century, a sound basis for effective, ethical practice must be laid.

Since the "public" element of public administration gives taxpayers, interest groups, and reporters, special motivation to be vigilant and indignant about violations of the public trust, it is reasonable to expect government to assume responsibility to clarify and encourage ethical behavior in the civil service. One cabinet officer pointed out, "A certain amount of unethical behavior must be expected. The only way that it can be dealt with is by institutionalized countermeasures." There are essentially three approaches to accomplish this: individual acts of leadership, codes of conduct, and legislation. All have been tried with varying degrees of success; all are useful and necessary for further advances to be made.

With respect to individual acts of leadership, there is little doubt that superiors can play a significant role in upgrading ethical conduct. As an executive in the Department of Interior said, "Ethical standards drop rapidly when employees see their supervisors engage in questionable managerial practices. What is needed more than anything else is leadership!" In the context of the traditional American suspicion of politicians, however, exemplary behavior by itself does not seem sufficient to meet contemporary needs. In the post-Watergate era, the example set by even the most scrupulous officials must be fortified by other methods of fostering ethical behavior.

The value of codes of ethics to govern managerial actions is controversial. Opinions range from the idea that they are virtually worthless to the view that they can serve to preserve and promote high standards. While advocates of written codes do not claim that they provide easy solutions, critics appear to offer few alternatives, which is hardly a justifiable position today. Therefore, one method of reinforcing honorable behavior of leaders is for that behavior to be a personification of a code of ethics which they have the responsibility of enforcing. A middle manager in the Department of Transporation explained:

> Standards can be maintained through leadership, indoctrination, and administrative controls such as impersonal reviews, supervision, and agreed-upon standards of conduct. A more rigorous administrative atmosphere should be more conducive to ethical behavior than a relaxed one.

The federal government does, of course, have an official, written code of ethical conduct which was most recently set forth by President Johnson in 1965. What it does not have is effective enforcement. For example, its existence brought no mention throughout the long Watergate inquiry. It is this situation that has stimulated proposals for a National Ethics Commission to enforce the code by recommending or initiating proceedings when necessary.

Finally, some commentators argue for appropriate legislation. Although many argue that "You can't legislate morality," Watergate, local scandals in half a dozen states, and a national digust with political practices, seem to have overcome the politicians' traditional abhorence of these laws. Since 1972, forty-six states have passed legislation aimed at cleansing their political processes. While it is unlikely that all aspects of this protean problem can be dealt with by statutory rules, it is probable that employees will be less likely to violate explicit legal standards than they would be to depart from unwritten understandings and practices.

In short, although acts of leadership, codes of ethics, and ethics legislation are not foolproof, a renewed institutional emphasis on professional conduct does offer the opportunity for conscientious public servants to clarify behavior and to make codes and regulations effective. It is important that public officials have adequate and authoritative guides through the ethical perplexities of situations which they will undoubtedly encounter. At this juncture of history there is a widespread and profound loss of confidence by the public in popular government. To do nothing in the face of this predicament is an abdication of responsibility.

The subject of ethics, in conclusion, is and will remain an area of controversy. Therefore, the principles on which government is conducted should be well-known by political leaders, civil employees, and the public. As Roy S. Webley of the British-North American Research Association has argued, these principles should not be subject to frequent change to suit the circumstances; situational ethics, though superficially appealing, can never be an adequate basis for human behavior. What should change is the application of the principles to the problems that arise in modern government and such questions will not always be simple or quickly resolved. While governmental ethics doubtless deserve more acclaim and less attack than they have been receiving, if the corruption that continues to be exposed is not vigorously dealt with, many cherished American traditions will be jeopardized. The search for appropriate standards for the conduct of popular government will not be an easy task. It is hoped that the analysis presented in this paper will contribute to this effort.

11.
Is The Ethics of Business Changing?

Steven N. Brenner and Earl A. Molander

What would you do if

• The minister of a foreign nation where extraordinary payments to lubricate the decision-making machinery are common, asks you for a $200,000 consulting fee? In return, he promises special assistance in obtaining a $100 million contract which would produce at least a $5 million profit for your company. The contract would probably go to a foreign competitor if your company did not win it.

• As the president of a company in a highly competititve industry, you learn that a competitor has made an important scientific discovery that will substantially reduce, but not eliminate, your profit for about a year? There is a possibility of hiring one of the competitor's employees who knows the details of the discovery.

• You learn that an executive earning $30,000 a year has been padding his expense account by about $1,500 a year?

These questions were posed as part of a lengthy questionnaire on. . . ethics and social responsibility completed by 1,227 *Harvard Business Review (HBR)* readers—25 percent of the cross section of 5,000 U.S. readers polled.

Our study was prompted by the same concern that Raymond C. Baumhard had in 1961 when he conducted a similar study for HBR: The numerous comments on. . . ethics in the media contained little empirical evidence to indicate whether large numbers of business executives shared the attitudes, behavior, and experience of those whose supposedly unethical and illegal conduct was being represented (or denied) as typical of the business profession.

In updating and expanding his study, we designed our survey around three main questions: Has...ethics changed since the early 1960s, and if so, how and why? Are codes the answers to the ethical challenges business people currently face? What is the relationship between ethical dilemmas and the dilemma of corporate social responsibility?

Here are some of the highlights of our study.

1. There is substantial disagreement among respondents as to whether ethical standards in business today have changed from what they were.

2. Respondents are somewhat more cynical about the ethical conduct of their peers than they were.

3. Most respondents favor ethical codes, although they strongly prefer general precept codes to specific practice codes.

4. The dilemmas respondents experience and the factors they feel, have the greatest impact on...ethics which suggest that ethical codes alone will not substantially improve business conduct.

5. Most respondents have overcome the traditional ideological barriers to the concept of social responsibility and have embraced its practice as a legitimate and achievable goal for business.

6. Most respondents rank their customers well ahead of shareholders and employees as the client group to whom they feel the greatest responsibility.

TODAY vs FIFTEEN YEARS AGO

Like other professions, business is continually scrutinizing its behavior relative to its own standards and those of the society around it.

What do business executives see when they look at themselves? One thing we found was that they see their profession as less ethical than the professions of professors and doctors, but more ethical than those of government agency officials, lawyers, elected politicians, and union officials, in that order.

Common Dilemmas

Of course, the ethics of business includes not only the moral values and duties of the profession itself, but also the existing values and expectations of the larger society. Because ethical systems are created by fallible people, they generally have some inherent contradictions. Further, the values and ethics of various organizations differ from those of other sectors of society in which business people participate (such as the family, religious institutions, and political parties). For these reasons executives inevitably face some ethical dilemmas in their daily work.

To learn how chronic a problem such ethical dilemmas are in the contemporary business environment, we asked our respondents if they had ever experienced a conflict between what was expected of them as efficient, profit-conscious managers, and what was expected of them as ethical persons. Four of every seven of those who responded (399 of 698) say they have experienced such conflicts, compared with three of four respondents in 1961 (603 of 796)—a substantial decrease of 19 percent.

One possible explanation for this decrease is that the internal pressures for profit and efficiency are not as great as they once were. Since we can find no evidence of such a change, two other possible explanations must be considered: Ethical standards have declined from what they were, or situations that once caused ethical discomfort have become accepted practice.

We did find that the *nature* of compromising circumstances has changed. Honesty in communication is a significantly greater problem in 1976 than it was in 1961. This includes honesty in advertising and in provoding information to top management, clients, and government agencies. We found number manipulation to have become a particularly acute problem.

Dilemmas associated with firings and layoffs are significantly less of a problem in 1976. Either terminations and their related problems are becoming accepted as routine in today's business world, or they are being handled more equitably when they occur. Undoubtedly because of government prosecutions, price collusion is also far less of a problem.

We feel it particularly noteworthy that relations with superiors are the primary category of ethical conflict. Respondents frequently complained of superiors' pressure to support incorrect viewpoints, sign false documents, overlook superiors' wrongdoing, and do business with superiors' friends. Either superiors are expecting more than subordinates in 1976 or subordinates are less willing to do their boss' bidding without questions, at least to themselves. Both possibilities suggest a weakening in the corporate authority structure and an attendant impact on ethical business conduct that deserves future study. The following examples demonstrate ethical dilemmas being faced in business today:

• The vice-president of a California industrial manufacturer "being forced as an officer to sign corporate documents which I knew were not in the best interest of minority stockholders."

• A Missouri manager of manpower planning "employing marginally qualified minorities in order to meet Affirmative Action quotas."

• A manager of product development from a computer company in Massachusetts "trying to act as though the product (computer software) would correspond to what the customer had been led by sales to expect, when, in fact, I knew it wouldn't."

• A manager of corporate planning from California "acquiring a non-U.S. company with two sets of books used to evade income taxes—standard practice for that country. Do we (1) declare income and pay taxes, (2) take the "black money" out of the country (illegally), or (3) continue tax evasion?"

• The president of a real estate property management firm in Washington "projecting cash flow without substantial evidence in order to obtain a higher loan than the project can realistically amortize."

• A young Texas insurance manager "being asked to make policy changes that produced more premiums for the company and commission for an agent but did not appear to be of advantage to the policy holder."

Accepted Practices

Clearly, that ethical dilemmas do exist and are too often resolved in ways which leave executives dissatisfied seems to be a matter of substantial concern for today's business people. And too often unethical practices become a routine part of doing business. To determine just how routine, we asked:

"In every industry there are some generally accepted business practices. In your industry, are there practices which you regard as unethical?"

If we eliminate those who say they "don't know" we see that two thirds of the responding executives in 1976 indicate that such practices exist, compared with nearly four fifths who responded in 1961.

Could this decrease be a sign of improvement in ethical *practices*? Perhaps, but it is also possible that such practices are now less visible than they once were. Even more disturbing is the possibility which we raised earlier—that ethical *standards* have, in fact, fallen in business so that practices once considered unethical are now not viewed as such. Further, these figures say nothing about the conduct that all agree is both unacceptable and unethical.

Nearly half (540) of all respondents and 84 percent of those indicating the existence of such practices, were willing to tell us which practice or practices they would most like to see eliminated. Both the changes and similarities in these "most unwanted" practices in the past 15 years are interesting.

As in 1961, the practice that most executives want to eliminate involves "gifts, gratuities, bribes, and call girls." Typical examples given by the 144 respondents in this category are:

• "Payoffs to a foreign government to secure contracts." [The vice-president of an Oklahoma oil exploration company]

• "Egg carton contracts with grocery chains can only be obtained by kickbacks—the egg packers do not have the freedom of choice in buying, thus stifling competition." [A young southern consumer goods executive vice-president]

• "Loans granted as favors to loan officers." [An Indiana bank vice-president]

• "Dealings with travel agencies that involve kickbacks, rebates, or other pseudonyms for 'bribes.'" [A Florida transportation industry executive]

Of the 80 respondents who mentioned practices which included cheating customers, unfair credit practices, or overselling, typical comments are:

- "Substitution of materials without customer knowledge after the job has been awarded." [A young New York salesman]
- "Misrepresenting the contents of products." [A Texas vice-president of engineering]
- "Scheduled delivery dates that are known to be inaccurate to get a contract." [A California director of engineering]

Both the sharp drop from 1961 to 1976 in concern over "price discrimination and unfair pricing" and "dishonest advertising" and the increase in concern over "unfairness to employees and prejudice in hiring" and "creating customers" are probably attributable to government enforcement and higher legal standards.

Economic Pressures

We have confirmed the continued existence both of ethical dilemmas inherent in everyday business, and of generally accepted practices which individual managers feel are unethical. To observe the impact of such an environment on our respondents' ethical beliefs, we turned our attention to a number of issues of general ethical concern.

Simply returning our questionnaire reflected, we think, a general concern about...ethics among our respondents. Nevertheless, 65 percent of them feel that "society, not business, has the *chief* responsibility for inculcating its ethical standards into the educational and legal systems, and thus into business decision making."

Another important aspect of the debate over ethics focuses on whether any absolutes exist to strive for or whether ethics should be purely "situational" or "relative." Four out of five respondents agree that "business people should try to live up to an absolute moral standard rather than to the moral standard of their peer group."

Not only do executives believe in ethical absolutes; they also believe that "in the long run, sound ethics is good business." As in 1961, fewer than 2 percent of the respondents disagreed with this statement. Yet, in practice, many of these same executives see their associates losing sight of this standard. Again, as in 1961, close to half of our respondents agree that "the American business executive tends not to apply the great ethical laws immediately to work. He is preoccupied chiefly with gain."

Our results suggest two explanations for this failure. First, despite its long-run value, ethical conduct apparently is not necessarily rewarded. Within the business organization, 50 percent of our respondents feel that one's superiors often do not want to know how results are obtained, as long as one achieves the desired outcome.

Second, competitive pressures from outside the organization push ethical consideration into the background. Of our executives, 43 percent feel that "competition today is stiffer than ever. As a result, many in business find themselves forced to resort to practices which are considered shady, but which appear necessary for survival."

Societal Forces

In the period since Baumhart's study, American business has seen some significant changes. A sustained period of economic euphoria which began in 1961 has been replaced by recession, inflation, and resource scarcity. Charges of corporate irresponsibility relative to critical issues of the 1960s and 1970s (minority relations, consumerism, and the environment) combined with the recent disclosures of corporate wrongdoing at home and abroad, have raised serious questions about the trend in business's ethical standards.

To determine if any such trend existed, we asked our HBR respondents:

"How do you feel ethical standards in business today compare with ethical standards 15 years ago?"

The old French proverb, "The more things change, the more they stay the same," seems appropriate in describing the responses. Rather than reporting a clear-cut shift in either direction, our respondents split fairly evenly; 32 percent (388) feel standards are lower today, 41 percent (492) feel they are about the same, and 27 percent (325) that they are higher.

But among those respondents who sense a more extreme change, a trend is identifiable with the 12 percent who believe ethical standards to be *considerably* lower outnumbering the 5 percent who believe them to be *considerably* higher by a 2.4-1 ratio.

We asked our respondents to describe "the single factor which has most influenced (or caused) the shift (you) observe in ethical standards." By splitting responses into two groups, those who see today's ethical standards as lower, and those who see them as higher, it is possible to isolate which factors our respondents feel gave influenced ethical standards in business.

The fact that 95 percent of the 713 respondents who see some shift in ethical standards provided further explanatory factors in brief sentences confirms our earlier assertion that ethics is an important personal concern to executives.

It is noteworthy that of the six major factors seen as causing *higher* standards, only two are subject to any significant measure of direct business influence and control—the education and professionalism of management and business's greater sense of awareness and responsiveness.

And of the six major factors seen as causing *lower* standards, only one is subject to such influence and control by business—pressure for profits in the organization.

Our respondents seem to be sending us three clear-cut messages:

1. Public disclosure and concern over unethical business behavior are the most potent forces for improvement in ethical standards.

2. Hedonism, individual greed, and the general decay of social standards, are the factors which most influence a decline in ethical standards.

3. The elements which influence shifts in ethical standards are ones over which they have little direct control.

Growing Cynicism

The situation, then, is that today's executive often faces ethical dilemmas and observes generally accepted practices which he feels are unethical. At the same time he is more likely to attribute questionable conduct to his business colleagues than he is to himself.

In 1961, Baumhart found his respondents to be quite cynical when comparing their own ethical decisions with what they expected the "average" executive to do in the same circumstances. To measure cynicism, we presented four case situations in two different ways. We asked half of our sample, "What would *you* do?" and the other half, "What would the *average* executive do?"

The two groups' answers differ more than Baumhart's respondents'. In Case 1, current respondents report themselves as less willing to pad their own expense accounts ands report others as more willing to do so than did respondents in 1961. This perception spread (between "I feel it is unacceptable" and "the average executive feels it is unacceptable") grew from 26 percent in 1961 to 36 percent in 1976.

In Case 2, while the spread is nearly the same (22 percent in 1961 versus 23 percent in 1976), the respondents indicate that both they and the average executive would be more inclined than 1961 respondents to hire a competitor's employee to get a technological secret.

The real magnitude of such cynicism is shown in Case 3's international situation where facilitative payments could help land a large contract: 42 percent of the respondents said they would refuse to pay a bribe no matter what the consequences, while only 9 percent felt that the average executive in the same situation would refuse to pay. Even more disturbing, seven eights of the respondents who report that the average executive would see such payments as unethical, also feel that he would go ahead and pay them anyway! And more than one third of the respondents who themselves see such payments as unethical, admit a willingness to pay them to help cement the contract award. Apparently, economic values override ethical values.

Case 4 illustrates another aspect of cynicism. Here we presented a potential conflict of interest and asked half of our respondents what an inside director would do and half what an outside director would do. The results suggest that executives expect outside directors to be more likely than inside directors to find fault in this situation (64 percent versus 45 percent) and to be more overt in their opposition when they do (30 percent versus 16 percent).

Our respondents apparently are cynical not only when they compare their own motives and actions to those of others, but also when they consider how business people with different organizational perspectives handle identical situations. This makes sense; organizational loyalty tends to inhibit an employee's perception of an ethical dilemma and to constrain his actions when ethical dilemmas are recognized.

Could our results be simply a flaw in our sampling method or in our analysis? This possibility is unlikely. We split our sample at random into two equal groups. Demographically, our groups were virtually identical. So, too, were their responses to the other questions we asked. So the differences must indicate that while executives see themselves as being faced with ethical dilemmas and as handling them correctly, they are not so confident about their peers' reactions.

GUIDEPOSTS AND CODES

What can be done to restore this confidence? And what can help reduce unethical acts?

We asked our respondents what factors they feel influence executives to make unethical decisions. They believe that the behavior of one's superiors is the primary guidepost, with formal company policy a somewhat distant secondary influence.

In other words, when faced with ethical dilemmas, people first refer to their immediate organizational framework for guidance. If the unethical acts of others and the lack of formal company policy provide a rationale for unethical behavior, would a formal policy, that is, an ethical code, be beneficial? The current popularity of ethical codes would seem to suggest as much.

When we asked our respondents for their feelings about ethical codes for their industry, 25 percent said they favor no code at all. Of those who favor a code, 58 percent prefer one dealing with general precepts while only 17 percent prefer one delineating specific practices. Despite this lack of enthusiasm for specific codes, the majority of respondents expect that such a code would help executives to (a) raise the ethical level of their industry, (b) define the limits of acceptable conduct, and (c) refuse unethical requests.

While respondents in 1976 are less certain of a code's efficacy than were their counterparts in 1961, these expectations support an argument many observers have made: The mere existence of a code, specific or general, can raise the ethical level of business behavior because it clarifies what is meant by ethical conduct. However, to an even greater extent than those in 1961, our respondents think a code is limited in its ability to change human conduct: 61 percent feel people would violate the code whenever they thought they could avoid detection, and only 41 percent feel the code would reduce underhanded practices.

Appropriate Enforcement

The single most negative response to our questions about a specific practice code concerns its enforceability: 89 percent of our respondents feel a specific practices code would *not* be easy to enforce. Anticipating this result since Baumhart's 1961 study had produced a similar response, we asked our respondents to identify an appropriate body for enforcing a code and the problems they foresaw in its enforcement.

In their choice of enforcement bodies, our respondents follow essentially the same pattern as Baumhart's did. Slightly more than a third favor self-enforcement at the company level, a third favor enforcement by a combined group of industry executives and members of the community, and slightly less than a third prefer enforcement at the industry level—either a trade association or a group of industry executives. Only 2.5 percent favor enforcement by a government agency.

Respondents foresee two major problems confronting all of these enforcement groups—getting information about violations and uniform and impartial enforcement. They feel that a third problem—lack of power and authority for enforcement—would be common to all groups except self-enforcement, which, understandably, they see as less of a problem. One young manager from Iowa hit on all three problems when he said, "You'll have problems with access to records, exceptions to the rules (and some may be legitimate), and punishment enforcement."

Our respondents feel that self-enforcement at the company level, the form of enforcement currently in widest use, has both substantial advantages and disadvantages compared with external enforcement.

Among the advantages they mentioned are:

1. Greater power and authority for those responsible for enforcement.
2. Easier access to information and detection of violations committed.
3. Easier interpretation when rules have been violated.
4. More natural definition of and execution of penalties to fit violations.

At the same time certain disadvantages exist:

1. Uniform and impartial enforcement.
2. Difficulty of securing the full-fledged commitment of the enforcers (top management).
3. Greater tendency to ignore or wink at the rules.
4. Greater difficulty in resolving profits-versus-ethics conflicts.
5. Continuous worry over actions of companies not covered by a code.

As a system sales representative from California rather curtly put it, "Self-enforcement won't always work, because those who make 'em, break 'em."

The enforcement problems inherent in ethical codes led us to question their potential effectiveness. We reexamined the data concerning (1) the dilemmas our respondents have encountered, (2) the practices they would most like to eliminate, and (3) the factors causing shifts in standards, and we asked, "In which of these areas could ethical codes have an impact?"

In general the responses suggest that codes can be most helpful in those areas where there is general agreement that certain unethical practices are widespread and undesirable. Ethical codes do not, however, offer executives much hope for either controlling outside influences on...ethics or resolving fundamental ethical dilemmas. This is not to minimize the potential for codes to have an impact in narrow areas of concern. It is to emphasize that regardless of form they are no panacea for unethical conduct.

NEW VIEW OF SOCIAL RESPONSIBILITY

The current revival of interest in...ethics coincides with a renewed focus on corporate social responsibility. To provide some insight into how our respondents see the relationship between "social responsibility" and " business ethics," we asked:

Is social responsibility an *ethical* issue for the *individual business person,* or is it an issue that concerns the *role* the *corporation* should play in society? The overwhelming response we got is that it is *both*—65 percent agree with the former statement and 83 percent with the latter.

But can it be both? The answer is, of course, yes. Whereas responsibility, for both the individual and the corporation, tends to be defined in the social arrangements and obligations which make up the structure of the society, ethics concerns the rules by which these responsibilities are carried out. As in numerous other settings, it is often difficult to separate the rules of the game from the game itself.

Erroneous Caricature

One important finding of our study is the rejection of the traditional ideology that says business is a profit-bound institution. Only 28 percent of our respondents endorse the traditional dictum that "the social responsibility of business is to 'stick to business,'" most often associated with Milton Friedman, in *Capitalism and Freedom.*

Further, only 23 percent agree that "social responsibility is good business only if it is also good public relations and/or preempts government interferrence." And 38 percent agree that "the social responsibility debate is the result of the attempt of liberal intellectuals to make a moral issue of business behavior."

By contrast, 69 percent agree with George Cabot Lodge's observation that "'profit' is really a somewhat ineffective measure of business's social effectiveness," in *HBR.*

Not only do those in our sample reject the traditional idological barriers to corporate involvement in social responsibility, but they also reject the practical ones. Of our respondents, 77 percent disagree with the idea that "every business is in effect 'trapped' in the business system it helped create, and can do remarkably little about the social problems of our time."

Have business executives abandoned their traditional profit orientation? Not necessarily. We still found strong support for long-term profit maximization among our executives. But these findings do indicate that the American business executive has incorporated a new view of his role and potential, and those of is company, into his profit concerns.

Those critics who continue to characterize the American business executive as a power-hungry, profit-bound individualist, indifferent to the needs of society, should be put on notice that they are now dealing with a straw man of their own making.

Before we go as far as to predict a revolution in corporate behavior, however, a word of caution is in order. First, the corporate organization still resists specific measures when trying to put social responsibility into practice. Of our respondents, 75 percent feel the rhetoric of social responsibility exceeds the reality in most corporations. And 58 percent agree that "the socially aware executive must show convincingly a net short-term or long-term economic advantage to the corporation in order to gain acceptance for any socially responsible measure he might propose."

A second major barrier is uncertainty—uncertainty as to what "social responsibility" means. Almost half (46 percent) of our respondents agree with the assertion that "the meaning of social responsibility is so vague as to render it essentially unworkable as a guide to corporate policy and decisions."

This uncertainty as to meaning is further amplified by an uncertainty as to consequences. Our respondents were almost evenly split on two statements:

1. Social responsibility invariably will mean *lower* corporate profits in the *short run*—41 percent agree, 16 percent are neutral, and 43 percent disagree.

2. Social responsibility invariably will mean *higher* corporate profits in the *long run*—43 percent agree, 22 percent are neutral, and 36 percent disagree.

The nearly even split and the high number of neutral responses on these statements, together with the feelings of vagueness about the meaning of social responsibility, suggest that bringing social responsibility to the operating level is an objective which its advocates have yet to realize.

Customer's Servant

To further clarify our respondents' concept of social responsibility, we asked them to rank the various groups whose relations to the corporation define the corporation's place in the social system.

The group to whom executives feel the greatest responsibility comes through clearly and unmistakably: *the customers.* Stockholders and employees are a clear second and third, and the interest of society at large and its elected governments—

the "public interest"—appears to receive the least consideration.

This rather surprising result—the primacy of customer interest—suggests that we need to reexamine the thesis that the guiding principle of American business and the justification for its power is service to stockholders. We may be observing a return to the original capitalist doctrine of the customer as the client whom production is intended to serve and the replacement of the doctrine of "long-run profit maximization" with the "long-run customer satisfaction" doctrine.

The primacy of customer interests also raises some serious questions about any unethical conduct at the expense of customers which is rationalized on grounds of profit maximization. If the assertion of customer primacy is valid, it follows that business should also make ethical conduct in dealing with customers a first priority, a condition which our data suggest does not currently exist.

Societal Obligations

How do these attitudes affect policy and decision making on specific issues? We asked HBR readers to express the degree of responsibility they felt in each of nine areas along a scale of 1 (absolutely voluntary) to 5 (absolutely obligatory). The third-place standing of "maximizing long-run profits," confirms our observation that it is no longer perceived as the primary responsibility of today's executives.

But we were surprised to find two areas of general responsibility to *society*— "being an efficient user of energy and natural resources" and "assessing the potential environmental effects flowing from the company's technological advances"—are first and second. The strong feeling of obligation toward these areas, together with "using every means possible to maximize job content and satisfaction for the hourly worker," demonstrates the desire of the business person to define his responsibility in those areas which involve externalities directly associated with his operation, areas where he can see clearly the internalized benefits of his "socially responsible" actions, either in reduced costs or preempted government regulation.

By contrast, the strong voluntary rankings for the United Fund and hardcore hiring indicate that executives do not feel a significant obligation concerning social problems of a remedial or welfare nature whose benefits to the company are not readily apparent.

Voluntary Measures

Perhaps not surprisingly, our respondents favor those measures for improving corporate social conduct that are both general in nature and leave room for voluntarism over those that involve compulsion and outside interference in corporate affairs. This result could be expected given our respondents' uncertainties about what social responsibility means and about its consequences, as well as their natural reluctance to accept any further constraints on the traditional freedom of the business decision maker.

We have already seen that respondents feel the media have had a powerful impact on . . . ethics simply by virtue of publicizing unethical conduct. They also feel that "endorsement of 'social responsibility' by the business media" would have the greatest positive influence on corporate social behavior. Altogether, 72 percent feel that such an endorsement would have a "positive impact," 55 percent believe that there would be "some positive impact," and 17 percent believe that the impact would be "very positive." Only 4 percent think it would have a "negative impact," while 24 percent think it would have "zero impact." Clearly executives look to the business media, not only for information and education, but for guidance in areas of uncertainty as well.

About 62 percent of our respondents also agree that "the equalization of managerial rewards and punishments for social performance with those for financial performance" would have a positive effect in making corporations more socially responsible. This view is corroborated by our earlier observation that most executives support the view that proposals for corporate social action must convincingly show a net economic advantage to the company.

Polling stockholder opinions on sensitive social issues (part of "shareholder democracy"), public interest representation on boards of directors, educating the average citizen to the realities of corporate operations, and corporate social audits have all been advanced, and debated, in business and academic circles. Our respondents' generally positive view toward these measures—no more than a fourth think any of them would have a negative impact—suggests that, if properly conceived and advanced, these measures might also be acceptable to most executives.

This willingness to accept outside inputs does not include input from government, however. Less than one sixth of our respondents see anything positive in federal chartering of corporations, strongly endorsed by Ralph Nader among others, while 39 percent feel that such a measure would be deleterious. And our respondents are least sanguine about increased governmental regulation: 64 percent fear it would have a negative impact, and 14 percent say it would have none, while only 21 percent feel it might be beneficial.

FREEDOM AND CRITICISM

At the outset we posed three basic questions for our study. The generous response of HBR readers has allowed us to answer them in this article. Now a fourth question is in order: "What do the results mean for managers and students of ethics?"

Our results suggest changes are necessary in two primary areas: managerial outlook and managerial actions.

The four aspects of change in managerial outlook indicated are:
- You will face ethical dilemmas, created by value conflicts, for which there

may be no totally satisfactory resolution. But don't use this condition to rationalize unethical behavior on your part.

• Don't expect ethical codes to help solve all problems. Codes can create a false sense of security and lead to the encouragement of violations.

• If you wish to avoid external enforcement of someone else's ethical code, make self-enforcement work.

• Don't deceive yourself into thinking you can hide unethical actions.

The five aspects of managerial action suggested are:

• Fair dealing with customers and employees is the most direct way to restore confidence in business morality.

• Corporate steps taken to improve ethical behavior clearly must come from the top and be part of the reward and punishment system.

• If an ethical code is developed and implemented, have an accompanying information system to detect violations. Then treat violators equitably.

• Test decisions against what you think is right rather than against what is expedient.

• Don't force others into unethical conduct.

It seems to us our respondents are saying that managers facing ethical dilemmas should refer to the familiar maxim, "Would I want my family, friends, and employers to see this decision and its consequences on television?" If the answer is yes, then go ahead. If the answer is no, then additional thought should be given to finding a more satisfactory solution.

Business executives and the companies they serve have a personal and vested interest in the resolution of ethical and social responsibility dilemmas. Our respondents recognize these dilemmas and to some extent appear willing to accept generalized guidance for their resolution in the form of general precept codes and statements from the business media. Although such measures will help in this regard, they are obviously no panacea for the continued strain arising from challenges to...ethics and responsibility. They also are not as action oriented as specific practice codes or government regulation.

The manager appears to prefer uncertainty and tension to the loss of freedom and complications that would accompany these more rigorous measures. In making this choice, he has to realize that he must continue to bear the criticism of the larger society in both the ethics and corporate social responsibility areas.

COMMENT ON STUDY

My interpretation of Professors Brenner's and Molander's data and the signs of the times indicate that business behavior is more ethical than it was 15 years ago, but that the expectations of a better educated and ethically sensitized public have risen more rapidly than the behavior.

This is the sixth, and most creative and extensive, replication of the series of questions I first asked in 1961. Each time the results have been remarkably similar, especially in the respondents' attitude that: I am more ethical than the average manager, and my department and company are more ethical than their counterparts; and a written code of ethics would help to improve business practices in my industry.

It is good to see the evidence that business managers accept the corporation as a social, as well as an economic, entity.

To me the most surprising finding of this study is that the 1,227 respondents rank responsibility to customers ahead of responsibility to stockholders and employees. What has happened to *caveat emptor?* Now it is the government and suppliers who should beware.

Raymond C. Baumhart, S.J.,
President of Loyola University

Selected Readings
Part IV.

Baumhart, Raymond. *An Honest Profit: What Businessmen Say About Ethics in Business.* New York: Holt, Rinehart and Winston, 1968.

Bowman, James S. "Managerial Ethics in Business and Government." *Business Horizons.* 19 (October 1976); 48-54.

Cooper, M.R., et al. "Changing Employee Values: Deepening Discontent." *Harvard Business Review.* 57 (January/February 1979); 117-25.

Dagher, Samir P., and Spader, Peter H. "Poll of Top Managers Stresses Education and Leadership by Example as Strong Forces for Higher Standards." *Management Review.* 69 (March 1980); 54-57.

England, George W. *The Manager and His Values: An International Perspective from the United States, Japan, Korea, India, and Australia,* Cambridge, Mass.: Ballinger Publishing Co., 1975.

Erskine, Hazel. "The Polls: Corruption in Government." *Public Opinion Quarterly.* 37 (Winter 1973-74); 628-44.

Ewing, David W. "Who Wants Employee Rights?" *Harvard Business Review.* 49 (November/December 1971); 22-35, 155-60.

———. "Who Wants Corporate Democracy?" *Harvard Business Review.* 49 (September/October 1971); 12-21, 24-28, 146-49.

Sikula, Andrew F. "The Values and Value Systems of Government Executives." *Public Personnel Management.* 2 (January/February 1973); 16-22.

"Special Section: Honesty/Ethical Standards." *Gallup Opinion Index.* 150 (January 1980); 7-29.

U.S. Merit Systems Protection Board. *Whistle Blowing and the Federal Employee: Blowing the Whistle on Fraud, Waste, and Mismanagement— Who Does It and What Happens?* Washington, D.C.: The Board, 1981.

Wynia, Bob L. "Federal Bureaucrats' Attitudes Toward Democratic Ideology." *Public Administration Review.* 34 (March/April 1974); 156-62.

Part V.
Conclusion:
Actions to Deal With
Ethical Problems

Recognizing that human beings are not faultless, it is critical to try to live up to the best kinds of standards that can be realistically established. The test for the administrator, then, is to understand just what she/he confronts, and to devise ways to making that reality manageable. Executives, as moral custodians of collective goals, are strategically placed to recognize factors that promote and inhibit appropriate behavior. As James Owens pointed out earlier in Chapter 5, ethics is a practical necessity for managers today. Accordingly, they should be held responsible for providing a basis for professional conduct.

Taking an oath of office or reading a company's code of conduct, therefore, is only the beginning, not the end, of an executive's ethical responsibility. The citizenry deserves greater assurance that government and industry can be depended upon to conduct the nation's business according to high ideals. For institutions so central to society, public confidence should not be left to chance. The principle question is, "How to provide that assurance?" If corruption cannot be prevented, how can it be responsibly controlled? Is it possible, in short, to catch the conscience of the manager?

In developing a strategy for ethical action in this, the final part of the book, the following assumptions are made:

1. The maintenance of a high level of trust and confidence between the public and societal institutions is essential in democracy.

2. Since each group in society is governed by a written or unwritten code of behavior, efforts to encourage ethical action must be "culture based," and

germane to the performance of the organization.

3. As humans are at least partially knowing beings, and knowing is not an automatic process, the potential for learning exists. Modifying behavior, however, is a difficult task, and miraculous transformations should not be expected.

4. On the premise that any significant organizational activity must be integrated into the mainstream of operations or it does not get done, ethics programs must be infused into the everyday life of the organization.

5. In an institution where ethics is taken seriously, an atmosphere of trust, mutuality, and credibility will exist.

6. Under appropriate circumstances, ethical programs can result in a different standard of conduct than would be achieved by the spontaneous development of group standards.

Since ethics asks questions about broad public purpose, an analysis of these problems mandates change. Until the executive speaks and acts decisively and sincerely, he behaves unethically. Ethics is a matter of doing; it cannot survive in a neutral, "no comment" environment. The conclusion of moral agreement is action.

It should come as no surprise, then, that no less than six of the previous eleven chapters contained suggestions for change. Among the many strategies outlined (see the article by Archie B. Carroll), the authors in this section evaluate two internal and three external reforms for organizations.

If the moral pattern of the institution is not explicit for each individual, the prospects for making ethical decisions and accepting responsibility on behalf of the organization are diminished. It is, therefore, imperative to develop a widely shared organizational vocabulary concerning issues of morality and honesty. A standard of practice is inherent in the very concept of professional life.

Studies indicate that most executives propose the Golden Rule as a code of conduct. Developing T. Edwin Boling's comments about codes (Chapter 7) in further detail, John Donaldson and Mike Waller (Chapter 12) argue that principles and standards can be starting points for action internal to organizations (see also James Owens, Chapter 5). That is, without some precepts of morality to guide behavior, it is impossible to mediate competing claims in organizations. It is not necessary to suggest that codes are universally obeyed. It only needs to be recognized that there is a strong presumption that a professional is going to perform with the individual's welfare in mind.

If codes are the central instrument in making ethics operational, the litmus test is to make then living documents; any creed worth having is worth enforcing. One method of implementation internal to the organization is offered by Theodore V. Purcell in Chapter 13. He proposes that institutions should have ethical advisors just as they now have legal and financial experts. These persons could serve as ethical "devil's advocates" in decision-making, formulate ethical impact statements, design employee bill of rights, serve as an ombudsman, provide space on standard forms for dissenting opinions, and/or chair review boards.

However much help internal mechanisms may be in improving management and fostering professional behavior, their limitations must be acknowledged. Any such procedures are dependent upon the goodwill of management, the very lack of which may be the cause of ethical concern in the first place. External checks on organizations are, therefore, desirable.

Thus a third way to regain public confidence and restore credibility in business and in government in the 1980s, is to recognize the critical role of dissent in organizations. Unenforced codes of conduct or ineffective ethical advisors can contribute to "blowing the whistle" or disclosing organizational misdeeds to the public. Given pervasive group norms in bureaucracies, whistle blowing is not a common occurrence. It is, as John A. Rohr and Deena Weinstein noted in earlier chapters, a departure from business as usual. Yet, it may be indicative and symbolic of problems frequently encountered in contemporary management. Ethics cannot prosper unless people speak their conscience when it really matters, when internal mechanisms prove inadequate to the situation.

Blowing the whistle will continue as organizations grow larger, as expectations of work rise, as more females, with fresh perspectives on work, enter the labor force, as America increasingly becomes a nation of employees, and as corruption persists in bureaucracies. Lea P. Stewart's chapter is one of the first systematic studies of organizational dissent (Chapter 14). It should be recognized that the situation of the whistle blower will only be marginally improved unless the questions he raises are dealt with. The need to blow the whistle will remain until basic issues about employee rights, managerial prerogatives, and social problems— the substance of dissent—are addressed.

In the next reading, Ralph C. Chandler points out that a popular remedy for ethical problems is legislation. While it may be true that "you can't legislate morality," the repeated incidents of scandal in recent years has led lawmakers to seek statutory remedies. Chandler identifies one of these efforts in state government that promises to be effective. No doubt not all aspects of this protean problem can be dealt with by statutory rules, but it is probably that people will be less likely to violate legal standards than unwritten understandings.

The last contributor, Jarold A. Kieffer, contends that despite recent legislation, strong, systematic arrangements do not exist in government to provide a regularized means to address untoward actions. Nonetheless, he retains faith in legal reforms not shared by others (for instance, Deena Weinstein, Chapter 8), by recommending the establishment of an external, independent inspector general authorized to investigate corruption in agencies.

The Selected Readings parallel and expand upon the five selections in this section. Several useful discussions of codes of conduct are Charles E. Harris, Robert N. Holt, and Kenneth Kernaghan. See Thomas Fletcher, Paula Gordon, and Shirley Hentsell, for practical programs to implement changes internal to organizations. For an introduction to the significant issues in whistle blowing, see James S. Bowman concerning the public sector, and Kenneth D. Walters concerning the private sector. Interesting ideas and trends in legal reforms can be found in Stanley S. Kreutzen, Christopher D. Stone, and Alan F. Westin and Stephen Salisbury. Joseph Nocera, writing before and in contradistinction to the Kieffer chapter, debunks the concept of inspector generals, at least as currently institutionalized within agencies. Readers interested in self-diagnostic exercises should consult Herman Mertins, Jr., and Patrick Hennigan as well as and Lowell Rein.

Examples of the failure of reform efforts are not hard to find, and cynics delight in recounting them. They fail when they are but window dressing from the outset, meant to please or exhaust employees, or when they are turned into manipulative management tools (Part V, Selected Readings, Sissela Bok; Daniel Feldman). A great deal of energy is expended in bewailing the impossibility of combatting waste, corruption, and mismanagement in government. Such energy would be put to better use in employing the techniques discussed here. These steps, and others like them, will not in and of themselves build a moral community. They can, however, serve to set a new tone and mood in which administrators will be more willing and able to restore public faith in American institutions. Ignoring the problem will not only not make it go away, but may well make it worse; substantial improvement can be expected only if organizations and their members act.

Business and government must, in their own interest, come to grips with the complexity of their operations that seem to make it possible for many questionable practices to flourish. The problem of administrative ethics is one of discretion in the pursuit of the common good. Executives are obliged to plant and nourish a standard of ethical performance which takes into account the realities of everyday management.

The challenge is to instill in organizations a program of action that builds upon the basic need for people to lead moral lives. Fortunately, many remedies are known—the problem is not so much ignorance of what needs to be done, but doing it. The resources which business and government have to bring to bear are substantial. It seems evident that American institutions cannot expect to regain public support and confidence until they adopt the essentials of management discussed in this book.

12.
Codes of Conduct and the Golden Rule

John Donaldson and Mike Waller

THE JUSTIFICATION OF BEHAVIOR,
FUNCTIONAL RELATIONSHIPS
OR PRESCRIPTIVE STANDARDS

The holding of responsible jobs or positions of trust in organizations often presents moral predicaments. To varying extents, acts of omission or commission can bring heavy costs to others, in terms of income, health, well-being, or life. Current interest in "The Quality of Working Life" could be indicative of some of these predicaments. Granted that some people are showing concern in this area, there are many ways of setting about improving theoretical and practical knowledge, and improving practice, just as there are many ways of evading the very difficult issues involved.

From time to time there have been clear calls from practitioners for help, and it is our contention that theorists of organization and practitioners in industry could do more than we actually do, in clarifying the issues and improving practice. We argue in this paper for a set of criteria for improvement based on the traditional "golden rule," but it will be helpful first to present the problem as we see it.

The "Comment" feature of the June 1976 issue of the *Institute of Personnel Management* magazine, carried a thoughtful and cogently argued contribution from T.P. Kenny, the personnel director of the British Printing Corporation. Entitling his piece "The Asbestos Situation, or Whose Safety First?" Kenny pointed out that as early as 1931, there had been an awareness of the dangers to health posed by asbestos yet, for at least thirty years, managers and, in particular, personnel managers, appear to have tolerated the flouting of government regulations on the subject, presumably for reasons of personal survival within their own organizations. Kenny's concluding remarks warrant quotation in full:

> The good of the organization and the good of the individual or society all too frequently diverge. The personnel manager looks in vain for any positive help or guidance on this from his institute. We use the word *professionalism* often and glibly. The time has come either to stop doing so, or to speak out more clearly on what being *professional* might mean for the harassed and often vulnerable personnel manager.

We think that Kenny's contribution has not had the attention that is its due. The issues raised are much wider than that of the felt need of at least some members of a professional body for a code of practice. In this article we attempt to raise some very general issues, and to identify the principles according to which codes of practice can be drawn up and evaluated. The natural place in which to find guidance for professional associations or individuals in this enterprise is in the literature on organizational behavior, but here too, the diligent searcher will largely look in vain. We believe that this state of affairs is unsatisfactory since much work in this area explicitly or covertly has the character of justifications of behavior and practices. Although much distinguished work has been done to identify functional or causal relationships between identified variables (that is, relations between overtime and absence), much has been prescriptive, using arguments from, supposedly axiomatic, "first principles." Routines for scheduling would be examples of this kind of work. At best, this is neutral between moral values, but it is often the case that apparently objective work, purporting to describe how some organizations are and can be, ends up as prescriptions for the running of all organizations.

Much of this work is of a nature that seeks to evaluate, usually in accordance with an economic efficiency criterion, different means of achieving what are implicitly assumed to be agreed ends. It has long been recognized, however, that questions of moral value which are an inevitable core component of "end" choices, cannot be so easily disposed of. The search for a "positive" organization theory or economic theory is in principle mistaken. Quite apart from the pervasive intrusion of technical values and norms, attempts to postulate a situation in which basic values are absent can never be coherent. One in which they are universally agreed and understood is likely to have no empirical referents, unless the value concepts are hopelessly vague: We can all agree that one must do the right thing—whatever that means. Sir Isaiah Berlin, in *Philosophy, Politics, and Society,* for example, argues persuasively for the proposition that "The idea of a completely *Wertfrei* theory (or model) of human action (as contrasted, say, with animal behavior) rests on a naive misconception of what objectivity or neutrality in the social studies must be." Berlin rightly points out in this context that unwillingness to consider alternative ends or interpretations is characteristic of dire emergencies and of totalitarian regimes, yet it is characteristic of many styles of management. Technical descriptions of behavior and technical prescriptions are thus useful and value-laden, but they do need to be guided by moral value systems, which are capable of rational and logical treatment. It seems to be commonly taken for granted that moral codes or value-sets cannot be subject to logical and moral evaluation, presumably on the grounds that they are "subjective." This position results from a whole set of confusions, as R.N. Hare in *Freedom and Reason* has demonstrated. There are many examples in the literature of sound, objective, impartial and just principles. Our concern is the elucidation of the best principles and practice, and not the ascription of praise or blame. Clearly, this is the stuff of moral philosophy. It is a matter of the profoundest regret that for historical, cultural, and emotional reasons, there has been some tendency to ignore (in the field of management), or at best to isolate, the distinguished work that has been done in the area over thousands of years.

It should be emphasized at this point that the historical origin of particular codes and the causal explanations of their continued existence are irrelevant to our argument. Values cannot be derived from the facts and vice versa. This is an essay in applied moral philosophy and not a sociological essay, but Hume's value-fact distinction applies to both. Quite apart from the radical ambiguity of causal notions, we are concerned with the *justification* of the continued existence of codes, and not in their origin, utility in defending group interests, or their maintenance by strategic or tactical arguments at the level of interests. We are concerned with their moral evaluation, and the present essay offers a criterion for achieving such an evaluation.

Thus moral codes are capable of moral evaluation. Their historical origin, or strategic use is irrelevant to our argument. The so-called indexicality or context-bound nature of codes is not an issue that need concern us.

In the specific case of Kenny's appeal, the only responses that the authors have been able to discover, are two letters published in the August 1976 issue of *Personnel Management*. One of these warmly welcomed Kenny's initiative and suggested that he might stimulate the production of a draft code (of ethics). The other took the form of a strong rebuttal. The latter was written by a senior personnel manager from within the asbestos industry and contained the assertion that "I have never felt that my personal moral standards, my duty to my company, my duty under the law, and my responsibility for the safeguarding of people at work have ever been in conflict or in need of reinforcement by a professional body." As Kenny pointed out in reply, this is clearly a state of grace for which "(m)any personnel managers, particularly those with safety responsibilities will be very envious of him." The Health and Safety Executive's Report for 1976 on manufacturing and service industries provides evidence of the patchiness of provision in complying with existing law. It is a commonplace that the law's demands represent minimal requirements: Responsible citizens, individual or corporate, are expected to do much more. Overall, we are inclined to feel that Kenny is to be congratulated for so clearly articulating a potent and enduring source for concern to many industrial managers.

"RESPONSIBILITY" AND "PERSUASIVE LABELING"

In exploring this area, the first difficulty is the extraordinary ambiguity in both popular and academic usage of most key terms in organizational behavior and management. In an extreme form, this may be demonstrated by contrasting the expressions *professional killer* and *unprofessional conduct*. With the former, there is the clear implication that the individual so described acts in a manner which is generally considered deplorable, and does so without feeling, and in return for material reward. In the second case, the behavior described is viewed has having fallen short of a standard set by the profession concerned. Thus we appear to use the same word to describe behavior which at best may be viewed as amoral, and behavior which is in accordance with an explicit code, which normally has a powerful ethical element. With the liberal professions, in theory, at least it is clear which description applies. Doctors, lawyers, priests, and so forth, normally have explicit codes of behavior and seek to regulate their membership in accordance with them. (However, the widely noted "professional" unwillingness to criticize the performance of a fellow professional even when such an unwillingness may lead to a serious and unjust loss to a third party, has clear "gun-man" connotations.) It is worth noting that to find nonmoral causal origins of a practice is not to free it from ethical critiques.

Speaking of moral codes, K. Prandy in *Professional Employees,* puts the point, "It is no argument against the importance of a moral code to show that the motives inspiring it are not necessarily altruistic" and that "The label 'professional' has become one of prestige and status, and the problem [of understanding and defining 'professional'—authors' note] has arisen out of a desire to prevent groups of lower status from using this prestige label."

Speaking of scientists and engineers, he adds that the "differing employment situations in which scientists and engineers are placed influence their attitudes and behavior in the direction of a class or status ideology, represented on the one hand by trade unions and on the other, by professional associations."

Now it is possible to accept that terms, such as *professional,* are used as persuasive labels (to adapt Stevenson's expression—*Ethics and Language,* 1945). Equally, it is possible to argue that the granting or withholding of such labels can be effective moves in power, status, or income struggles. One can concede that beliefs and attitudes are in fact influenced by situational variables. However, as Hare (and Kant) point out, "is" does not imply either "ought" or "has to be." One can argue with Bernard Shaw that professions are conspiracies against the laity. None of this, however, can prevent their moral evaluation, unless one subscribes to an extreme subjectivist account of ethics—as we shall show.

For the moment it is important to point out that *persuasive labeling* is very common indeed and that since most key terms are radically ambiguous the validity of a moral argument can easily be broken by slipping between different uses of the same term—the trick that is usually used in the process of persuasive labeling.

Much the same ambiguity appears to apply to industrial management. Are professional managers those who show a single-minded determination to pursue the interests of their employers, or are they those who use an ethical code of behavior either implicit or explicit as a guide to their actions? In the past, at least, it has not been unfair to suggest that the former has been the predominant usage. Clearly, in theoretical terms, there is a sound functional explanation for this being the case. In capitalist economies, managers have traditionally worked for capital at its interface with labor; and presumably in every "managed" society, they work for the powerful in "managing" the less so. Inevitably, this will on occasion involve acting against the real or perceived interests of the latter and, in our society at least, there is a general tendency to acquiesce to harsh treatment if we can grasp the rationalization that the agent is "only doing his job," for example, the bailiff. Thus the powerful are more likely to achieve their ends if they work through a surrogate, rather than invite challenge by appearing physically both as agent and instigator.

The same functional argument would suggest that it would be advantageous to make a virtue of such obedience by terming it *professionalism*. Certainly, one suspects that in the asbestos situation described by Kenny, any manager who had taken a stance against one of his employers on ethical grounds, might well have found himself accused of unprofessional behavior. The persuasive labeling process here works precisely because of the moral overtones imported surreptitiously in the service of what is clearly a prudential and restricted group interest.

FUNCTIONALISM AND ETHICAL RELATIVISM

Such an analysis raises the central question of whether ethical codes or ideologies have an independent existence apart from their usefulness as a means of legitimating the action of those who hold them. Clearly, if ethical codes are to be anything other than *post hoc* rationalization, they must be logically prior to acts, and provide standards or criteria for measuring acts.

To avoid misunderstanding it is important to point out at this stage that logical priority does not entail temporal priority. Logic is concerned with the forms of valid inference, and is timeless. Temporal priority is thus contingent. It is logically possible for values to precede codes in time. But it is also logically possible for codes (but not ethical codes) to precede values for individuals and groups. For example, codes which began as mere whims, commands, or prudential guides, can become ethical codes if they are acceptable as such. Of course, codes can also be vague or confused. Rival codes can enshrine different value-sets. There are, however, circumstances in which rival value-sets can be reconciled. On these points, Ryle has pointed out that to predict an event does not cause it to happen. To say that action X is morally correct is to say that action X is justifiable as a case of the general value Y, and is acceptable as a morally justifiable act *as* a prescription for future relevantly similar circumstances *by virtue* of being a case of value Y, irrespective of actual motives at a particular time in the past of the performer. As a *state of affairs,* it may be *good* (in very many senses of the word) irrespective of motives, as for example when someone performs some action that is in fact helpful, though intended not to be (an own goal in football is an example that springs readily to mind).

In cannot be the case that acts express value preferences which are then enshrined in a code. Codes must be logically prior, since *post hoc* justification is of the same logical form as *post hoc* prediction. The values of those who are subject to the codes *may* vary only at the level of absolute presuppositions (which are very general notions reflecting the most deeply held beliefs about nature and man's place in it). We can reasonably say that justification is a matter of radically "subjective" preferences and choices only when all reasoned arguments have been put and all evidence weighed, and a fundamental cleavage in values and beliefs is unbridgeable; but many value positions are taken well before this limit is reached. Up to this level, codes and actions can be accepted or rejected on grounds of objective argument and evidence. Thus genuine moral codes are independent sources of justification or rejection of actions; those which serve as rationalizations are limitations of them. To take the view that codes cannot be logically prior to actions is to embrace a most pessimistic view of human nature, but the at least partial instrumentality of most managerial (or other) ideologies must be recognized. As Fox in *A Sociology of Work in Industry,* observes:

> Managerial ideology often tends understandably to stress a unitary conception of the organization; to favor the view which sees it as having but one proper correct authority and one focus of loyalty. In this form the ideology serves three purposes. It is at once a method of self-reassurance, an instrument of persuasion, and a technique of seeking legitimation of authority.

Even the contemporary willingness to question the propriety of such ideologies, of which this article is an example, might be viewed as part of that painful process by which old instrumentalities are rejected, and new ones—more appropriate to the dramatic changes in the real-politik of industrial relations— are forged.

However, it is our belief that appeals such as that articulated by Kenny are made at least in part from a genuine desire to "do what is right," rather than arising entirely from the need for a more sophisticated set of rationalizations tailored to fit the complexities of modern industrial life.

We have drawn attention to an aspect of organizations which does not seem to have had the attention which the following factors would suggest it merits.

First, moral codes are important influences on behavior (that is, on observable events, states, and processes) within organizations. This influence also extends to relationships between organizations, and between them and individuals who are not members of them: clients, customers, and the public. Moral codes (real and proviso) are sources of commitment and are therefore sources of power and control. They can be used to exploit others, partly because they are ambiguous and partly because genuine commitment is difficult to distinguish from lip service. The language, if not the substance, of morals seems to be used more frequently by the most powerful and by those with the least power. Its richness in the British culture is legendary ands the tone and content of speeches at TUC debates and of managers' and strikers' representatives is testimony to this. For all that, groups of workers are quite capable of "exploiting" their fellows, as witnessed by the maintenance of some indefensible differentials, while using mock ethical arguments in justification. To be a member of a group that views itself as the target of unfair discrimination does not guarantee impeccable behavior (or prevent it). Of course, in addition to ethical consideration, behavior is influenced by rules, both formal and informal, written and unwritten. It is also influenced by taboos, tacit assumptions, presumptions, presuppositions, beliefs about law, and beliefs about custom and practice. It is sometimes (but perhaps less often than is commonly supposed) influenced by what they think they can get away with.

None the less, it is our firm contention that beliefs about rights, duties, obligations, and prerogatives, do have a significant influence, although not as significant as we would suggest is desirable. Evidence for this contention is to be found in the increasingly common references—especially in industrial relations practice—to justice and precedent with a consequential and proper movement into jurisprudence and legal studies.

Secondly, ethical problems frequently appear complex and are only sometimes resolved by the use of professional codes of practice. The number of actual and potential reasons for action is infinite. Moral codes can legislate only for a few. There is necessarily a trade-off between specific rules for action and general guidelines. The more precise the rule, the narrower the range of cases it covers.

In consequence, so-called ethical principles should be treated with the same circumspection as those of administration. To the extent that attempts are made to use them indiscriminately, they become mere routines with the obvious danger of being inappropriately applied. Certainly, the poverty of such an approach is shown in cases where the satisfying of one principle entails the breaking of some other. This problem cannot be solved by using a predetermined hierarchy of principles. The literature on moral theory abounds with dilemmas showing conflicts of principle. The promise to tell the truth to a dying man pitted against the compassionate urge to shield him from anguish, is but one common example. Basically, all moral behavior is situation-dependent. To say this is to use the notion of situation-dependency in a different sense from its use in the quotations from Prandy in the previous section. The present use is best explained by saying that for any moral law, rule, or prescription, there are genuine cases and ones which are substandard, or are cases of something else.

Many acts are examples of more than one law or principle, and a great deal of moral argument consists of differing views as to which principles are relevant, and which should have priority. The facts of the case provide the minor premises. But the situation here is not logically different from that facing the physicist or historian in deciding what laws an observastion is a case of; or what laws apply to a particular observation. Thus, whether or not an act is moral, is determined by an evaluation of the intention which motivated it, the correct ascription of principles (which are prescriptive) and the accurate account of the facts of the matter. This applies both to individual acts and to continuing practices. However, as the proverb puts it, the road to hell is paved with good intentions. It is not enough that the intention should be benevolent in a general sense; it must be rigorously thought through. Nor is it enough that the actor acts according to his own accepted code and values: These, as we shall show, can and should be subject to scrutiny. This is in part the distinction commonly made between "justice according to law" and "the justice of the law."

Moral behavior is necessarily the product of conscious choice, not social convention; otherwise it would not be moral. It might be, for example, prudential or "traditional." Similarly, doing the right thing for the wrong reason may produce a desirable outcome, but it is not ethical in our sense simply because it is not done for ethical reasons. The critical point here is that there are different kinds of codes. They are all normative, but not necessarily moral, because *moral* values are a subclass of values.

Nor can the issues surrounding moral and behavioral codes be settled by surveys of people's beliefs, attitudes, or opinions, even when these methods are capable of eliciting useful information. These issues, are to a considerable extent, matters of logic and evidence, toward which people may indeed have attitudes or beliefs; but the attitudes and beliefs are not unchallengeable; there is more objectivity in the matter than is usually supposed, and it is of a different order than that of counting the number of people who answer in a particular way. It is simply not the case that any code of behavior or any act is as good as any other. Up to the point where evidence, reason, and consistency are not satisfied, codes or action are morally questionable.

ETHICS AND THE BEHAVIORAL SCIENCES: SOME EXAMPLES

Much of the literature on organizational behavior has drawn attention to the psychology which underpins it. Many studies and particularly the participant observer studies of the anthropologists have attempted, often with considerable success, to provide sound "behavioral" reasons for many practices which casual observers had hitherto tended to treat in moralistic, usually condemnatory terms, and still do. It is an advance, for example, when T. Lupton in *On the Shop Floor*, and D. Roy in *Payment Systems*, explain what others have seen as "bonus fiddles" and "restriction of output" in rational, causal terms. There are lessons yet to be learned from this work, in view of the vast output of organizational behavior texts of the human relations type. These studies go a long way toward correcting what is now widely acknowledged to be managerial bias in much of the literature. It is an advance also when W. Baldamus in *Efficiency and Effort* refers to the "effort bargain"—a concept which draws attention sharply to the one-sidedness of much of management thinking on these matters.

It is true that the human relations literature frequently has an evangelical flavor, and that, as Grigor McClelland put it, much of the classical literature is replete with "orgies of avuncular pontification." Joan Woodward's comment that this may be functional given the cacophony of prescriptions for approaching the management of organizations, is still apposite; also given that theory inevitably has a justifying (or, as some might put it, *ideological*) nature. No doubt a manager of classical or Taylorist persuasion might be astonished at the thought that the content of the "contract of employment" is not properly left to the discretion of the owner of the business. Moral and political theorists from Plato to Mill have all pointed out that justice according to law, is a different question from that of justice of the laws themselves.

We still discern a tendency in some quarters to blur the moral issues by offering accounts of industrial or organizational situations which suggest a prescription in the form that has neatly been described (by Tom Lehrer) as "doing well by doing good." If, (so it is argued, or more commonly *assumed*) employees or customers are treated in such a way that their interests are looked after; and if people are allowed to participate in decisions, then their commitment to the organization—and its practices—will be enhanced; and the organization cannot fail to be a high performer, and a pleasant place to work in. The moral way to behave seems to turn out to be the most profitable. But closer examination of such approaches tends to suggest that moral responsibility extends only to those who are in a position to articulate their moral rights (for example, members of powerful T.U.'s), but not to those who lack much power (for example, citizens of Third World primary producers). It is true that there are some researchers who are skeptical about the universal profit-generating character of participative schemes or of paternalistic schemes, but there is little treatment of the ethics of all this, other than by implication. We recognize that there are radical critics who hold the whole industrial framework to be biased toward the interests of a minority of high status, highly paid people, and that there are authoritarian approaches, which argue on the lines of the outlook caricatured by MacGregor as "theory X," that a stiff dose of industrial discipline administered by those whose superiority is demonstrated by the fact that they have achieved senior positions, would be "good" for all. These come close to ethical arguments and raise a forest of moral issues, but they are still arguing at the level of individual or group interests, or of prudential or efficiency reasons for preferring this course of action to that one, or some other.

Kenny's example of the asbestos situation is one of the more dramatic examples of moral issues. Speaking specifically of personnel managers, he asks, "Is not the personnel manager constantly in the 'asbestos' situation, even if not so obviously or so tragically? The good of the individual or society all too frequently diverge."

We suggest that we are *all* confronted with divergencies between individual, group, and organizational "goods," with varying levels of seriousness.

Our argument so far has been somewhat abstract. It is important to steer a course between pontification and causistry. It is not our function or purpose to prescribe what practices are or are not permissible in business management, any more than to prescribe what the rule books of trade unions should contain. No doubt there is enormous diversity of practices which individuals would nominate as proper subjects for the content of moral codes.

Our own list would certainly include the asbestos situation as described by Kenny. We certainly believe that some firms have an impeccable record on this matter. We would also argue for a set of principles governing actions and relationships which it would be futile to enshrine within specific codes. We would include:

- Scapegoating.
- Transference of risk from strong to weak individuals (for example, it is common to justify the position of owners of businesses in terms of risk, but to transfer the risk to employees in the form of redundancy).
- Maintenance of power positions by improper means, for example, the denial of access to information.
- Prejudice, stereotyping, argument evasion (*cf.* tax evasion).
- Insistence on adherence to group norms.
- Suppression of dissent or of alternative views.

These are all techniques available and used in conflict management, and in the exercise of or struggles for power. They will happen whatever moral theorists say and try to do. They all occur in voluntary organizations, in pressure groups, and in trade unions, as well as in managerial and "professional groups," in firms, the Church, and many more.

But to say that these are all moves in power games is not to provide a unique categorization: they are also moral issues. To explain behavior in terms of such moves is to provide only a partial explanation (or better—to satisfy only one of many *uses* of the word explanation).

Moral arguments are sui generis and it is an illusion to suggest that they can be explained away as psychological arguments or notions or instrumentality.

THE NATURE OF MORAL BEHAVIOR

Why has there been this fairly general tendency to avoid direct confrontation with moral issues or, at a minimum, to treat them as highly esoteric matters to be debated in isolation, and without conclusion, by ivory-towered academics? The answer, we suspect, is deceptively simple. The conclusion of a moral argument is an action. The lack of such an outcome is indicative of a mere intellectual exercise. Unfortunately, actually doing one's moral duty (that is, acting) may well be at a high personal cost. Indeed, on those happy occasions, when doing what is seen to be right aligns with what is seen to be expedient, the moral component is easy. If moral codes can increase the incidence of these, then so much the better. There will never be a shortage of hard choices. This is the nub of Kenny's example. We doubt that in such cases there is much uncertainty in which way moral duty lies. If a largely ignorant workforce is being denied the minimal protection to its health afforded by the law, presumably as a means of optimizing the return to shareholders, most people would feel a degree of moral obligation to speak out against it. Of course, there may be some moral counterweight such as genuine feelings of obligation to dependents and, possibly, employer. But it is improbable that feelings such as these could provide an entirely moral justification for silence. The central difficulty is that to act in the way most people view as morally correct (if foolhardy) will be at considerable personal cost.

Clearly, the central attraction of an institutionally backed professional code is that it would enable individuals to follow the dictates of their consciences at freatly reduced personal risk. However, although such an outcome is highly desirable, if only for the practical consequences of reducing the incidene of death (for example, from asbstosis), it is difficult to see that it reflects much moral credit upon those who are only prepared to act when supported by such an established, power-backed code. The morally "strongest person" is one who in Ibsen's terms *stands alone,* that is, who has the courage to act without institutional support and frequently in the face of it. A statement which at least in part applies to Kenny.

It is this capacity of moral issues to push us in directions that we do not wish to take that makes them such an embarrassment. In consequence, administrators seem to be inclined to avoid them, using a variety of excuses: they are theoretical or insoluble or impracticable. There may be other reasons for this. Among them we would offer the following possibilities. Many administrators do not receive much (or any) training in ethics. As a result, they frequently fall back on home-spun or intuitive principles or on to arbitrary choices; some administrators are prisoners of their own past decisions, or of practices inherited from predecessors, or simply of "custom and practice rules." Freedom to act in preferred ways may be circumscribed by budgetary or allocation systems; some administrators may have genuine "theory X" convictions, or believe themselves to be capable of making better decisions than can be made by "the democracy." Some may simply be Hobbesians and determined to pursue their interests at all costs; *some* may be genuine hypocrites. These are pitfalls that other people beside administrators fall into; but the latter, in our view, have a special responsibility.

This is not of course to deny that there are not some genuine moral dilemmas. The classic medical example comes readily to mind: whom to save, given that only one of two patients can be saved, with the resources available (which could be increased at the cost of something else).

In such cases the problem facing the practitioner is simply the technical one of how to implement his genuine desire to do what is right. But we would suggest that in most cases so-called moral problems are in fact a mixture of arguments or issues concerning duty, prudence and efficiency. Throughout the history of moral thought, various schools have emphasized one of these elements rather than another. Very rarely have people attempted to combine them, because in hard cases, they are irreconcilable. In Kenny's example, it would be our view that a moral code should specifically place people's life and health before profit. However, economic considerations clearly dictate otherwise. Examples could be multiplied in almost every sphere of activity. In road traffic regulation, cases of accident black spots come to mind, requiring expensive road works blocked for reasons of expense and traffic flow, and in the political sphere many choices entail weighing the relative merits of items such as tax cuts, defense considerations, and kidney machines.

HOW TO IMPROVE PRACTICE

In exploring this area, it is not our contention that a mere awareness of ethical criteria will encourage individuals to behave in a more acceptable manner. Again, it is important to emphasize this point. It is probable that awareness alone of ethical criteria will not affect behavior. We recognize that in ethics, as in all the disciplines, there are different schools of thought. These schools, however, do have many points of agreement. Some action may be inadvertent, and awareness of this may be useful—as Wittgenstein put it, a role of philosophy is to assemble reminders for particular purposes. We do claim that an examination of moral philosophy should be able to provide a means of making a clear distinction between ethical behavior and prudential behavior. If we can furnish an unambiguous moral criterion, we may reasonably ask those who do not accept it to offer an alternative, and we enable those who do accept it squarely to face the nature of their own behavior.

We should say, by way of an interim summary, that moral arguments do not compel action in any physical or even psychological sense. Positively, they can point to alternatives and, negatively, they can remove the moral aura (or air of correctness) surrounding improper, or improperly thought out actions. These are important functions in their own right. If people have the legal right, or the power to perform or omit some action, they might do so anyway, and no moral argument or code can force or prevent action. It can remove the semblance of correctness or can show that the act or omission can or cannot be justified. Insofar as moral codes have any persuasive force, they will persuade only those who subscribe to them.

THE CONTRIBUTION OF MORAL PHILOSOPHY:
THE GOLDEN RULE AS CRITERION

We have argued that moral codes can be used to exploit people as well as to protect them. We have shown that they are logically prior to particular acts in that if we were to make up the codes as we went along, there could be no codes: The notion is self-contradicting. The codes represent relatively general and relatively permanent values. We have shown, also, that to operate a code uncritically is to act at best amorally. Circumstances and beliefs change, the ranking of values changes, the values themselves and their meanings change.

It is now appropriate to reconcile the apparent contradiction between these propositions and the proposition that the code is logically prior to the act, or to the specific moral value (we are not concerned with nonmoral values, such as prudential or technical norms). The short answer is that just as codes are logically prior to specific acts or values; the codes themselves are "corrigible" in the sense that their appropriateness depends upon the extent to which they embody more basic and permanent values. These in turn are related to basic beliefs and presuppositions concerning nature and man's place in it. This, too, is the stuff of moral philosophy. It has all been said before, over the last two thousand years or so, but the persistence of the dilemmas and the persistence of situations in which duty can be done only at high personal cost testifies to the need for it to be restated with a much greater frequency than has been the case. These basic beliefs and presuppositions provide the next step in the argument. If they change substantially, we might expect a major change in the content or interpretation of codes. This is the basic justification of moral codes, their evaluation and revision.

Thus, it is simply not true that any code is as good as any other. It might be objected that the evaluation of codes is nevertheless not *moral* evaluation, because what passes or a "moral rule" always reduces to a statement of the interest of the dominant group, or ruling elite. This objection is incoherent. If there were no genuine *moral* obligation, there could not (logically) be a pseudo-moral obligation.

We cannot have the concept of false belief unless we have the concept of true belief. "All that glisters is not gold" could not make sense unless there were such a thing as gold, so that if people never behaved morally (always prudently for example), then they could never be taken in by false moral arguments.

If people made more explicit appeal to moral codes, we guess that more people would be able to achieve, at least to some degree, the job satisfaction that many researchers (and managers) seek to understand or provide. We think that this would probably increase commitment and release more productivity growth (or economic growth in general), but this is an empirical matter and, even if it did not have the expected effect, there is a great deal to be gained by the language of rights, duties, prerogatives, and obligations. *The proper conduct of relationships* is, in our view, as important as economic growth.

It is part of the task of organization theory to explain behavior in and out of organizations. The process of explanation includes describing, analyzing, and identifying causes. Much of this work quite properly implies justification.

This, like explanation, can take many forms and operates at different levels. That an action or practice is held to be profitable, or efficient, and in the interests of all concerned would normally be taken to be sufficient justification, but there can be cases in which an action can be all of these things, but still remain unjustified. This is, in general, where some individual's rights would be infringed. But *profit,* efficiency, or the pursuit of interests, are all *values* and, logically, any person involved may subscribe to a different value set from that of the majority, or of the most powerful people. In such cases something more is needed in justification for pursuing one value-set rather than another. Democratic theory contains many successful attempts at such justification. Many organizations, however, do not even purport to be democratic, so logically *arguments* are needed in justifying industrial practice. Law is not sufficient: That someone has the "legal" right to do such and such does not entail that he has also a moral right to do so.

Here again, particular codes of practice are of service: They provide justification over and above the provisions and permissions of the law. We must ask why anyone should be held to be bound by the practices of such codes: the grounds for obligation to obey company rules or custom and practice rules, for example. In organization theory, it seems to be widely assumed that the grounds for obligation *are* basically prudential. This would explain the significance attached to the practice of "binging"—the use of physical force to gain compliance with group output standards at Hawthorne. However, such explanations cannot provide a complete answer. Even if, in most cases, people comply with rules and codes because it is in their interests to do so, it still does not explain obligation: That can only come from consent. In the Lockean version of this doctrine, in John Locke's *Second Treatise of Government,* tacit consent is sufficient to provide grounds for obligation. Thus, if people have not specifically objected to a practice or act, then they are said to have consented to it. But this implies that people at all times are provided with a means and opportunity for registering objections, and such provision is by no means a sine qua non of organizations.

There are then very many ways in which the legitimacy of administrative acts or organizational codes can be lost, even if all concerned share a set of substantive values and understand the same things by them. This does not mean that the proper conduct of organizational relationships is unattainable or fragile. All that is required is an adequate procedure for checking decisions, for changing rules, and for recognizing and correcting improper practice, and many organizations achieve this.

The most difficult case is that in which substantive values are not shared. We remarked earlier that democratic theory has had some success in dealing with cases of this kind. But what should we say of organizations which do not purport to be democratic? How might we answer someone who, like Thrasymachus in Plato's *Republic,* maintains that "justice is the interest of the stronger" or asks "Why should I obey the moral law, if I can get away with not doing so?"

THE GOLDEN RULE

Our contention is that the traditional "Golden Rule" is still capable of providing a compelling answer to these questions. In order to show that this is so, it is necessary to give a reminder of the nature of the "Golden Rule" (GR) and to draw out its main implications. The Golden Rule is, of course, the injunction from the Sermon on the Mount: "Thou shalt love they neighbor as thyself. " Kant's version is "I ought never to act except in such a way that I can also will that my maxim should become a universal law." A third statement of the GR is taken from Thomas Hobbes, in *Leviathan,* although our reasons by no means coincide with his.

Hobbes expresses the GR as follows: "Do not that unto another which thou wouldst not have done to thyself." This Golden Rule has lately had a revival in J. Rawls in *Philosophy, Politics and Society,* and in R. M. Hare in *Freedom and Reason.*

To put this in our own more prosaic terms: The legitimacy of administrative acts and organizational codes is related in specific ways to the values of the persons concerned with them and to the arrangements for ensuring that these values are taken seriously and are given due consideration. At its simplest, the argument is that the ethical legitimacy of the behavioral relationships between A (an administrator) and B (a person subject to A's administrative rules and decision) in the case of an issue which only affects them can be tested by a role-reversal method. The legitimacy of the relationship does not depend on A's imagining himself in B's position with A's own values; it does depend on A's imagining himself in B's position with B's values. We transfer B's values to A, and vice versa, because their respective values are part of the structure of the situation. This can be generalized to an indefinitely large number of people. As it is sometimes put, each person should be treated as an end and not as a means, and each person should count as neither more nor less than one. To seek to be exploited has no more merit (on this criterion) than the exploiting of others. This is well recognized in law in many contexts. It is sometimes suggested that managerial organizations are founded upon the necessary treatment of people as means and not as ends. It often seems to be assumed that management is (and ought to be) the direction of subordinates so as to achieve ends willed by managers. There are, of course, no necessary treatments of people, and how some people think that organizations *are* (constitutionally), has no bearing on how others *ought* to see them, except in the context of our value-transference criterion. As Russell points out (in the context of nation states), such institutions are logical constructions out of individuals. The fact (if it is a fact) that we live in a stratified society (or economy) does not imply that any stratum has any moral right to initiate or dominate. Such rights as do occur can be there by virtue of the law (which is not beyond criticism), by default, or by conscious agreement. Only the last of these, we argue, can give a genuine moral correctness.

The kind of action which according to our criterion is not legitimate would be that based on the ascription of values to B which B does not in fact possess. The following example is illustrative. In hierarchical organizations a hierarch A wishes to gain the compliance of an underling B in raising B's work load. B's promised formally or tacitly a reward (bonus or promotion), or B is simply expected to comply. B considers himself to be overloaded as it is and refuses. A then imposes sanctions on the grounds that he (A) is responsible for the overall running of the organization and that B has a duty to comply. The onus is upon A to show that in selecting a given course of action, he has placed equal weight upon his own interests and principles and those of B and other interested parties. Consider another example. There are people, some of whose values are in fundamental conflict with "the capitalist system," or with "liberal democratic systems." Included under this heading would be a heterogenous group with heterogenous values, holding perhaps no values in common.

It is possible that a radical critic of the modern political economy may work in a potentially dangerous production plant.

Should we say, in this case, that the critic should be *forced* to comply with A's (the *manager*'s) judgment on how to apply (say) safety regulations? Suppose the critic (B) is wholly opposed to the production of the product itself (for example, where the particular product is one of many)? A case of the manager using sanctions (force) to gain compliance *by virtue* of the fact that he is a manager? This is not enough.

According to the GR, there is a more potent source of authority: If the manager can show that *his* views and those of the critic have been considered, with those of other interested parties, all being assigned equal weight, then the sanction can be justified (if an appropriate sanction is used). In a democratic organization the action would be justified by reference to accepted law and internal constitutional principle, such as acceptance of a majority decision or expressions of confidence in the executive. A nondemocratic organization needs special provision to be able to get the same result. In this case an attempt by the "critic" to stop the job would be opposed with legitimate sanctions on the grounds that the "critic" sought to have his views count as *more than one,* and those of his opponents as less than one.

According to our rule, if the organization does not purport to be democratic, then the onus is upon *A* to show that *B in fact* freely chose to be subject to changed requirements such as those in question. If this cannot be shown, then *A* does not satisfy our ethical criterion, and has no moral grounds for expecting *B*'s compliance. There are, we suggest, so many ways in which breaches can occur that it is very unlikely indeed that many industrial organizations do satisfy our criterion, which is not weakened thereby.

Similar arguments can be raised against the contention that the source of compliance is command, operating through prerogatives. It can be shown in formal logic that any pair of inconsistent statements jointly asserted implies all other statements, including all false ones. Similarly, if anyone in *B*'s position accepts the "command" model of organizations, then work overload or any incompatible "orders" or "duties" release *B* from all moral obligations to work or to comply. If *B* attempts to comply, the reasons are not to do with *A*'s hierarchical prerogatives and are more likely to arise from other sources of obligation, usually prudential. For all these reasons, nondemocratic organizations are unlikely to provide the conditions necessary for legitimacy in relationships at work.

It could be that this explains why business ethics is so underdeveloped as a discipline. Organizational moral codes are used in fact as power sources. That normative order occurs at all in organizations is due partly, we suspect, to moral and legal codes which originate and are validated outside the organization and partly to a mixture of behavioral (prudential and habitual) reasons. Frequent breakdowns of normative order, low morale, and destructive conflict, are in part explicable in terms of confusions about moral codes in organizations.

Whether these would disappear in the presence of more rigorously devised moral codes is a matter for conjecture. Our guess is that breakdowns and conflict would persist in different forms.

At the very least, though, ethical confusions would no longer be a major problem source.

THE GOLDEN RULE IN USE

We have shown that the GR is implicit in most concepts of equity and justice and that these are applicable to, and often form, the currency of democratic practice, and are applicable to procedures for collective job regulation and collective bargaining. We have tried to show also that the GR and its implications are more likely to be practiced in democratic organizations than in other kinds. A code or an act can be justified in our view, if and only if, it satisfies the Rule. The practical test for each case is the value-transfer, which enables the values of all concerned to be taken explicitly into account and enables relevant evidence to be available to all concerned, and rationally discussed by them.

It has been our intention to show that these genuine moral issues are an integral part of modern organizatinal life, and that they have not had the attention that their importance merits. We have argued for our own specified view that the Golden Rule is a serviceable criterion for *those* who wish to recognize the ethical issues for what they are.

We have not attempted to show that anyone who does not possess moral concepts, or who chooses to ignore "the moral law," or prefers to act in radically "selfish" ways can be compelled, logically or in any way, to change his attitudes or behaviors. If it were possible to do so, then paradoxically, it would cease to be moral behavior. This is the crux of the "Thrasymachus" case: to be moral is to choose freely, and to accept the implications of the choice. If Thrasymachus chooses to be inconsistent, we cannot compel him. But we can, if our analysis is correct, provide reasons why those who do choose to obey the law should withhold the credit of legitimacy to any moral claims which "Thrasymachus" tries to make agains them.

Consider a very simplified example. In peacetime there are many jobs that involve physical danger. In principle, there is free choice of jobs, but the design of jobs is not always wholly determined by technical considerations. On oil rigs at sea, it is judged to be necessary to design some jobs so that divers work in dangerous conditions. Assuming that there is no technical alternative and that every reasonable safety precaution has been taken, inducements of a financial nature are common, that is, people get high pay for this work. In this case the value-transfer test is satisfied—provided that the rate for the job (if any) is paid, and the persons concerned are in full possession of the evidence of alternatives, risks, and conditions.

And a more complex one... Should restrictive trade practices be regarded as prima facie wrong, as they are in the 1956 Restrictive Trade Practices Act? They are considered to be so for a variety of reasons. We are interested in the prima facie case. This case is based on the grounds that the economic system is based on the principle of consumer sovereignty, and on the technical grounds of production and distribution optima. It is, however, the case that there is a technical "optimum" for every possible distribution of income, and each of these is capable of being a valid state for at least someone. The factual evidence on the technical economic arguments, does suggest that the prima facie case does not in *fact* have the expected result in all cases. It is even argued by some economists that the perfect competition case (the paradigm for restrictive practices legislation) is itself inconsistent with a number of major and widely held values. Since the holders of these values are not always in a position to legislate, there is a duty (according to our criterion) on the part of legislators to ascertain the existence of these values. yet a great deal of argument is ignored—and the position is not noticeably different what what it was when Mill wrote his *Essay on Liberty.* Here the value-transference might well have produced different legislation. Whether or not it did so, it is capable of producing much more powerful arguments than those that commonly appear in the economics literature.

In practice, most moral issues in organizations are between these extremes. Thus, mere awareness of ethical criteria will not affect anything—but an awareness, *together* with a willingness to use them can do so. But the improvement is logically (and practically) impossible without the awareness of ethical criteria.

CONCLUSIONS

By way of conclusion, we attempt some shorter answers to a set of general questions relating to codes or to practices where other people's interests or ideals are involved.

To the question, "What should be *done?*" we offer the general answer: "Use the Golden Rule." Why should we be moral? To this, the answer must necessarily refer to the consequences of not doing so. We consider two classes of consequences.

1. *Utilitarian:* The classic statement of this position is by Hobbes: If we do not obey the codes, the consequence will be "the war of every man against every man." This is mainly a prudential answer, but there are other implications, such as

2. *Moral* arguments, though prescriptive, are still subject to the logical "principle of contradiction." Unless an act satisfies the Golden Rule, it cannot be said to be moral, just as a self-contradictory descriptive utterance cannot be said to be true. This is, we believe, essentially the same point that Hare makes when he describes moral judgments as both "prescriptive" and "universal." For those unfamiliar with the structure of this argument, we adopt Hume's method of challenge: Produce an alternative *moral* rule that is better than the GR.

Moral evaluations are prescriptive, but this does not mean that they are arbitrary. Nor are all prescriptions equally valid or appropriate. In the end they are intuitive, but only in the same sense as the minimum step in a logical or mathematical argument: Either you see it or you do not.

Moral evaluations are universalizable. Although some "universals" may be characteristics shared by only a few objects, any new ones like them would also "share" the same universal. This is asserted as a basic principle by Hare, but it follows from Russell's proof of the principle of contradiction: Incompatible imperatives imply *all* conceivable courses of action, and hence imply none at all.

"If the majority are foolish enough to follow moral codes, why should *I*, if I can get away with not doing *so?*" This is a standard objection to attempts to provide ethical criteria. It is, of course, physically possible to behave in this way. We *ought* not to do so, but those who do cannot logically claim "moral qualifications," and lose all moral claims. Moral rights imply (some) moral responsibilities. The evading of only some moral responsibilities does not entail the losing of all moral claims. However, it does follow that the making of some moral claims implies the unacceptance of the concept of moral obligation. It follows also that one cannot simultaneously and reasonably claim moral rights and deny the existence of moral obligations. It does not follow that it makes sense to speak—as so often occurs in management literature and practice—about an equality relationship between degree of responsibility and degree of authority.

SUMMARY

We are now in a position to draw the conclusions together and to point to some implications:

1. There is no act which may not have a moral dimension. This is simply not a matter of arbitrary selection and analysis of values and norms: There are qualitative differencecs of a decisive nature between different kinds of values and norms.

2. Codes are hypothetical, provisional, rule of thumb—the first place to look.

3. If we are not to agonize eternally in a search for absolute certainty, we need codes: It is logically and practically impossible to justify *all* statements from first principles because some express the principles themselves. *Some* things must be taken on trust. Actions and beliefs are based on so many assumptions that they cannot all be simultaneously reexamined as a preliminary to all acts. One would never be able to do anything.

4. The codes express prima facie duties; an appeal to them must always be hypothetical in the sense of being contingent upon circumstances.

5. Codes do have a contribution to make towards efficiency, equity, criteria for action, stability, and predictability, but

6. No code is sacrosanct: Any and all provisions (except the Golden Rule) are

open at all times to revision. The status of the Golden Rule is equivalent to the "principle of contradiction." Not to use the Golden Rule is equivalent to using self-contradictory arguments.

7. The Golden Rule is the *criterion* for evaluation of principles.

8. If Golden Rule terminology is inclined to put people off from considering these issues, we can see no objection to finding a modern label for it—"The Prescriptive Groundrule" perhaps? Whatever we call it, it should be recognized for what it is.

13.
Institutionalizing Ethics in Public and Corporate Governance

Theodore V. Purcell

This paper does not primarily discuss ethics as applied to economics but rather ethics as a needed input into...decision-making. Economic thinking is already one component of such decisions, along with law, politics, technology, finance, and so forth. But our treatment should also have relevance for economic theory and research.

Why should managers explicitly ask ethical questions? The post-Nixon *corporate* Watergate, followed by sensational investigations of international payoffs, aroused unprecedented distrust of big business and further stimulated the so-called ethical investor movèment. Therefore, it becomes plain good strategy...and for individual managers to be concerned with ethics, if for no other reason than "to keep the restless natives quiet."

Of course there is a much deeper reason than that. Most people want and need to be ethical persons not only in private life, but also in business, where a manager's decisions may affect many thousands, perhaps hundreds of thousands of persons. Also, individuals normally want to be part of an organization whose purpose and activity they believe is beneficial to society.

WHOSE ETHICS?

One hears doubts raised about the wisdom and feasibility of introducing ethics into the executive suite—doubts revolving around the question: Whose ethics are you talking about? To be severely brief, this paper takes ethics as a practical science based on reason, concerned with the rightness and wrongness of human action. Ethics means that each person should act according to his nature and dignity, as a free human person. Ethics means that each institution, as a collection of persons, should act to preserve an advance human dignity and freedom. Ethics is not necessarily a matter of religion or revelation, though it is certainly inspired and guided by Christian, Jewish, Moselm, or other religions or theologies. There is obvious pluralism in philosophy today with fundamental differences between such schools as existentialism, Aristotelian-Neo-Thomism, analytic philosophies, utilitarianism, and so forth. We shall not discuss here the philosophical underpinning of ethics, or metaethics, as it is called, because there is considerable consensus about the general and middle principles of ethics we are going to present, even though there remain big differences about their underlying philosophical explanations.

There are at least two objections about introducing ethical thinking formally into executive decision making: Some people say that ethics is too personal, too individual for corporate use, or that personal and private ethical preferences should not affect the public policy decisions. . . . One may answer that indeed ethics does concern person-to-person honesty and fairness. But one cannot draw a hard and fast line between the manager's personal family life, for example, and his business decisions. The normal manager is not a schizophrenic; his private ethical values inevitably affect his corporate decisions for good or bad. Like Miliere's M. Jourdain, the manager in his business decisions is writing ethical prose whether he knows it or not.

Furthermore, ethics also asks questions of *public* purpose. For example, could ever-increasing economic growth in the West (not in the Third World) become a kind of GNP fetish? Should we examine the effects of competition on the quality of life, with either too much competition or too little competition being harmful? Are Americans wastefully consuming too much of the world's energy and resources with too little concern for development of the Third World? Should the corporation respond only to groups with power or should it respond also to the surrogate advocacy of the powerless? True, these are economic, political, and legal questions, but at bottom they are also *ethical* questions. At the core of ethics is the notion of justice, and justice by its very nature concerns more than merely individual behavior.

Second, ethics is often described as too variable and too situation-bound to have a role in management decision making. This view is based on the belief that ethics varies from person to person, from case to case, from time to time, from culture to culture.

Of course ethics is influenced by culture and time. For example, the Middle Ages condemned *all* interest taking as usury. But as J. Broderick, in *The Economic Morals of the Jesuits* points out, this proscription changed as commercial society evolved, as capital became productive and as the science of economics developed. There is and must be adaptation over time in ethical thinking.

But ethics also has an immutable core. Solomon Asch, a social psychologist, in *Social Psychology,* makes this point when he says, "We all feel that we value a thing because it has value, and not that it has value because we value it."

Clyde Kluckhohn, an anthropologist, in *Toward a General Theory of Action,* went through the literature of anthropology in 1951 and came out with this conclusion:

> Contracy to the statements of. . . extreme cultural relativity, standards and values are not completely relative to the cultures from which they derive. . . No culture fails to put a negative valuation upon killing, indiscriminate lying, and stealing within the in-group. There are important variations, to be sure, in the conception of the extent of the in-group, and in limits of toleration of lying and stealing, under certain conditions. But the core notion of the desirable and nondesirable is constant across all cultures. . . To the extent that such. . . imperatives are universal in distribution and identical or highly similar in content, they afford the basis for agreement among the peoples of the world.

We have an expression of that agreement in the thirty propositions of the *Universal Bill of Human Rights* of the United Nations (even though not all of the UN members observe those rights). Ethics is not totally subjective, like a taste for lobster tails or a fancy for bow ties.

WILL CODES HELP ETHICAL BEHAVIOR?

Many professional associations have not found ethics so subjective or so fuzzy that they were afraid to set up their own ethical standards. The American Institute of Certified Public Accounts (AICPA) describes its code of professional ethics "as a voluntary assumption of self-discipline above and beyond the requirements of the law." It further states that in general usage the word *ethics* means "the philosophy of human conduct, with emphasis on right and wrong, which are moral questions." The AICPA then cites many examples and applications of ethics in the accounting and auditing professions.

The American Psychological Association drew up its ethical code for psychologists from practical problem cases drawn from professional-client relationships.

The American Bar Association has a detailed code and canons. Of course, we know that Watergate brought the legal profession into serious self-questioning and subjected it to public skepticism; yet it is also true that some Watergate lawyers have been disbarred.

Especially, it is not easy to draw up an ethical code for doing international business among countries with very different values and customs. Yet the Organization for Economic Cooperation and Development (OECD) has recently drawn up such a code. Time will tell how much it helps.

It is important to stress, however, that ethical codes are not a panacea, even when they can be enforced on association members, something not too common. Though they often merely relate the profession to individual clients rather than to the collective public, codes nonetheless can help clarify ethical thinking and encourage ethical behavior.

IS IT POSSIBLE TO BE BOTH ETHICAL AND PROFITABLE?

The debate about...ethics always seems to get confused over the issue of profits and self-interest versus doing good for society. Obviously, profits are important. Unless a reasonable proportion of company's returns on sales are segregated as profits the firm cannot grow or even maintain itself. This fact is just as true in a socialist or communist society as it is in America—whatever name is given to the word profits.

But the myth that business decisions are *uniquely* made for profits or personal gain dies hard. As James Worthy, former vice-president of Sears, Roebuck and Company put it in the *Journal of Business* (October 1958):

> It is amusing to observe the extent to which the businessman will sometimes go in his efforts to explain in terms of self-interest an action which he wants to take for perhaps quite different reasons, some of which may be definitely...unselfish....Because unselfishness (is) explicitly outside the frame of reference within which the businessman, as a businessman, is supposed to operate, he feels it necessary to explain himself in other terms...Furthermore, in critical situations society is very likely to take business at its word that it acts only in its own self-interest and turn for leadership to others, such as government or unions, whose norms of conduct at least *pro forma,* include concern for the general welfare.

In his classic study, *Ethics in Business,* Raymond Baumhart examined the motives behind businessmen's decisions. Of the managers he interviewed, 56 percent recalled occasions when they acted on moral principles in preference to financial gains. Aware their answers could be self-serving, Baumhart had the managers describve these cases in some detail; his research methods gave considerable assurance that those he interviewed were speaking honestly. Baumhart concluded that his findings "explode the myth that profit is always the determining factor in business decisions." Incidentally, Baumhart's studies have been replicated six times with basically similar findings.

Let us take a recent example involving General Electric. GE found that most of its middle and top managers had professional degrees in engineering, finance, business, and so forth. They knew that blacks, for example, constituted only about 1.5 percent of present engineering graduates. Therefore GE, along with a coalition including other companies, unions, and the federal government, stimulated a national effort to get more minorities and women into the engineering and other professional pipelines from grammar school on. There was cost in this, with no immediate return. In my judgment it was not only a creative business decision but an ethical action on the part of management, going beyond the law's requirements.

Whether or not we accept as valid the cliche that "good ethics is good business in the long run," we know that is not always true in the short run. However difficult the tradeoffs, ethics must prevail if our free market system is to survive.

ETHICS VERSUS THE LAW

Some people say ethical motivation and profit motivation are incompatible. Therefore: "Forget about ethics and social responsibility. Just talk about the law." Laws are necessary, of course. The Civil Rights Act of 1964, to take one example, was absolutely essential. But there is a danger in all this. Some years ago, Douglass Brown's presidential address for the Industrial Relations Research Associaiton warned that excessive legalism was harming industrial relations.

We now find the field of equal employment opportunity going this same route of legalism and litigiousness. We cannot have laws, government agencies, lawyers, and courts, involved in every management decision. The country would soon be bogged down by a legal bureaucracy and could ultimately produce a contempt for law. We may be seeing something of this now in the medical malpractice mess.

Furthermore, many management decisions involve social issues about which no laws provide guidance and probably no viable laws can be written. What then? Social awareness and conscience can be the only guides.

A PRACTICAL THREEFOLD ETHICAL PROCESS

How can you "do" ethics at the top management level? You can do it if you handle ethics as a threefold ethical process:

- Examination of general ethical principles.
- Examination of middle level ethical principles.
- In-depth study of cases and classes of similar cases.

These three tools are interacting and should be used *simultaneously,* each reinforcing or clarifying the other.

A. *General ethical principles.* Ethical inquiry can yield valid and basic principles such as the following:

1. People should maximize value and minimize disvalue in their actions.

2. Human life ranks much higher than animal life.

3. Certain human needs are more necessary for life than others and therefore a person should not try to satisfy luxury wants without practical concern about the life needs of others.

4. Persons and institutions should be just and honest in their dealings.

5. The morality of an action is determined by analysis of the values and disvalues present in the act, the circumstances inseparable from the situation and the intention of the agent.

Most people would agree with those general principles. They are important because they are absolutely fundamental, the foundation on which ethics is built. But being general, they have no practical value until they are specified by middle principles and case analyses. On the other hand, judging cases has no ethical meaning unless judgments are based on fundamental ethical principles. This is where the simultaneity comes in.

B. *Applied or "middle" ethical principles.* These ethical principles are middle in the sense that they are in between the more general principles and specific cases. They stem from a study of general principles and specific case situations. Practical experience, therefore, is important in formulating them. They should be held firmly as long as they promote justice; they should be modified when new situations demand it. Most of the thirty statements of the United Nations *Universal Declaration of Human Rights* are middle ethical principles. Here are seven other examples:

1. *Greater power requires greater social responsibility.* This was brought out in the hearings a few years ago for the confirmation of Nelson Rockefeller as Vice-President.

2. *The rule of law is central, but unjust laws can exist; and there are times when a higher moral cause may justify breaking the law, provided the violator is willing to accept the consequences.* Example: the civil disobedience of the Montgomery, Alabama, bus riders.

3. *Property is a vital private right, but it has a social aspect.* Example: I may not build any kind of building I want regardless of my neighbors.

4. *Private power need not be based on property ownership to be legitimate.* Take the power of union leaders and corporate managers, for example. *But such power (and indeed all private power) carries the obligation of public accountability.*

5. *The firm does not exist solely for its own corporate prosperity or even survival; it also has social responsibilities to its various publics.* Witness the growth of public interest organizations.

There are two other kinds of middle principles more logical in character that can guide us in applying the other five:

6. *There is a difference between a precept or commandment, saying what must be done, and a counsel, recommending the better or more saintly action.* Examples: I must fulfill a contract; I may give half my income to the poor.

7. *When action has both a good effect and a bad effect (a common conflict situation), one may morally perform the action provided (a) he does not directly intend the bad effect; (b) the bad effect is not a means to the good end, but is simply a side effect; and (c) the good involved is not outweighed by the bad effect.* An example: A pharmaceutical company may market a needed drug (that might in some cases have harmful side effects) provided the good and bad effects are carefully weighed and consumers are encouraged to take all reasonable precautions. A consideration for the company: Is there another drug that would achieve the same benefits with less risk?

c. *Specific case analyses.* While essential in the process of ethics, these middle-level principles are not fully usable unless we apply them to specific cases.

Take the middle principle just cited: "The rule of law is central, but unjust laws can exist that there are times when a higher moral cause may justify breaking the law." Immediately one must ask: When does individual conscience justify violating the law? Who has the right to determine when a law is "unjust?" What about laws that grant rights to people to take actions which others consider immoral?

Another example: "Property is a vital private right, but it has a social aspect." An issue related to that principle is covering over strip mines for the benefit of the people in Kentucky and West Virginia versus the resulting higher cost in electric power and perhaps fewer urban jobs in Chicago or Pittsburgh. The tough trade-off questions between the different groups in our society cannot be solved by principles alone but must also involve the continuous and careful analysis of cases and classes of cases along with the principles. The student of ethics must work closely with economists, lawyers, sociologists, psychologists, engineers, and others.

One class of cases is "acceleration/preferential practice" in the hiring and promotion of minorities and women. Are such practices morally justified to correct the injustices in our society, provided certain careful provisos are met such as whether the minority group member is clearly qualified for the job, or can acquire the qualificaitons in a reasonable time? Are they necessarily and always reverse discrimination? The author thinks that such practices are ethically justifiable under certain conditions.

Another set of cases involves the employee's obligations of loyalty and confidentiality toward his employer versus his conflicting right and obligation to "blow the whistle" and reveal (leak) to the public the misconduct of his employer if he feels this is the only way to correct abuses. Philip I. Blumberg, vol. 24, No. 3, *Oklahoma Law Review,* treats these cases very well in terms of law. Much of his reasoning can guide the student of ethics. Management needs to provide its employees with a reasonable right of dissent. At the heart of the matter is the balancing of the ethical rights of the individual and the ethical rights of the organization.

Still another case class involves multinational corporations bribing foreign officials or making political contributions abroad. Going along with bribery to meet competition downgrades the business climate for everybody. But first we must determine whether such actions are in fact bribery, middlemen's commissions, local-custom-public-relations or sheer extortion. Only a careful study of each case and of classes of cases, along with principles, will give valid ethical answers here. You can start from what is legal in the host country, but recognize that there is a moral minimum across all cultures not to injure, not to harm people at least, even when honesty is not valued by those very cultures.

THE NEED FOR...ETHICS SPECIALISTS

The threefold ethical process described previously is practical and workable for...management, but it calls for a certain degree of expertise. Is it not time to appoint a small number of directors and also perhaps officers to be...ethical "devil's advocates" or better yet, their ethical "angel's advocates?"

We should institutionalize ethical expertise at the board of directors and top management levels, perhaps focusing on one director but with responsibilities shared by a committee of the board. These director/ethical advocates need not be philosophers in the field of ethics but they should keep up-to-date on the extensive literature of ethics as applied to business. A number of companies such as General Mills and General Electric already have public responsibility committees. Could not such committees also take on an explicitly ethical function? According to Fred T. Allen of Pitney Bowes: "...A moral dimension should be added to the board's criteria for judging a CEO (chief executive officer) and his principal subordinates."

About 28 large companies now have on their boards of directors committees that are explicitly designated as ethics committees: the Norton Company of Massachusetts, the world's largest manufacturer of abrasives, and the Consolidated Natural Gas Company headquartered in Pittsburgh.

The director/ethical advocates proposed here might also include corporate officers, perhaps the general counsel, as suggested by William Gossett, former president of the American Bar Association and vice-president of Ford Motor Company. Such an appointment admittedly would be controversial. One top management team of a major corporation warn that: "Any officer with marketing, financial, legal, staff, or whatever responsibilities, can scarcely be expected to step back in complete objectivity and to perform the role you envisage."

They may be right. But a firm could well have ethical advocates on its board if not among its officers. However, there is no neat formula here. Much depends on the top managemewnt personalities of a given company, their management styles, the structure of the corporation, and related characteristics.

A principal function of the ethics committee would be to identify generic questions of an ethical nature that should be asked routinely along with the usual legal, financial, and marketing questions. For example: A strategic planner might ask, "If we take certain actions, what would our market share be and will we run afoul of antitrust laws? What would our discounted cash flow be?

The ethics advocates might want to know how a given decision will affect the rights of employees versus the rights of the corporation. Or will an action help or hurt the long run general welfare of the cities or countries (South Africa, for instance) where our plants are located? Or, how shall the firm balance the public's right to know about minority hiring with the company's right to keep competitive information confidential? Or will a new product help or hurt the environment, the conservation of energy, the quality of life, or the safety of consumers?

The...ethics advocates would need to be socially sensitive enough to phrase such questions in generic terms but still keep them sufficiently practical and thus manageable for specific top-management decisions. It would be up to this committee to cooperate where necessary with ethics committees from other firms for that watchdog committee that Secretary of the Treasury Michael Blumenthal suggests. They might help develop an ethical code for thier company and encourage ethics seminars for top, middle and lower managers in their mid-careers, when their experience will lead them to see more clearly the ethical implications of their decisions. They might encourage the study of ethical principles and cases in schools of business administration, some of which could perhaps help them and their industry with the ethical problems that they face.

If the committee is entirely composed of corporate officers, its secretary will need to be a strong and able manager who has the backing of the chief executive officer. The CEO will be a prime force in the succcess or failure of the ethical advocacy idea. But a board committee is better.

The committee and its secretary should expect to encounter strong resistance. They will have to win over operating managers—no small assignment when ethical considerations compete with immediate profits or personal power. Their policies may have to persuade managers not by talking ethics, but by focusing on long-range business problems. (For example, an inner-city plant may have to hire and promote minorities if it is going to have any work force at all. Furthermore, if it makes a consumer product, the inner-city could provide an important market.) But at times the ethics committee should also appeal to a sense of ethics, because operating managers may turn out to be more receptive than one might expect. In any case, the problems of the ethics advocates may be only a little more difficult or different from the problems of any other corporate officers, such as the equal employment director, who has to deal with managers in the field. At the start at least, the main function of the ethics committee will be to ask questions rather than to impose the answers.

WHAT CORPORATE MANAGMENT THINKS

So far, top management executives seem mostly cool to this ethical advocacy idea. Their objections may be put into about four categories:

1. The "Tokenism" argument.
2. The "Ethics is Everybody's Business But Especially the CEO's Business" argument.
3. The "Ethics is Too Subjective and Variable" argument.
4. The "Our Only Hope is Law" argument.

The tokenism. One chief executive officer writes: "If one person is worrying about ethics, others will feel less constrained to do so on their own." But that result need not occur. While ethical advocacy might be focused on one board member as secretary of the committee, the responsibility should be explicitly shared by a committee of the board.

The second objection, "Ethics is everybody's business, especially the CEO's business," can be answered by saying, "What is everybody's business usually becomes nobody's business." The corporation has already institutionalized functional experts in law, finance, marketing, public relations, research, and so forth, to assist the chief executive officer. The CEO does not regard law or finance as "everybody's business," so why should the CEO not have at least a part-time expert in ethical analysis or a small committee? Ethics is not "fuzzier" than law or economics or finance. Furthermore, in these days economists and lawyers have been known to differ with each other.

We have already opposed the argument that ethics is too variable and subjective, or that law is our only hope.

No one denies that seriously organizing ethical expertise into top management with a board member (or perhaps an officer) and a small ethics committee is going to be a difficult and perhaps even a risky task, at least if the committee takes strong positions. We don't really have a blueprint for it yet, but the concept is a creative idea that demands exploration.

Applying ethics to complex business decisions will be difficult. At times this may be due to ethical pluralism. But mostly it will be due to the complexity of the facts. We all know that two honest, ethical persons sometimes take opposite sides on the same issue. The manager (and for that matter, public interest and religious groups) should be cautioned against coming up with dogmatic moral judgments when the facts are not clear. But they should also be cautioned about failing to take a moral position when the facts are not perfectly clear—but yet are sufficiently clear—for the facts will almost never be perfectly clear.

This calls for a mixture of both prudence and courage. Each manager, as he contributes to top level decision-making, will have to follow his own conscience both as an individual and as a member of a management group. And in so doing he will find agreement with associates in many, but not all, cases.

We are certainly not talking about window dressing here, but about realistic and serious management concern for ethics. . . . This concern will do much to bolster confidence in the American system. Many Americans are cynical about government, labor, and the professions and medical and academic institutions. But business management can take the lead in tapping the reservoir of good will that still exists for American institutions.

Ethical considerations can enter practically and systematically into executive decision-making at the policy level if management is willing to experiment, to take some risks and to be creative.

14.
Whistle Blowing in Organizations

Lea P. Stewart

There is a growing tendency for employees of organizations, especially scientists and engineers, to challenge management decisions, either protesting within the organization, or to the public. This latter avenue of protest, often called whistle blowing, is occurring more frequently or at least is being more widely reported. But researchers have been slow to focus upon the determinants, forms, or outcomes of whistle-blowing incidents.

There appear to be three reasons for this neglect. First, organizational phenomena have typically been looked at from the point of view of management; whistle blowing is, by definition, an antimanagement act. Second, there are no specific or well-developed treatments of whistle blowing from which to draw generalizations and conclusions. Third, information about specific whistle-blowing events is difficult to obtain. Although some cases, such as A. Ernest Fitzgerald's exposure of Air Force cost overruns, are well documented, many are described very briefly in general discussions of organizational problems.

This article examines whistle blowing as an organizational phenomenon, and analyzes fifty-one reports of actual incidents to derive a model of the steps through which whistle-blowing incidents progress. From this model it is possible to generalize about the nature of whistle-blowing incidents and how they fit into patterns of communication in organizations.

Americans do not have the same rights, such as freedom of the press, freedom of speech, and due process, at work as they do at home. This lack of rights is most conspicuous for employees who do not belong to unions, such as scientists and engineers and stems, in part, from the idea that the employer and employee are, as David W. Ewing notes in *Freedom Inside the Organization,* "equal partners to the employment agreement. Just as the employee is free to resign whenever he wants, so the employer is free to show him the door whenever it [sic] desires." The assumption behind the "legal notion of freedom of contract" is that an employee can leave a firm and find comparable employment with little difficulty. Nonethless, as Lawrence E. Blades vol. 67 of the *Columbia Law Review,* points out, "it is the fear of being discharged which above all else renders the great majority of employees vulnerable to employer coercion." He maintains that "only the unusually valuable employee has sufficient bargaining power to obtain a guarantee that he will be discharged during a specified term of employment only for 'just cause.'" Employers view the great majority of employees as expendable. Thus, an employee's threat to quit his job has little power in effecting change in an organization.

Nonetheless, society depends on the professional integrity of the experts in an organization to ensure that management decisions will not harm society. Professionals are often bound by an explicit code of ethics such as that of the National Society of Professional Engineers, which states that the engineer "will regard his duty to the public welfare as paramount." The engineer is instructed to "notify the proper authority of any observed conditions which endanger public safety and health" if "his engineering judgment is overruled by nontechnical authority." Thus, as Gerry E. Morse vol. 45, *Journal of Engineering Education,* notes, "engineering ethics, from the viewpoint of industry, will rise or fall on the decisions of the engineer himself. Application of engineering ethics in actual cases may, however, result in "gray areas" since engineers are also technically bound to uphold their clients' best interests in all cases. Such a resulting dilemma would be especially acute for older engineers who might find job security in competition with ethical interests.

Whistle blowing is based on the assumption that employees who disagree on ethical grounds with their employers about organizational policy should not quit, but should speak out.

According to Ralph Nader et al. in *Whistle Blowing: The Report of the Conference on Professional Responsibility,* whistle blowing is "the act of a man or woman who, believing that the public interest overrides the interest of the organization he serves, publicly 'blows the whistle' if the organization is involved in corrupt, illegal, fraudulent, or harmful activity." Thus, whistle blowers challenge organizational heads "who appear to be engaged in illegal, immoral, or irresponsible activity." A whistle blower is "the muckraker from within, who exposes what he considers the unconscionable practices of his own organization," or "the insider who feels compelled to tell all to the outsiders." In general, the whistle blower "believes he can best rectify unethical behavior in business or government by making his charges and identity public." According to Kenneth D. Walters, 53 (4) *Harvard Business Review,* the whistle blower, "having decided at some point that the actions of the organization are immoral, illegal, or inefficient,. . . acts on that belief by informing legal authorities or others outside the organization." Thus whistle blowers, whether federal employees or employees of corporate organizations, put their duty to the public above their loyalty to the organization. Whistle blowing is an indication that "the rules and guidelines for resolving disputes and failures within an organization have been insufficient" and that the situation is so serious it demands public attention.

A large number of whistle-blowing cases have involved professionals employed by industry and government. In a survey of 800 members of the National Society of Professional Engineers, Frank von Hippel, October 1977, *Physics Today,* found that most of the respondents had at one time or another felt obliged to question some of the activities in which their organizations were involved. "When asked to work on a product or project they believed not to be in the public interest," 7 percent of the respondents said they had sought transfer within the organization and another seven percent said they had resigned. Over 20 percent refused to work on a project or on a client's commission or to accept a job offer for this reason; and 60 percent had "expressed their disapproval of a project to their employer or client." The force of this disapproval is unknown. Von Hippel and others believe that known cases of whistle blowing may only be the tip of a rather large iceberg.

Potential whistle blowers are forced to weigh the seriousness of their claims against the likely consequences of making such claims public.

In the spring of 1975 the Committee on Scientific Freedom and Responsibility of the American Association for the Advancement of Science (AAAS) issued a report urging scientists and engineers to blow the whistle on their employers when they saw their work being used for "morally dubious ends." In the same year, Senator Edward Kennedy "sponsored hearings. . . to publicize the cause of government employees who spoke out against illegal or immoral actions in their agencies."

Although the AAAS and the Kennedy hearings encouraged conscious acts of whistle blowing, Helen Dudar, *New York Times Magazine,* October 30, 1977, maintains that "most people who wind up in the fraternity [of whistle blowers] begin almost accidentally, expecting gratitude and encountering, instead, a stone wall of either indifference or hostility." Apparently, much of the whistle blowing which does occur is a result of organizations' unresponsiveness to employees. In a study of university students, Ralph H. Turner, vol. 36, *Sociometry,* reports students "believed their freedom of expression was impaired, not because anyone actively prevented them from speaking, but because no one would listen, understand, or care." Similarly, whistle blowers feel that management will not listen to what they view as legitimate concerns. There is some evidence to substantiate this belief. For example, Isidore Silver claims most employee complaints are "insubstantial," while Kenneth G. Thompson claims most managers feel employees will see that management is "right" if they are given "the facts." Walters believes managers should respect employees' rights to disagree with organizational policy not because it is the employees' fundamental right, but because it is in the best interest of the organization.

In an often-quoted statement, James M. Roche, chairman of General Motors Corporation, claims in the March 26, 1971 issue of the *New York Times:*

> Some of the enemies of business now encourage an employee to be disloyal to the enterprise. They want to create suspicion and disharmony and pry into the proprietary interests of the business. However this is labeled— "industrial espionage," "whistle blowing," or "professional responsibility"— it is another tactic for spreading disunity and creating conflict.

Even when managers recognize the legitimacy of blowing the whistle, they may note how difficult it often is "to distinguish between those who are blowing the whistle and those who are crying wolf" and maintain that employees who make a "public attack" on their organization should be willing to resign.

Thus, Larry L. Boulden, 22 (3) *Automation,* warns engineers that "any effort to. . . speak out against company practices, will be interpreted by your employers and fellow workers as disloyalty and near treason." He maintains whistle blowing almost never has a positive effect on an engineer's career, and the "odds are that management will not only attempt to brand your statements as falsehoods, but may also attack your veracity and competence." Charles Peters and Taylor Branch in *Blowing the Whistle: Dissent in the Public Interest,* describe the "typical" response to a whistle-blowing attempt:

> A whistle blower's antagonists will probably do something like the following: Hand the press a 2,000-page computer-blessed study by experts in support of their position; cite national security, job protection, or economic emergency as the justification for their actions; inpugn the person with the whistle as an unqualified, self-seeking, disloyal, and moderately unbalanced underling who just doesn't understand the complexities that converge at the top; call for further study of the problem; and retire to dinner with their lawyers.

An article in *Time* notes that most employees who oppose corporate policy are fired, demoted, or forced to resign.

Robert N. d'Aprix in the *Believable Corporation,* maintains that "in a highly traditional organization,. . .there is considerable emphasis on communication up and down a chain of command. The worker is not permitted to air his grievances to his boss's boss without first seeking permission and approval." Larry L. Boulden warns engineers that they should always speak first to their supervisor when they have information about an unsafe product or condition within the company. Most employees usually do seek such approval first, but they are most likely to go directly to the public with their concerns when their criticisms have met with "bureaucratic runarounds, deaf ears, or hostility" in the past.

Often, the whistle blower will be subjected to what Blades terms "abusive discharge" in which the employee is "discharged as a result of resisting his employer's attempt to intimidate or coerce him in a way which bears no reasonable relationship to the employment." The "abusive discharge" is apt to be malicious because as Ewing, in *Freedom Inside the Organization* notes: "When a competent employee with years of service is fired for refusing to submit to a boss's improper or overreaching demands, the boss feels guilt in a way not experienced when firing an employee for incompetence or laziness. Christopher D. Stone in *Where the Law Ends: The Social Control of Corporate Behavior,* suggests: "People who feel. . . threatened by whistle blowing will inevitably seek to 'make an example' of the whistle blower: by firing, demotion, or harassment." The whistle blower is seen as a threat to the hierarchical organization. An organization may pay some price for the loss of an employee, but an employee is likely to pay a still higher price. Ewing cites a sociologist who has called "abusive discharge" the "organizational equivalent of capital punishment."

As a result of such attitudes, Nader et al. maintain the most vulnerable whistle blower is the one who speaks out from within an organization. Accordingly, most whistle blowers are those who have reached what Peters and Branch call a "career plateau," because blowing the whistle may lead to expulsion from the organization, and often the end of a career.

Thus the potential whistle blower must call for help loudly enough to receive public attention, without appearing to be seeking ego gratification. Whistle blowers are more likely to be heard and believed if they appear clearly to lose from their act. Some whistle blowers may find comfort in the fact that nearly all whistle blowers who have been punished for their views win their cases when they challenge their punishment in court.

An examination of 51 separate whistle-blowing events reveals
consistent patterns of events in "pure" whistle-blowing incidents
(when the whistle blower is still an employee of the organization)
and in "alumnus" whistle-blowing incidents (when the whistle blower
is no longer a member of the organization).

Although information on specific whistle-blowing events is limited, I was able to collect information on 51 separate incidents. The amount of information available on these events ranged from one paragraph descriptions in general overviews of whistle blowing, to extensive discussions of cases which were well publicized.

In pure whistle-blowing incidents, the events occur in the following order (although some steps may be omitted):

Step 1: An organizational member becomes aware of an organizational product or policy which he feels is unethical, immoral, or illegal, and/or will endanger the public.

Step 2: The organizational member expresses his concerns to his immediate superior(s). The member perceives that his superior(s) is not going to act upon his concerns.

Step 3: The organizational member expresses his concerns to administrators higher up in the corporate or governmental hierarchy. The member perceives that the administrators are not going to act upon his concerns.

Step 4a: The organizational member takes his concerns to the regulatory body (such as a Congressional subcommittee, the courts, or the Atomic Energy Commission) which is charged with overseeing the organization or government agency. This step, by definition, makes the member's concerns public.

and/or

Step 4b: The organizational member takes his concerns to the public press, which then publicizes them.

Step 5: The organizational member is isolated by his superiors (for example, his assistants are taken away and other organizational members are instructed to avoid him).

Step 6: The organizational member is expelled from the organization; he is either fired or forced to resign.

In the 25 cases of pure whistle blowing examined, only two deviated from this pattern. In one case, Step 5 occurred before Step 4b; in the other case, Step 5 occurred between Steps 4a and 4b.

There are two types of alumnus whistle blowers: those who voluntarily resign from an organization before blowing the whistle, and those who are expelled (fired or forced to resign) and then blow the whistle. The following stages typically occur in alumnus whistle blowing incidents (although some steps may be omitted):

Step 1: An organizational member becomes aware of an organizational product or policy which he feels is unethical, immoral, or illegal, and/or will endanger the public.

Step 2: The organizational member expresses his concerns to his imediate superior(s). The member perceives his superior(s) is not going to act upon his concerns.

Step 3a: The organizational member resigns voluntarily. His resignation may or may not be publicized.

and/or

Step 3b: The organizational member is expelled. He is either fired or forced to resign.

Step 4a: The organizational member takes his concerns to the regulatory body (such as Congressional subcommittee, the courts, or the Atomic Energy Commission) which is charged with overseeing the products or services offered by the organization or government agency. This step, by definition, makes the member's concerns public.

and/or

Step 4b: The organizational member takes his concerns to the public press, which then publicizes them.

There may be a lapse of time between Step 3a and Steps 4a or 4b. In one case, an organizational member voluntarily resigned and waited 21 years before completing Step 4a.

In the 26 cases of alumnus whistle blowing examined, only two exceptions to the above order were noted. One case occurred in the following sequence: Steps 1, 2, 4a, 3a, 4b. In the other case, the organizational member was isolated before Step 3b.

The response of superiors to the strategies which employees use to deal with their concerns can be explained, in part, in terms of superior-subordinate communication in general.

It is commonly believed that communication in organization can be "improved" by increasing the *amount* of communication that occurs. But some restrictions on communication are inherent in organizations.

To be in an "organized state," random and diffuse communication must be restricted so that various groups and specialists will receive the information that is most relevant.

Communication overload occurs when there is "an excess of 'input' over the ability of the message-receiver to 'handle' such input." One mechanism to reduce overload is the "exception principle," which holds that "only significant deviations from standards, procedures, and policies should be brought to the attention of the superior; [that is, only] matters of exception and not of standard practice [are brought to the attention of superiors]."

Procedures and practices such as the exception principle create problems for organizations, however. Too much information cannot be allowed to travel up the organizational hierarchy; yet decision makers must receive the information they need. G. March and M.A. Simon posit the concept of "uncertainty absorption" to indicate that there are progressively increasing omissions of detail as a message travels up an organizational hierarchy.

All complex organizations, by definition, involve superior-subordinate relationships, and the communication occurring at these crucial junctions has received much research attention. One area of superior-subordinate communication that is relevant to whistle blowing is upward communication. When potential whistle blowers attempt to take their concerns through an organizational hierarchy, they may be attempting to increase, or at least alter, the upward flow of information. They express their concerns directly to the public when they feel they cannot alter the flow of information or get a suitable response from the organization. This feeling may result because their superiors will not pass their concerns to the next level of the hierarchy or because their superiors do not respond to the concerns as the subordinates wish them to. Thus, the crucial concern becomes the superior's decision to transmit information through an organizational hierarchy, to act upon the information in the way the subordinate wishes.

Subordinates are likely to pass information to their superiors if the information is seen as important and favorable to themselves. Potential whistle blowers often consider their information to be favorable because they feel they have discovered an organization problem which needs to be remedied; thus their concern shows that they are conscientious employees. Their information is unlikely to be passed up the organizational hierarchy by their superiors, however, because this information, be definition, is unfavorable to their superiors. Superiors are also unlikely to pass such information upward because they view messages which are favorable to subordinates as less accurate than messages which are unfavorable.

The problem of passing information upward may be confounded by a large "semantic/information distance," P.K. Tompkin's term for the "gap" in information and understanding which exists between superiors and subordinates on specified issues. R.L. Minter notes that serious semantic differences between superiors and subordinates are quite frequent, occurring approximately 60 percent of the time. Such a gap might exist, for example, when the superior is a nontechnical manager or an engineer with a different specialty than the subordinate.

Given this framework, there is a potential for whistle blowing any time a subordinate communicates to a superior information perceived to be unfavorable to the superior. Of course, in many instances, when a superior stops a subordinate's message, the subordinate decides the information was unimportant and gives up. Occasionally, however, the subordinate feels that he has discovered something immoral, unethical, or illegal, and refuses to keep silent. A subordinate who feels this way is likely to bypass the communication channels normally associated with the organizational hierarchy—sometimes by going directly to the public. Members of the organizational hierarchy are likely to react against such a person, in part, because he has publicly demonstrated the ineffectiveness of the organizational communication system.

The dilemma of the potential corporate whistle blower thus stems from one of the dilemmas faced by all complex organizations—how to restrict the flow of information up the organizational hierarchy and, at the same time, ensure that *all* the necessary information reaches the organizational decision makers. This dilemma could perhaps be eased first by encouraging communication "openness."

An "open" communication relationship exists between superiors and subordinates when "both parties perceive the other interactant as a willing and receptive listener, and refrain from responses which might be perceived as providing negative relational or disconfirming feedback." Openness is an essential element for an effective organizational climate. Employees are more satisfied with their jobs when communication openness exists between superiors and subordinates.

Whistle blowing often occurs in research laboratories which employ scientists and engineers. Boyden C. Sanders, Jr., in *The Management of Scientists,* maintains that a combination of technical ability and judgment with administrative ability and judgment is rare in scientists, but essential for managers of scientists. Organizational communication specialists can help managers of engineers develop administrative ability and judgment and perhaps, thereby, obviate the need for whistle blowing.

A second principle that might help alleviate the whistle blower's dilemma involves a special technique for accomplishing more efficient upward communication—the use of ombudsmen. According to Silver, Vol. 45, *Harvard Business Review,* a political ombudsman is "a person of some eminence, learned in law, who is appointed by a legislative body to inquire into complaints against administrative officials and to make periodic reports about his findings." A corporate ombudsman would hear an employee's complaint, decide whether or not the complaint was warranted, investigate the dispute, and suggest a solution. Silver maintains that an ombudsman could explain to an employee why the employee's complaint was unwarranted. He contends that

> one of the great problems of corporate life, and a cause for frequent grievance, is not the unfairness of management action, but the inexplicability of it. . . . Often. . . decisions appear to be arbitrary when in fact they are not. Equally often, work discontent is caused by a lack of understanding as to reasons for such apparently unfavorable decisions.

On the other hand, a corporate ombudsman will not be successful in answering the grievances of professional employees if he automatically assumes that decisions made by management are correct, especially when those decisions affect professional employees.

Dissent in organizations has not been studied from a communication perspective. Dissent occurs, at least in part, through the communication of information which organizational members consider negative. More systematic research needs to be conducted to determine the nature of this information and how it is acted upon by organizational members.

Whistle blowing is both a constructive and a destructive phenomenon. It is constructive because whistle blowers often reveal unethical practices or defects which would cause danger to the public, and it is destructive because whistle blowers often suffer personal and professional harm and/or create suspicion within organizations. As a result, the public may begin to distrust the motives of all complex organizations. Understanding whistle blowing may make it possible to reduce its destructive effects while at the same time protecting public safety and encouraging ethical behavior in organizations.

15.
Ethics and
Public Policy

Ralph C. Chandler

A VIEW FROM HISTORY AND PUBLIC ADMINISTRATION

During the past seven years public attention has been focused on the problem of ethics in an unprecedented way. Forty-six of the fifty states have enacted new ethics legislation in this period, or they have significantly amended existing laws. Three of the four remaining states, Nevada, New Hampshire, and Vermont, have ethics legislation pending before their legislative houses. Only Mississippi has taken no action in this regard.

So active have been the states in the ethics area, in fact, that the National Municipal League has established a clearinghouse in New York just to collect, classify, and distribute legislative acts and executive orders now appearing on the subject.

At the federal level the House of Representatives on March 2, 1977, overwhemingly adopted House Resolution 287, described by Speaker Thomas P. O'Neill, Jr. (D.-Mass.) as "the toughest ethics code of any legislative body in the country."

Seven days later the House by a vote of 410-1 adopted a resolution to establish a Select Committee on Ethics to implement and write the code into statutory law. Thus what began as a series of amendments to the House rules is now intended to subject violators to criminal penalties and permit investigations of alleged abuses by federal law enforcement agencies.

On April 1, 1977, the United States Senate adopted an ethics code even broader than the House version, extending it by the end of the first session of the

95th Congress to cover all federal employees. Majority Leader Robert C. Byrd (D.-W.Va.) argued on the floor that "the necessity of the times," and the "climate created by the errant actions of a minority of public officials," demanded the Senate adopt such a code to restore public confidence in Congress.

Some would argue from history that this apparently unprecedented attention to ethics in government is not unprecedented at all. An influential new book entitled *Corruption in the American Political System*, maintains, for example, that corruption has been so systemic in the United States for so long that the reformers who not infrequently arise should be less interested in correcting the "evil man" the system occasionally produces than in restructuring the system itself.

It can also be argued, looking through a theological window, that since complex governmental systems such as ours are changed only incrementally, and since a basic restructuring of the American political system is hardly possible short of an unlikely revolution, we are left to live in the short run of trying to achieve approximate justice, and that we must work out even approximate justice in ambiguous circumstances.

In this view the existential question comes to be: How can public administrators properly plant, bring to flower, and keep weeded a *personal* code of ethical performance which both meets the requirements of the law and adequately takes into account the complexities of situations they encounter almost daily in the real world: situations which demand discretion and sometimes demand decisions on the margin of the law.

Two books might occur to the reader at this point. One is Joseph Fletcher's *Situation Ethics*, published an intellectual millennium ago, in 1966, and the other, the book of the prophet Jeremiah, written more recently in the seventh century B.C. Fletcher agrees with Alfred North Whitehead that "the simple-minded use of the notion of 'right or wrong' is one of the chief obstacles to the progress of understanding," and Jeremiah summarizes the accumulated wisdom of ancient Israel in the thirty-first chapter of his book, in which he represents Yahweh as saying God's law would be planted deep within his people; it would be written not on their law books, but on their hearts.

The historical record sustains the view that corruption is endemic in the American political system. From the Yazoo land fraud in the 1790s, to the bribery of members of Congress by officials of the Second United States Bank in the 1830s, to the scandals surrounding land acquisition by the Union Pacific Railroad in the 1870s, to Teapot Dome and Elk Hills in the 1920s, to the revelations of kickbacks in tax settlements by collectors of internal revenue in the 1950s, to the Watergate phenomenon of the 1970s, and many other instances in between, our national history can be read as a litany of avarice and greed. Carl Snyder in his book *Capitalism the Creator*, calls the characteristics of the sharpdealer the great forces in the building of America.

Consider the opinion of Henry Steele Commager. In an article entitled, "A

Historian Looks at Our Political Morality," he prefers not to address individual culpability in our national past, but to inquire into certain presuppositional questions of national policy. These have to do with our collective responsibility for what he describes as "the conquest and decimation of the Indian," slavery defended as a moral good, the child labor of the Industrial Revolution explained as the necessary price of progress, and the Vietnam War pursued as the logical result of "better dead than Red." Commager concludes that ". . . we must square our conduct with principles of law and of morality. . ."

Carl Sandburg in his role of poet as well as historian has a kinder indictment. He says we're all liars, just different kinds.

> People lie because they don't remember
>   clear what they say.
> People lie because they can't help
>   making a story better than it was
>   the way it happened.
> People tell white lies so as to be decent
>   to others.
> People lie in a pinch, hating to do it,
>   but lying on because it might be worse.
> And people lie just to be liars
>   for crooked gain.
> What sort of liar are you?
> Which of these liars are you?

Although Snyder, Commager, and Sandburg are competent historians and base their value judgments on lives of scholarship and reflection, other jurors may prefer to have relevant facts laid before them for their independent determination of the prevalence of corruption in American government. The following data represent part of the basis for the contention by historians that modern legislators are dealing with an endemic problem.

Alexander Hamilton had written in the *Federalist Papers* in 1788 that

> The aim of every political constitution is, or ought to be, first to obtain for rulers men who possess most wisdom to discern, and most virtue to pursue, the common good of society; and in the next place to take the most effectual precautions for keeping them virtuous. . .

The ink was hardly dry on the *Federalist Papers*, when the Yazoo land fraud case came to light in 1795. The state of Georgia, its legislature bribed by New England financiers, sold to private speculators most of what is today the states of Alabama and Mississippi at one and a half cents an acre. Involved in the graft were two United States senators, including Robert Morris of Pennsylvania, two congressmen, and three leading jurists, including Associate Supreme Court Justice James Wilson.

The story is celebrated and involved and eventually resulted in a major Supreme Court decision, *Fletcher* v. *Peck* (1810). The speculators won out, finally, because the Marshall Court held invalid an act of a subsequent Georgia legislature repealing the sale. The bribers kept their profits largely through the efforts of their sagacious lawyer, one Alexander Hamilton.

During this same period the Speaker of the House of Representatives, Jonathan Dayton (1798-1800), was driven from office for embezzling some $15,000 from the pay and travel allowance of members.

In 1833, United States Senator Daniel Webster sent the following message to the president of the Second United States Bank, whose charter was before Congress for renewal:

> I believe that my retainer has not been renewed or *refreshed* as usual. If it be wished that my relation to the Bank should be continued, it may be well to send me the usual retainer.

Bank President Nicholas Biddle came across with "loans" of $17,782.86 for Daniel Webster. Biddle also refreshed the bank accounts of 54 other members of Congress, including Henry Clay and John C. Calhoun.

Throughout the second half of the nineteenth century there was a near fusion of economic and political power in the United States as railroad and other economic interests largely controlled several state legislatures, notably that of Iowa, and influenced a working majority in the United States Senate.

Most remarkable among the schemes of the agents of the Union Pacific Railroad was the creation of a bogus construction company, the Credit Mobilier, which distributed its stock to members of Congress in exchange for congressmen looking the other way as the profits of the company reached enormous proportions. A major source of profits was congressional grants to the railroad for completion of the final 667 miles of the Union Pacific.

Another low point in the administration of public affairs in the United States came in the Harding administration when Secretary of the Interior Albert B. Fall was charged with accepting over $385,000 from the oil companies leasing the Teapot Dome reserves in Wyoming and the Elk Hills reserves in California.

And as a final example, in 1951 the Douglas Committee on Ethical Standards in Government disclosed a decade of kickbacks in tax settlements by collectors of internal revenue in New York, Boston, Detroit, St. Louis, and San Francisco. In the same year Senator J. William Fulbright said of his investigations of the Reconstruction Finance Corporation:

> As our study of the RFC progressed, we were confronted more and more with problems of ethical conduct. . . How do we deal with those who under

ETHICS AND PUBLIC POLICY • 181

the guise of friendship accept favors which offend the spirit of the law, but do not violate the letter? What of the men outside government who suborn those inside it?. . . Who is more at fault, the bribed or the bribers?

One might wonder if the revelations of the Douglas committee in 1951 would have produced the spate of ethics legislation apparent today if the news media had in fact covered those hearings as assiduously as the Ervin committee was covered 22 years later. In his book, *It Didn't Start With Watergate*, that unobjective journalist Victor Lasky quotes Fulbright as saying

> The Watergate was ballooned up into an enormous issue. People like those two reporters who uncovered it for the *Washington Post* and the *Post* itself—they had discovered a whole new world. People make reputations overnight discovering some new scandal. They're still doing it, they just love it.

Lasky further quotes former Representative Jerome R. Waldie (D.-Calif.) a leader of the anti-Nixon forces in the House, as saying he doubted whether the President would have been forced out of office "if the press had not desired it."

Is Watergate unprecedented?

Or is the press coverage the only thing different about it. Is the Watergate scandal so precedented in American history that indeed it exists on a continuum of scandal, and may not be qualitatively different from other scandals? If Watergate *is* different, is the difference only in the magnitude of the President's personal involvement in it, and in the lies he told?

But Carl Sandburg said we're all liars.

Watergate is different, but not primarily for these reasons. Put in simple terms, previous corruption was about money. Watergate was about power.

It is as though the United States has finally come to Plato's discussion of the foundation of political authority. In the *Republic* the sophist Thrasymachus said the foundation of political authority is power. Socrates said that politics is also a system of obligations and a system of values. Have we reached the point in our national history at which this is no longer a theoretical discussion?

Theoretical discussions bore us. The expanse and abundance of America are largely responsible for that. We didn't have time for theory. We had before us in the nineteenth and early twentieth century the practical problems of nation-building, moneymaking, inventing, fighting wars, technologizing, and doing right; and these were all proper activities of Puritan ethics. They so subsumed the more modest interests of our founding fathers and an occasional jurist, however, that the processes of defining probity and managing scarcity were mental and administrative exercises we didn't get much experience at.

We were not entirely unprepared for the current tasks of public administration, however. We do know how we feel in this country, and we did not like the feel of the sophist position at Watergate. Politics is not just a power game. It's not okay to play dirty. Dirty play may continue, and the smart players may not get caught, but the *definition* of politics as a sordid business did not receive the sanction of the commonweal.

And so legislative bodies all over the country, embarrassed and quickened by an historical record of scandal culminating in Watergate, have acted to bring politics and ethics back together again. Is the corrective legislation hitting the mark? Is it about the right problem?

A VIEW FROM PUBLIC ADMINISTRATION

Historians point to the systemic nature of corruption in the government of the United States. Public administationists have looked at Watergate and related shenanigans for four years now and concluded in some quarters that these events also represent a breakdown of public administration theory.

Reflecting on the lessons of Watergate for public administration, James L. Sundquist noted that the profession devoted 40 years to aggrandizing presidential power. Rather than believe Lord Acton, that "power tends to corrupt, and absolute power corrupts absolutely," public administrationists preferred to believe Louis Brownlow when he said,

> During the whole history of the thirty-two presidents, not one has been recreant to his high trust—none has used his power to aggrandize himself at the expense of our settled institutions.

That was a marginal statement even in 1947.

Public administration's emphasis on a strong executive did not start with Luther Gulick, but this professor of Municipal Services and Administration at Columbia University, certainly articulated the doctrine in a way which admirably served the disposition of Franklin Roosevelt, as well as the needs of the nation at that time.

In 1936 he wrote "It is clear from long experience in human affairs that...a single directing executive authority" is mandatory for solving the problems of governmental organization. From the time the Brownlow committee on Administrative Management, of which Gulick was a member, recommended to President Roosevelt the establishment of an Exeuctive Office of the President, the movement toward the President's increased command and control was also a movement toward the imperial presidency.

The White House staff grew from 37 members under Herbert Hoover, to more than 500 under Richard Nixon, and the Executive Office of the Presidency, with its proliferation of boards, committees, and special groups, mushroomed from 1,175 in the late 1950s, to roughly 5,000 at the end of 1976. The changing attitude of the staff, with its steady accretion of command and control power, was described by George Reedy, President Johnson's press secretary, as "the heel click at the other end of the wire." It fitted naturally, he said, with the style of a royal court provided with a swimming pool, masseur, telephone in every bathroom, and a helicopter at the push of a button, all to serve the needs of a single man and shield him from ordinary discomforts.

The administrative tools the chief administrator was given to use for the aggrandizement of his office: budgeting, legislative clearance, and the preparation of government reorganization plans, for example, were supplemented in the 1950s with a development public administrationists could not have foreseen: the rise of the political technician.

These technicians are the people who know how to package and sell a candidate. They are the public relations men, advertising men, television directors, fund-raisers, speechwriters, and organizational experts who make up a personal campaign coterie. . . . If the candidate is successful, they accompany him into the corridors of power.

That this should be so—that the Haldemans and Ehrlichmans should be the ones to help the President see that the laws are faithfully executed—is a direct result of the Pendelton Act. Where there is no patronage in the public service, there is no effective party machinery. This has proven to be a two-edged sword in American history.

Patronage and its twin, corruption, were countenanced in the big city machines of America because, in the words of Martin Lomansey, the political boss of Boston in 1915:

> I think that there's got to be in every ward somebody that any bloke can come to—no matter what he's done—and get help. Help, you understand; none of your law and justice, but help.

This is not entirely an unethical position.

If the machine was a fount of favors which generated political obligations paid on election day, it also generated something else; respect toward the public on the part of the practicing politician. That's why he balanced his ticket, secured advantages for his constituents, and served the "public interest" as he scented it. He stayed in office that way.

The political technician, on the other hand, typically has no such experience in democratic politics. His experience is not so much in service as in manipulation. His loyalty is not to party or a principle but to the leader in whose entourage he serves. The law for him is instrumental. It can be bent or broken when necessary.

When Luther Gulick and other public administrationists transposed the literature of business administration into the service of public institutions in the 1930s they had no idea that political technicians would eventually transpose the philosophy of corporate life into public administration as well. This is the philosophy that in a corporate struggle the victorious faction takes over the company.

The issue hung in the balance for some months in 1973 and 1974 as to whether the press and the United States House of Representatives would successfully remind the technicians that the people still own the company.

But what of the structure of things now? A political candidate still must practice the public relations game of image manipulation. He still will be tempted to fall victim to the arrogance of the technicist world view, especially if he is successful.

The legislative responses are appropriate enough. At the federal level, however, neither of the stringent ethics codes passed by the House on March 2 or by the Senate on April 1 of 1977 speaks across the separation of powers to be aggrandized by presidential power.

Again, public administration theory is of doubtful help. Many practitioners would still agree with Paul Appleby's judgment about presidential power in 1945: "Through Congress, and through elections, it is a power popularly controlled." In this view it will take a long time before a President will again embark on any such headstrong foreign adventure as Lyndon Johnson undertook in Vietnam, or on any such exercise in megalomania as Richard Nixon undertook at Watergate.

The modesty of Jimmy Carter's initial days in office support this view. *New York Times* correspondent Hedrick Smith has written the following vignette to illustrate the sensitivity of the new President to the cult of the presidency which has developed since the early 1960s.

> A few days after his election in November, Jimmy Carter boarded the airborne palace called Air Force One for a flight to a vacation hideaway and declared with obvious relish: "This is the one I've been waiting for."
>
> After he was publicly chided for so quickly abandoning the populist propensities of his electoral campaign in favor of the seductive perquisites of Presidential power, the chastened Mr. Carter passed up the return flight on the presidential jet and flew home on a more humble commercial aircraft. In that hasty retreat and in other ways, the new President has shown he understands that informality and openness are needed in his administration...

Sundquist rightfully observed that public administrators can point with pride to the fact that career civil servants were tarnished very little by Watergate. The Federal Bureau of Investigation, notably the Criminal Division, the Internal Revenue Service, and the Central Intelligence Agency, in fact acted as a restraint on the President. This is why the "plumbers" were forced to operate directly out of the White House.

But dependence upon bureaucratic restraints to assure ethical behavior on the part of the chief administrator is a thin reed indeed. We must simply admit at this point that there is no general rule of law save impeachment proceedings which can restrain a President from the abuse or misuse of power.

The houses of Congress, however, have not only passed comprehensive codes for their own members, but are currently taking steps to have the provisions of these codes enacted into statutory law to cover all federal employees.

President Carter has asked Congress to require annual public financial disclosure statements from top executive branch officials and to prohibit them from lobbying their former agencies for at least one year after leaving government. He also asked that a special prosecutor's office be created to prosecute misconduct by high-ranking executive branch officials and that an Office of Ethics be established within the Civil Service Commission.

In the House and Senate codes, office accounts are banned; outside income from speaking engagements, articles and other sources is limited; gifts from lobbyists are restricted; travel by lame duck members is prohibited; financial disclosure is widened; and so forth. Representative David R. Obey (D.-Wis.), chairman of the commission which drafted the House code, said it was designed to assure that "members are not cashing in on their positions of influence."

Likewise the states have acted vigorously to elevate their standards of public service. The state legislation generally falls into four categories: (1) The specification of acts which are prohibited to public officials, candidates and employees; (2) The enumeration of codes of ethics applicable to public servants; (3) The requirement of certain procedures to prevent conflicts of interest; and (4) The requirement of public disclosure of the financial interests of public officials, candidates for office, and certain government employees and members of their immediate families.

"Public officials" are of basically two types in the legislation and in practice. These are elected officials and professional administrators. The former often delegates discretion to the latter. If this were not so, legislatures would be paralyzed by interest group conflict. Few laws could be written in broad and vague terms, leaving details to be worked out later. The bureaucracy, then, in working out the finer points of policy, often enters into the same kind of bargaining process as characterized the original policy discussion. The question of how much discretion should be permitted civil servants, and how to make its exercise responsible, occupies a thoughtful place in current public administration literature.

In discussing ethical guidelines for professional administrators in the *Public Administration Review*, George A. Graham has pinpointed the problem of discretion:

> Where there is discretion, there is uncertainty, and there may be confliciting obligations and loyalties. In dealing with this situation, the administrator is subject to a double heirarchy of authority, one impersonal

and one personal, which defines his obligations. The heirarchy of law (constitutional, statutory, administrative) is impersonal. The chain of direction or command, into which he fits somewhere, is quite personal.

Graham goes on to say that general law must be *interpreted*, and that the courts seldom get around to definitive interpretations on the vast majority of issues which arise administratively. Thus administrators must delineate the law. Their policies, programs, instructions, rules, procedures, and day-to-day decisions may not always agree with the intent of the elected officials who broadly structured the law in the first place, or the courts who are too busy to define it.

This no man's land of what is lawful, or what is wise, or what is in the public interest, is where the difficult ethical issues lie for public administrators.

It is against *this* reality that the ethics legislation in the states ought finally to be measured. Forty-three states, for example, have legislated on conflict of interest and financial disclosure for public administrators.

California, in mandating the formulation of ethics codes by each state agency, enumerate the positions within the agency which could affect outside financial interests. The occupant of each such position must file an annual statement of his financial status to show it has not been improved by agency decisions. New York has a similar requirement for selected state employees, and has a Board of Public Disclosure to monitor compliance.

The student of public administration might ask at this point: Do these rather onerous reporting requirements with their resulting deprivation of privacy really address the ethical dimension of the job of the public administrator? Is the real ethical problem about money? It is tempting to formulate laws about conflict of interest and financial disclosure and feel that the ethics job has been done. In many ways, however, this represents a retreat into legalism.

The problem of administrative ethics continues to be one of discretion, of judgment, of interpretation, of definition of the public interest and pursuit of the public good. Good ethics legislation will facilitate solutions to these and other conundrums of statecraft.

A piece of legislation which appears to appreciate some of the dilemmas of public administrators is Michigan's Public Act 196, enacted in 1973.

The act established a state board of ethics which renders both decisions and advisory opinions. The former occurs when there has been a formal complaint filed with the board against a public official or employee. The latter occurs when a public official finds himself in a questionable position regarding what constitutes propriety in handling the public's business. Without an adversary proceeding he can receive guidance.

This kind of procedure is flexible, and it sems infinitely more fair to the public administrator. It is probably more consititutional, as well. The Michigan experience has been evaluated as follows:

The mere fact that a public official might be evaluated against ethical criteria may result in many officials avoiding the risks of improper conduct because of the difficulty of carrying it off without disclosure and public censure.

The types of problems that come before the Board of Ethics are not of venal people attempting to take advantage of their public trust, but rather conscientious public servants who have real questions about the propriety of their actions... The people who present requests to the board are honest people with real problems.

A view of ethics from American history leaves the question of whether federal legislation has attacked the right problem: aggrandized presidential power. A view from public administration leaves the same kind of question about federal and state legislation from another perspective: Does the reform movement understand the bureaucratic and human context of the administrator's discretionary choices?

Please do not misunderstand me. I favor ethics legislation, including legislation about conflict of interest and financial disclosure. It sets a tone and a level of expectation which permeates the governmental organization. But ethics is much more than legislation. If it is *only* legislation, in fact, it is decidedly unethical. For ethics presupposes a context of personal principle and of moral commitment which rules and rulesmakers cannot touch.

As Frank Getlein wrote in *Commonweal* in response to the new ethics codes in the House and Senate:

> A code of ethics, after all, is something one believes in, or something the members of a given society subscribe to; it is not something imposed, it is something observed because it is thought to be right. Least of all is a code of ethics something drawn up by a committee. God knows what the Ten Commandments would have looked like if composed by a committee of proto-Talmudic scholars...

The reason Jesus got into considerable trouble with the theocracy of his day was that he maintained the law did not necessarily have anything to do with ethical behavior. One could be steeped in the law and not love. And love, Paul Tillich was to add sometime later, is the ultimate law because it is the negation of law; it is absolute because it concerns everything concrete.

Is there anything practical in this theological jargon? Its truth doesn't have to lie in its practicality, but it does happen to be practical. It gives us a reason not to be cynical.

The ethics legislation recently enacted is not going to solve the problem of corruption in American government, for several reasons. One is that the historians are right: Corruption is endemic in the American system. Another is that the public administrationists are also right: Discretion is not a suitable subject for legislation. A third is that even if both were not true, most of the new ethics legislation misses the mark anyway. It is about money, while Watergate and the cult of the presidency have taken a quantum leap into a more insidious source of corruption than money.

So, practically speaking, let us not expect too much from the legislation. True, it will make potential violators more circumspect. It will make President Carter more humble. But whatever Mr. Carter's predilections toward humility, he will find in time that the presidency shapes him more than he shapes it.

And then, alas, there is original sin. There is the imperfectibility of man. But there is also American man's stubborn refusal to admit that the best he can do is to approximate justice in his institutions and in himself. His tolerance for ambiguity remains low; his struggle for the right remains his most obvious, and admirable, characteristic; and where is the respository of the right but in the law?

That eminent philosopher Garry Trudeau makes the point in a Doonesbury comic strip shortly after Watergate. A law professor is telling his class that law schools must do much more than simply teach the law. They must teach "its spirit, its moral essence," and then drawing himself up dramatically the professor adds, "Right and Wrong 10-A is one such stab in the dark."

There is a right and a wrong, of course, but most often there is something in between. There is freedom. Law tries to escape from it; love tries to embrace it; and for a very long time ethical and political systems have tried to reach some sort of compromise with it. There is only one sure thing about the moving target of ethical and political obligation: It is two sides of the same coin. Rousseau probably said it best when he said those who treat politics and ethics apart will never understand either one.

16.
Recent Reforms in Government and the Case for an Inspector General of the United States

Jarold A. Kieffer

Both the Congress and the executive branch in recent years have been trying to strengthen the processes by which wrongdoing in the federal government can be exposed and dealt with more effectively. We have seen the establishment of inspectors general in the departments and agencies. An Office of Special Counsel has been established in the new Merit Systems Protection Board, and telephone "hot lines" to this officer and to the General Accounting Office (GAO) are now available to executive branch employees who feel that they are being given improper orders, or wish to report wrongdoing, or that they are being punished for whistle blowing.

In the legislative branch, ethics committees in both the House and Senate have grappled with, or are now working on, a number of well-publicized cases involving alleged wrongdoing by members of Congress. A number of newsworthy bribery and conspiracy prosecutions involving members were undertaken by the Justice Department.

Several special counsels were appointed to conduct inquiries concerning questionable or illegal activities involving President Nixon and his closest White House associates, and judicial proceedings led to convictions and prison sentences for a number of those implicated. In the current administration a special counsel investigated charges of wrongdoing in connection with the President's private business affairs, and the activities of several top members of is official family have come into serious question or led to court action.

Most relevant to this paper, the 1978 Ethics in Government Act (Public Law 95-521, as amended by P.L. 96-19 and P.L. 96-28 in 1979) provides detailed financial disclosure rules ands procedures to help identify and avoid potential conflict of interest situations for personnel of all three branches of the federal government. Also, this legislation establishes nearly automatic procedures for starting investigative and follow-up action for dealing with evidence or charges relative to wrongdoing by certain high level officials of the executive branch.

This paper does not criticize any particular case or how it was handled or the objectives of the new ethics legislation and arrangements. Rather, it focuses on the still serious gaps that exist in the nation's efforts to deal more effectively with high level wrongdoing. Specific proposals are offered for closing several of these gaps. For definition purposes, high level wrongdoing, as used herein, refers to wrongful acts by members of Congress, the President, the Vice-President, and all appointed officials with the rank of deputy assistant secretary and above.

DEFICIENCIES IN PRESENT ARRANGEMENTS

The initial actions under the 1978-79 ethics legislation, plus the legislative and executive branch cases of actual or alleged high level wrongdoing already or currently being dealt with by the means just noted, including their outcomes to date, have helped illuminate the following deficiencies.

1. The U.S. Criminal Code still seems not to define adequately and make illegal coercive actions by members of Congress, often through hidden methods, to force high level officials (and they in turn to force their subordinates) to act in ways that violate established rules and regulations for making governmental decisions that confer, confirm, or take away rights, privileges, or advantages, or for making grants or contracts.

2. No systematic means exist to ensure early warning and prompt and unbiased investigative and corrective action in these types of coercive situations. Also, in the case of other forms of high level wrongdoing, the means for assuring early warning and prompt and unbiased investigative and corrective action either are only partially in place or responsibilities are too scattered.

3. High level wrongdoing of various types, when and however it surfaces in both the legislative and executive branches, tends to be handled belatedly, awkwardly, and often unproductively in terms of the public interest.

4. The actual scope of alleged high level wrongdoing too often is only

partially investigated and later partially dealt with in prosecution and legislative and executive corrective actions. Also, quite commonly, even key actors in such wrongdoings escape attention and punishment, and large amounts of critical evidence bearing on the methods and outcomes involved are left unused.

COERCION OF FEDERAL OFFICIALS BY MEMBERS OF CONGRESS

While federal statutes declare the illegality of many forms of wrongdoing, they remain weak in the area of coercion of federal officials by powerful congressmen. Congress itself has been notoriously unable to expose this kind of coercion and rarely deals with it promptly and effectively if such situations are exposed by other means. Also, high level officials who become parties to coercing lower ranking subordinates on orders from congressmen, seem to be unreachable by present laws, nor is their conduct perceived to be a violation of their oaths of office or agency codes of ethical conduct.

Historically, our presidents and the Congress have lacked early warning systems to alert them to this form of wrongdoing. Even when finally alerted, the presidents and the leaders of the Congress, for political, constitutional, or procedural reasons, or perhaps because of tactical needs of the moment, repeatedly seem to have found it inexpedient, awkward, or otherwise difficult to deal forthrightly and effectively with such cases.

No Effective Definitions

Neither branch has done an effective job of defining improper interactions between the two. Admittedly, the task inherently is a difficult one. However, that can be no excuse for failing to identify and make illegal specific improper actions that clearly are contrary to the public interest and are disruptive of sound administrative and funding arrangements, waste taxpayer funds, hurt employee morale, and weaken public confidence in government. In the absence of such corrective action, powerful members still are able to commence coercive maneuvers without the potentially deterring knowledge that their conduct would be illegal and subject to prompt and unbiased investigation and corrective action. In the current uncertain circumstances, high government officials, despite their oaths of office, feel they have to "go along" or look the other way. They tend to rationalize their conduct on the grounds that if they refused the members' demands their programs could face serious trouble because of the members' strong program, funding, or political leverage.

Actually, the whole structure and many of the operating practices of the Congress both encourage and help hide abuses of authority and role by congressmen, particularly powerful committee or subcommittee chairmen. Also, new constitutional barriers to the questioning of the actions of congressmen in connection with their legislative activities seem to be arising from recent court rulings.

No Effective Early Warning

Since the presidents and the Congress have not had effective early warning systems to alert them to coercion of government officials by congressmen and clear guidelines as to what types of conduct between the branches are improper have not been developed, the surfacing of allegations and evidence relating to wrongdoing of this nature has had to depend upon random causes and sometimes bizzare events. Examples abound. A member's assistant, charged with a felony, implicated his boss. A disappointed grant applicant found unexplained lapses in the regular procedural handling of the grants in question and in the application of program priorities and was able to point to evidence that the grant awards were influenced strongly by the coercion of a powerful congressman.

In another instance, a legislative employee caught on a felony count in one case, decided to bargain for a lesser sentence by implicating his boss and another congressman in taking bribe money from a man in a series of other cases in which allegedly the members' influence would shape government decisions in favor of the man. Finally, a troubled official who was forced to resign or be fired for not "going along" with coercive action by a congressman on behalf of a preferred grant applicant, decided to go public with the facts on what was going on.

While the GAO is commonly referred to in the press as a watchdog agency, this agency is a part of the legislative branch and gets many of its investigative instructions from committee chairmen. In practical terms, and perhaps even institutionally, the agency is unable to deal frontaly with charges that a powerful committee chairman has coerced government officials to take improper actions. It can and does investigate and report on the strange or wrongful behavior of government officials, but it is not really free to reveal evidence it has gathered that such behavior may have been compelled by the coercion of a powerful congressional chairman. Unfortunately, when the GAO has the need to engage in such partial reporting, it also becomes an unwilling accomplice in the cover-up of wrongdoing.

INADEQUATE CONGRESSIONAL FOLLOW-UP ACTIONS

The Congress not only lacks effective means of early warning about member wrongdoing, but when it finally becomes informed, it has trouble pulling itself together to act promptly and decisively. In several recent cases, lengthy delays developed before the House and Senate Ethics committees began to act. The progress seemed to lag or actually dissolve—as though they were waiting for something to happen elsewhere before they moved further, or as though they lacked the will or a strategy for proceeding. In other cases, such committees never did act, or they dropped interest when the offending member left Congress.

The reasons for these delays or lack of follow-through vary from case to case. Commonly however, neither the regular committes of jurisdiction in the areas of government where the alleged wrongdoing took place nor the ethics committees have suitable investigative staffs in being to do a proper job of fact-finding and assessment for the types of wrongdoing involved. Consequently, much time is lost in finding special counsels and staffs with the necessary skills and available time. Some of the investigations have been complicated further by jurisdictional problems between committees or with government agencies or by difficulties in gaining access to critical information. Also, the credibility of some investigations suffered from widely held public perceptions that the investigators were unduly restricted in their scope, either for political reasons, or because members wanted to avoid humiliating their colleague who had done the wrongful things.

INADEQUATE PRESIDENTIAL FOLLOW—UP ACTIONS

The new Ethics in Government Act is a direct outgrowth of the fact many of our presidents, going back to Grant, when confronted with allegations of wrongdoing in their personal or official families, failed to act promptly and decisively. The presidents involved (Grant, Harding, Truman, Eisenhower, Johnson, Nixon, and Carter, among others) reacted by defending the alleged wrongdoers and by delaying meaningful investigative and corrective action. Such postures lost these presidents a lot of plublic confidence, especially when, in most of the cases, the allegations later proved to be substantially correct.

In nearly every one of these instances, the press and the general public developed persistent doubts that the President at the time intended to deal objectively with the situation. Much time was lost in charges and denials, and long periods elapsed during which the public could not get clear whether the alleged offenders did or did not do the things charged. For unexplained and often suspicious reasons, investigative agencies sometimes failed to act in convincing ways. In some of the cases, systematic fact-finding, when finally begun, was forced on the presidents by progressively deteriorating public confidence, and then took place in well-after-the-fact conditions. Sometimes access to vital records was blocked and files, tapes, and other records reportedly were changed or lost. Allegations persisted that key witnesses were actively or passively coerced into silence or into "arranged" responses to questions.

During these long and confused periods, individuals who played the whistle blower role were not only often shunned by colleagues but proved vulnerable to retribution. In the meantime, the high level wrongdoers usually were left in their official positions, sometimes for extended periods, with the ability to cover their tracks and in some cases to continue doing the very things complained about.

ETHICS IN GOVERNMENT ACT OF 1978

As a means of reducing the types of problems just noted, Congress and the President, in the Ethics in Government Act, as amended, have been provided a procedure for eventually obtaining an unbiased review of evidence in cases where allegations of high-level wrongdoing surface. However, the law has a number of critical limitations. At the same time in at least one respect the law may create circumstances of overreaction and do harm to persons against whom allegations have been made.

On the limitation side, it should be noted that the whole investigatory-special prosecutor aspect of the legislation (Title VI) applied only to a few very high level government officials. All members of Congress and most subcabinet officials are not covered by the provisions of Title VI. Also, the law limits its investigatory-special prosecutor provisions to cases where violations of federal criminal laws are alleged. Other levels of wrongdoing are not subject to the Title VI procedures for triggering the attorney general's investigations or the court appointment of a special prosecutor.

Maybe an Early Warning

The functioning of the new law may help provide early warning of, and could serve as a deterrent to, some forms of high-level wrongdoing. The financial disclosure features could have positive values in both areas. On the other hand, the investigatory provisions have to be triggered by the attorney general, whose objectivity and speed may continue to be perceived with suspicion by the press, by the opposition party, and by the public, since that official is a key political appointee of the administration that may be the subject of the alleged wrongdoing. Moreover, several times in the past thirty years attorneys general themselves were the subject of charges of serious wrongdoing.

Title VI of the Ethics in Government Act directs the attorney general to start an investigation whenever that official receives specific information that the president or any of the other high-level officials specifically listed in the Title allegedly has violated a federal criminal law (other than a petty offense). The attorney general then has up to ninety days to determine whether the alleged wrongdoing violates a criminal law and whether the evidence is sufficient to warrant further investigation and possible prosecution. If he thinks not, he then is required to advise the judges of the District of Columbia Division of the U.S. Court of Appeals to this effect and supply them with a summary of the information he received, plus the results of the Justice Department's preliminary investigation.

If the judges do not agree with the attorney general's conclusions, they have no authority to appoint a special prosecutor or to take any other action in the matter. Moreover, in an understandable effort to protect high-ranking officials from destructive publicity growing out of unfounded charges, Congress provided that the attorney general's memorandum of conclusions cannot be revealed to anyone other than the judges and the Justice Department unless the judges allow it.

Congress Faced a Dilemma

Clearly, Congress faced a dilemma here. Remembering the suspicious delays and failures to act on the part of the attorney general's office in the Watergate affair, Congress sought to establish a fairly automatic investigatory process in cases of allegations of high-level wrongdoing. On the other hand, as just noted, Congress wanted to spare such officials needless harassment and damaging publicity. The outcome of this dilemma is a set of legislative provisions that probably will not secure either objective and may well open up some new problems that will force them to be changed.

In particular, the attorney general's authority to decide how seriously he will deal with allegations of high-level wrongdoing is a weak spot in the legislation. His decision in this instance is final, and his reasons may be kept from the public. Moreover, it is possible that the new law may be construed as not permitting any court to review either his decision to ask for a court-appointed special prosecutor or his conclusion that neither further investigation by him nor the appointment of a special prosecutor is warranted.

Another weakness in the law poses the danger not that the attorney general will be motivated to suppress allegations of wrongdoing, but that he will find himself compelled to act quickly and even blindly in order to avoid the charge of suppression. Some basis exists for this concern. It is likely that parties who allege high-level wrongdoing, whatever their motive, will not do so quietly. Most probably, the presentation of allegations to the attorney general will be accompanied by considerable publicity. From that moment on, the attorney general is on the spot. Even if his preliminary investigation leads to a conclusion that the charges are quite flimsy and are based upon the worst of motivations, he likely will find it prudent to let a court-appointed special prosecutor do the job of proving this to be so to the public's satisfaction. To do otherwise would be to tempt certain attacks by the opposition party and many others.

Credence to the Allegations

However, if the attorney general feels compelled to ask for a court-appointed special prosecutor as a means of dispelling doubts about his own integrity and independence, the very act of referral of the matter to the Court of Appeals will tend to lend more credence to the allegations of wrongdoing, whether they have any substance or not. Moreover, during the weeks when the attorney general is making his preliminary inquiry, and during the months when the Appeals Court and the special prosecutor it appoints are playing their roles, the suspected wrongdoer is subject to all manner of speculative publicity, and his ability to function in office could well be severely impaired. The dilemma is inherent in the language and action structure established in the law.

SPECIAL COUNSEL—MERIT SYSTEMS PROTECTION BOARD

Earlier mention was made of the establishment of an Office of Special Counsel in the Merit Systems Protection Board. While this official is supposed to function as an independent investigator and prosecutor who will protect whistle blowers, both the nature and scope of the office are quite limited in relation to high-level wrongdoing.

Both the board and the special counsel's office focus on alleged violations of the government's personnel laws, rules, and regulations. The special counsel could help illuminate and give early warning concerning a broader range of wrongdoing brought to light by a reprisal type of personnel action against a whistle blower. However, even then, he would have to concentrate on the offending personnel action, not on the basic wrongdoing that the whistle-blower complained about. Any information gathered about other possible law violations in connection with such personnel cases would have to be referred for follow-up action to the Justice Department or other appropriate law enforcement agencies and be subject to their policies, priorities, and workload constraints.

In any case, suspicions will persist that the special counsel is not positioned with sufficient independence from the administration of power. Indeed, the special counsel is appointed for one limited tour of duty. If the incumbent lawyer wishes to have an elective or appointive role thereafter that depends upon support from the President, then it follows that keeping in the good graces of the administration will be essential. In this connection, it needs to be noted that the first lawyer appointed to the post reportedly resigned prior to the completion of his tour so that he could campaign for the reelection of the President.

Furthermore, the special counsel has no jurisdiction relative to alleged wrongdoing involving members of Congress. Finally, this officer, whose functioning was supposed to be characterized by independence of action, nevertheless is an appointee of the President. As such, the special counsel cannot help to some extent being considered a part of the administration in power. Already press reports have developed that other appointees of the President in the departments have protested that the actions of the special counsel have the effect of embarrassing them in their official roles by giving aid and comfort to misguided complainers. Employee union representatives have expressed their concerns that the special counsel not be subject to pressure from the staff of the White House to show less zeal on behalf of whistle blowers.

FRAGMENTED AND INCOMPLETE HANDLING
OF WRONGDOING SITUATIONS

As noted earlier, the congressional ethics committees have a record of not acting quickly to check into charges of member wrongdoing. During the often lengthy delays, the members against whom allegations have been made can, if they choose, remain in their seats and continue to serve as chairmen of subcommittees or committees. While both houses resent being embarrassed by the wrongdoing of members, they seldom have acted in such a way as to discourage future member wrongdoing. As a matter-of-fact, punishment of offending members ranges from mild to nothing at all. In some cases, deals were made wherein the offending member gave up a chairmanship and perhaps received a reprimand. Some were defeated or chose not to run again or resigned their seats. In each case ethics committee investigations of their wrongdoing then stopped.

From time to time, congressional and government investigative units have referred charges of high level wrongdoing to the Justice Department "for appropriate action." However, such referrals have not always led to full and prompt action. The investigative and prosecution staffs of the U.S. attorneys and other Justice Department units have tended to be heavily overburdened. For workload limitation reasons, cases are shunted aside or are put on delayed timetables. In the meantime, alleged wrongdoers are able to shift their methods, lay low, or cover their tracks. In these circumstances, whistle blowers are left exposed and alone. Witnesses drift off and over the years become forgetful of the critical details that are important in court proceedings. Files and other records are shifted about, broken up, and even altered. Statutes of limitations run their course, and prosecution on some or all counts of wrongdoing becomes impossible.

In addition, prosecution staffs necessarily have to limit the scope of grand jury presentations to the parts of a total wrongdoing that have the best chance of securing an indictment, to the evidence that the judge will allow in his court, and to the things that could convince a trial jury. In many cases, for reasons of prosecution strategy, whole ranges of coconspirators and other persons involved by what they did or failed to do, were not brought to trial; either their roles were not judged to be indictable on the basis of evidence the prosecution felt it was able to use, or statutes of limitations had come into play. In some instances, prosecutors held back from one prosecution in order not to prejudice other planned prosecutions, or they found it easier to concentrate on the offender they had the best chance of getting convicted. Also, for strategy reasons, some wrongdoers, after plea bargaining, were considered more valuable as witnesses for the prosecution.

For some or all of these reasons, whole portions of wrongdoing are never systematically exposed or gone into by investigators, prosecutors, and the courts.

Consequently, the public rarely is able to have confirmation of the full range of allegations dealt with in press stories, and corrective action, where attempted, tends to be fragmented and inconclusive.

THE CONSEQUENCES OF THESE DEFICIENCIES

1 These deficiencies have led to the following practical outcomes:

1. The fragmented and incomplete arrangements and processes currently in place for exposing and dealing with wrongdoing do not and probably cannot effectively deal with cases involving alleged improprieties by: (a) powerful congressmen who place improper pressure on government officials; (b) the officials involved who submit to coercion and violate their oaths of office or agency codes of ethics in so doing; and (c) most subcabinet officials because they are not included in the list of high level officers covered under the Ethics in Government Act.

2. The attorney general, the special counsel in the Merit Systems Protection Board, the General Accounting Office, and the congressional ethics committees are ill positioned to act vigorously and independently in many of these types of cases. A system that depends upon their taking the initiative in investigation and follow-through in instances of high level wrongdoing is a system designed for failure.

3. Too much of the actual and potential value of such early warning machinery as exists is lost or narrowed by default on account of the long lapses of time and the gaps that develop in what actually gets investigated or pursued to prosecution. The value is shrunk even further by the practical requirements of a prosecution strategy and by the limitations of the judicial process, with all of its peculiar and arcane requirements that necessarily exist to protect those on trial.

4. The present fragmented whistleblowing arrangements and processes and the criminal code as now written do not constitute a meaningful deterrent to high-level wrongdoers in the legislative and executive branches of the federal government. Strong and systematic arrangements are not in place that provide a regularized means for prompt and unfettered investigation and effective closure of the wrongdoing issues and cases that somehow surface. Corrective actions often are not taken, or they hang too long in abeyance or are piecemeal. Wrongdoers often escape serious punishment by resigning their positions. Then wrongdoers with good lawyers can reduce the scope of punishment further by getting reductions in the counts to be tried in court. Smart courtroom tactics and judicial rulings as to which witnesses and what evidence can be used can narrow things still more. Finally, juries sometimes reject facts because they do not quite trust the witness stating them, or judges may soften a sentence for any number of reasons when the wrongdoer is a high-level and perhaps by now pathetic-looking

penitent. For some or all of these reasons wrongdoers can reasonably calculate that their chances of getting caught or, if caught, of getting seriously punished are not prohibitive. Indeed, much evidence argues that people who violate their public trust and rob the taxpayers are treated less harshly than people who steal in other ways.

5. These practical outcomes of existing ethics in government arrangements repeatedly teach lower ranking employees that it is not safe for them to try to expose high-level wrongdoing and that they must "go along" or look the other way. In a circular manner, this behavior of most employees then adds to the margin of safety accorded high-level wrongdoers to take risks. Despite the recent efforts to improve the situation for the potential whistle blower, employees faced with efforts by their superiors to coerce them, or who see wrongful things being done, still have inadequate defenses and are quite vulnerable to pressure and retribution.

THE PUBLIC'S UNRESOLVED DOUBTS

The public's business and the public interest require strong actions to deal with these weaknesses. Despite recent efforts to strengthen the machinery for exposing and dealing with wrongdoing in government, the public still believes that a double standard exists in the catching and punishing of high-level wrongdoers. This is particularly serious at this time when the requirements for high-level leadership to produce critically needed public responsiveness are especially high. Mitigation of the nation's energy and inflation problems requires the public to be willing to make real individual sacrifices. However, public confidence for a variety of reasons has become corroded by the belief that taxpayer resources are being wasted and that high-level wrongdoers abuse their public trusts, get away with it for long periods or entirely, or, if caught, finally escape serious punishment. In the circumstances, it can be no surprise that more and more people develop the feeling that it is smarter to try to satisfy their own needs and not make sacrifices for the general good.

Cynics will argue that the public always has accepted the fact of high-level wrongdoing. That is probably true. However, something is different now. During the 1970s, public confidence in both the legislative and executive arms of the federal government dropped disastrously. That sharp tilt downward was strongly influenced by repeated instances of high-level wrongdoing and by the inadequacy of the machinery for early discovery, effective investigation, and even-handed punishment of those involved.

WHAT SHOULD BE DONE?

The central need is to put in place regular on-going machinery for dealing with high-level wrongdoing in an independent and effective manner. The arrangements would have to be such that the mechanism would have a real chance to gain and hold public confidence that it can do the job, and, critically, that it would serve as a powerful deterrent to would-be wrongdoers. This need cannot be met through changes in existing institutional arrangements whose results are weakened by the limited jurisdictions of the officials and offices involved, by their conflicting priorities, and by the widely held perception that they do not and probably cannot function with true independence. These weaknesses are inherent in the present fragmented and incomplete approach to the problem. A new and different institutional approach is needed.

INSPECTOR GENERAL OF THE UNITED STATES

The core of the necessary changes should be the establishment of an independent office of inspector general of the United States. The incumbent of this office should be appointed by the President, subject to approval by a majority of those voting in each house of the Congress, for one fifteen-year term.

The inspector general should function in the limited area of law violations and other forms of prohibited conduct by high officers of the government or by members of the Congress. The types of wrongdoing and the types of positions that the inspector general's work would relate to should be described in the enabling law establishing the new office. Removal of the inspector general should take place only as a consequence of a vote by a two-thirds majority of those voting in each house of the Congress, after a special bipartisan, joint House-Senate commission has found the inspector general was:

1. Incompetent or grossly derelict in the performance of the statutory duties of the position, or unable mentally or physically to perform them
2. Grossly abusive of his statutory authorities and responsibilities
3. In violation of one or more provisions of the code of conduct included in the inspector general enabling act or any other provision of law (other than a petty offense)

INVESTIGATIONS AND PROSECUTIONS

The inspector general should have both investigating and prosecuting roles. He should have a core staff and should be able to request further assistance from the FBI, the Secret Service, the comptroller general, and other sources of data and investigative help. He could start an investigation if information has come into hand that suggests the strong probability that high officers of the government or members of the Congress have engaged in the types of wrongdoing covered in the code of conduct included in the inspector general enabling legislation or the criminal code of the United States.

The inspector general also could act upon the request of the President, the Speaker of the House, the president pro tempore of the Senate, the attorney general, or the comptroller general. The inspector general should not be required to make full and exhaustive inquiry into every allegation presented to him but should investigate sufficiently to determine if reasonable grounds exist for the allegations made. Notice to the public of the results of preliminary inquiries would be at the discretion of the inspector general.

In making investigations, the inspector general should be expected to avoid destructive competition or interference with the work of the Justice Department or other investigative and prosecutive bodies. However, in the event the inspector general is dissatisfied with the scope, focus, or pace of another agency's efforts, he could elect to gather evidence, question witnesses, use subpoenas, and otherwise develop the basis for independent findings and action.

In cases where the inspector general finds sufficient evidence to support allegations of wrongdoing, as defined in the code of conduct or the criminal code, he should have the authority to convene grand juries and make presentations with a view to securing indictments.

INFORMATION PROCEDURE

The inspector general enabling act also should authorize an alternative information procedure. This option would allow the inspector general to determine that the public interest would be served better in a particular case if the emphasis were placed on developing and understanding the whole structure, scope of participation, methodology, and implications of a conspiracy or attempt to violate the laws and regulations of the government or the code of conduct, rather than on the prosecution of the initially discovered offenders.

Using the power to grant immunity from prosecution or to reduce charges, the inspector general could encourage those first caught to provide evidence and background that could give the inspector general, the public, the President, and the Congress a full picture of the objectives, methods, and participation in connection with a planned or actual wrongdoing. Through this option the Congress, the President and the public would be in a good position to identify the need for, and scope of, corrective administrative and personnel changes that would both root out the offenders involved and make a repetition of the wrongdoing more difficult. In these circumstances of full disclosure, the subsequent failure of the Congress and the President to act responsively and objectively would stand out in clear public perspective.

WHY AN INDEPENDENT INSPECTOR GENERAL?
WHY A PERMANENT ONE?

Clearly, the public interest has not been served by existing investigative and prosecutive arrangements that let clouds of doubt persist over a long period about the integrity of and special favors accorded to one of the chief advisors to the president:

> • that leave a large number of congressmen tainted for several years by allegations that they were the subject of bribery and influence-peddling by a foreign agent;
>
> • that fail to investigate and clear up repeated charges that several powerful congressional committee chairmen allegedly threatened to cut agency funds unless special grants and contracts were given to favored persons and institutions; and
>
> • that proved unable to act with prompt and unfettered independence in dealing with persistent allegations that the president of the United States and several of his closest associates participated in the cover-up of evidence that other associates engaged in illegal break-ins, committed perjury, and did other wrongful things.

Unambiguous Independence

Under present arrangements, the public could not be assured that a prompt and fully independent process would be initiated to expose equally wrongful activities and to punish those involved. New institutional arrangements are necessary to assure the unambiguous independence of the officials who would be responsible for investigative and follow-up action. Although the attorney general from time to time will try to give the appearance of independence from the President and his colleagues in the administration, there is an inherent problem in that official being able to do so for very long. Moreover, the opposition party, the media, and the public do not perceive the attorney general as independent of the president and his administration and its necessary political, funding, and other linkages to powerful members of the Congress.

The Title VI arrangements in the Ethics in Government Act that authorize court-appointed special prosecutors to function in certain circumstances are deficient in that they do not extend to wrongdoing by members of Congress or by most of the subcabinet officers of the government. The arrangements provided in the recent civil service reform legislation that set up the Office of Special Counsel in the Merit Systems Protection Board, as noted earlier, are deficient in that the special counsel does not have adequate independence from the President, he is ill positioned to deal with wrongdoing by members of the Congress, and his charter really does not reach to the types of high-level wrongdoing issues and wrongdoers cited in this paper.

Honesty Cannot Be Legislated

As important as having more independent and adequate means for investigating and punishing high level wrongdoing, the nation requires better arrangements to help in deterring would-be high-level wrongdoers. Honesty cannot be legislated. Always some individuals will overreach. Always some will tempt others, and some will be tempted. Some will have the power to coerce others and will try to do so; others will be vulnerable to coercion. However, we can and should do more to raise the odds against the would-be wrongdoer. The keys to raising these odds are:

1. A strengthening and reformulation in understandable and unambiguous language of the particular U.S. Criminal Code provisions that bear on high level wrongdoing, with copies of this portion of the code given wide circulation

2. Stiffer penalties for high level officers of the government and congressmen who break the law, including longer jail sentences or larger fines, or both, minimum use of public service assignments in lieu of regular imprisonment, and fewer possiblites for reduction of sentences for good conduct for persons who abused their public trusts

3. A stretching out of the time periods before statutes of limitations take effect and thereby give immunity to people who abused their public trusts

4. Availability to whistle blowers of access to an independent official of long and protected tenure whose principal function is to go to the heart of allegations of high-level wrongdoing and pursue them without delay, and without interference from the President and his staff, agency heads, or members of Congress

5. A higher probability for would-be wrongdoers that both conspiracy to do wrongful things and actual wrongdoing will be promptly exposed, independently investigated, and effectively dealt with.

The functioning of the proposed inspector general's office would have another deterrent value. If government employees know that they have ready access to an officer in a position to commence promptly an independent investigation of high level efforts to coerce them in the performance of their duties, they will be better able to repel such efforts or otherwise discourage would-be wrongdoers. Would-be wrongdoers, in turn, will know more clearly the jeopardy in which they place themselves if they seek to coerce government officials or carry on unlawful activities. Thus, the establishment of the position of inspector general of the United States would both deter wrongdoers and strengthen the hand of officials to resist or expose wrongdoers.

Selected Readings
Part V.

Bok, Sissela. "Whistleblowing and Professional Responsibility." *New York University Education Quarterly.* 11 (Summer 1980); 2-10.

Bowman, James S. "The Management of Ethics: Codes of Conduct in Organizations." *Public Personnel Management,* 10 (1981); 59-66.

————. "Whistleblowing in the Public Service: An Overview of the Issues." *Review of Public Personnel Administration.* 1 (Fall 1980); 15-28.

Carson, Charles R. *Managing Employee Honesty.* Los Angeles: Security World Publishing, 1977.

Ewing, David W. *Do It My Way Or You're Fired!* New York: John Wiley and Sons, 1983.

Feldman, Daniel. *Reforming Government: Winning Strategies Against Waste, Corruption and Mismanagement.* New York: William Morrow & Co., Inc., 1981.

Fletcher, Thomas, Gordon, Paula, and Hentzell, Shirley. *An Anticorruption Strategy for Local Governments.* Washington, D.C.: National Institute of Law Enforcement and Criminal Justice, 1979.

Government Accountability Project. *A Whistleblower's Guide to the Federal Bureaucracy.* Washington, D.C.: Institute for Policy Studies, 1977.

Harris, Charles E. "Structuring a Workable Business Code of Ethics." *University of Florida Law Review.* 30 (Winter 1978); 310-82.

Holt, Robert N. "A Sampling of Twenty-five Codes of Corporate Conduct: Call for a Renascence." *Directors and Boards.* 5 (Summer 1980); 7-13.

Jasper, Herbert N. "The Merit System: She Ain't What She Used to Be." *The Bureaucrat.* 8 (Winter 1979-80); 25-33.

Kernaghan, Kenneth. "Codes of Ethics and Public Administration: Progress, Problems, and Prospects. *Public Administration* (UK). 58 (Summer 1980); 207-23.

Kreutzen, S. Stanley. "Protecting the Public Service: A National Ethics Commission." *National Civic Review* 61 (July 1972); 339-42.

Levy, Charles S. "On the Development of a Code of Ethics." *Social Work*. 19 (March 1974); 207-16.

Mertins, Jr., Herman and Hennigan, Patrick, eds. *Professional Standards and Ethics: A Workbook for Public Administrators,* 2nd rev. ed. Washington, D.C.: American Society for Public Administration, 1982.

Mitchell, Greg. *Truth...and Consequences: Seven Who Would Not Be Sentenced.* New York: Dembner Books, 1982.

Nocera, Joseph. "Inspectors General: The Fraud of Fighting Fraud. *The Washington Monthly*. 10 (February 1979); 31-39.

Proxmire, William. *The Fleecing of America.* Boston: Houghton Mifflin Company, 1980.

Rein, Lowell G. "Is Your Ethical Slippage Showing?" *Personnel Journal*. 59 (September 1980); 740-43.

Stone, Christopher D. "Law and the Culture of the Corporation." *Business and Society Review*. 15 (Fall 1975); 5-17.

"Uncle Sam's Fraud Hotline," *U.S. News and World Report*. 87 (August 20, 1979); 38.

U.S. Congress, Senate, Committee on Governmental Affairs, *The Whistleblowers: A Report on Federal Employees Who Disclose Acts of Governmental Waste, Abuse, and Corruption.* 95th Cong., 2d sess., 1978.

Walters, Kenneth D. "Your Employees' Right to Blow the Whistle," *Harvard Business Review*. 53 (July/August 1975); 26-34, 161-62.

Weisband, Edward, and Franck, Thomas M. *Resignation in Protest.* New York: Grossman Publishers, 1975.

Westin, Alan F., ed. *Whistle-blowing! Loyalty and Dissent in the Corporation*. New York: McGraw-Hill Books, 1981.

Westin, Alan F., and Salisbury, Stephan, eds. *Individual Rights in the Corporation: A Reader on Employee Rights.* New York: Pantheon Books, Inc., 1980.

Zemke, Ron. "Ethics Training: Can We Really Teach People Right from Wrong?" *Training*. 14 (May 1977); 37-41.